WAR TRAUMA
AND ITS AFTERMATH

*An International Perspective
on the Balkan and Gulf Wars*

**Laurence Armand French
and
Lidija Nikolic-Novakovic**

University Press of America,® Inc.
Lanham · Boulder · New York · Toronto · Plymouth, UK

Copyright © 2012 by
University Press of America,® Inc.
4501 Forbes Boulevard
Suite 200
Lanham, Maryland 20706
UPA Acquisitions Department (301) 459-3366

Estover Road
Plymouth PL6 7PY
United Kingdom

Library of Congress Control Number: 2011942458
ISBN: 978-0-7618-5801-0 (paperback : alk. paper)
eISBN: 978-0-7618-5802-7

Table of Contents

Chapter One

Introduction to Psycho-cultural and Historical Precedents to Classifications of Traumatic Stress

Psycho-Cultural Factors

The aftermath of war continues to be costly to those societies involved - both economically and psychologically. Bereavement for those killed, either by military action or suicide; medical costs associated with the treatment of wounded veterans and civilians; and the social-economic cost of a traumatized population are some of the unintended consequences and burdens of war. Even then, any analysis needs to take into consideration psycho-cultural factors. Most significant is the enculturation process and the societal perception of the person as either a culpable individual or a member of a collective/shared persona. The latter is most prominent in tribal-centric societies where one's identity is closely associated with the extended family or clan.

Our study focuses mainly on conflict analysis among Western cultures where the Protestant Ethic prevails along with its precept of individuality as well as that of contemporary Muslim societies such as those that exist in the former Yugoslavia. The period of study begins with two conflicts that began in the early 1990s. There was the First Gulf War which began on August 7, 1990 with the Iraqi invasion of Kuwait (Desert Shield; Desert Storm in Iraq, Saudi Arabia and Kuwait), a conflict that was kept active following the cessation of ground activities (in August 31, 1991) for the next twelve years through the United States of America (USA) and the allies' policy of maintaining "no fly" zones in Iraq and maintaining deployable forces in Kuwait. The second stage of the Gulf Wars (Operation Iraqi Freedom; Operation Enduring Freedom) began with the 2003 US-led invasion of Iraq and later involvement in Afghanistan as part of the *War on Terrorism,* a conflict that continues today. Also covered is the Balkan Wars which lasted from 1991 until 2002 with continued European Union (EU) and North Atlantic Treaty Organization (NATO) presence today. Both the Gulf and Balkan wars involved Western and Islamic cultural elements. These sub-cultural factors need to be taken into consideration, including the military culture and other tribal-centric elements of pluralistic societies such as gender, age cohort and racial, ethnic, religious or sectarian affiliations to best understand the dynamics involved in these co-occurring conflicts.

The sense of a strong group identity (collectivism) is often woven into the fabric of many Western societies notably those focused upon in this work – United States of America, Canada, Great Britain, and Europe, including the former Yugoslavia with its Muslim and Roma components. Indeed, group membership often transcends the socio-legal concept of individual culpability, so common in Western societies, during crises situations.

A person's cultural-specific identity often supersedes the larger societal norms especially during times of personal crisis while, on the other hand, a shared national crisis can actually solidify the population when it is dealing with a well-defined, often stereotyped, outside threat. Thus, while the entire population may pull together during the crisis itself (in-group cohesion), once the immediate threat (out-group hostility) subsides individualized crises emerge with a greater reliance on familial or sub-cultural affiliated resources.[1] Clearly, any attempt to adequately address unresolved clinical issues needs to take into account the group dynamics (*audience effect*) of those being treated. It is also necessary to determine if these group ties are strong enough to sustain the traumatized individual. Someone with a strong group affiliation would more likely be confronted with clinical issues associated with shame then someone who feels alienated from their reference group – the group they psychologically identify with. Isolation from societal and sub-cultural lifelines exacerbates a sense of normlessness (anomie/alienation) and guilt – the basic ingredients for suicide. By the same token, a sense of strong affiliation with a group is also conducive to suicide. These are situations whereby the person cannot separate his or her individuality from that of the cohesive cohort thus explaining phenomena such as suicide bombers and combatant willing to spare their life in order to save comrades.[2]

Emergence of Standards for Medical and Clinical Classifications

In order to have a better understanding of the current situation relevant to war trauma we first need to look at the historical antecedents of Western medicine as it pertains to clinical definitions of trauma. Although historical records trace the roots of Western medicine to the classical Greek era, efforts toward a systematic classification of medical/clinical diagnoses did not occur until the late 19th century with Euro-American efforts to document national records on death statistics. In 1893, the first international list of causes of death was established (*Bertillon Classification of Causes of Death*) and adopted by the International Statistical Institute located in Chicago, Illinois in the United States. Five years later, at a meeting of the American Public Health Association in Ottawa, Canada, the (Jacques) Bertillon Classification was adopted by the three North American nations – Canada, Mexico and the United States. France subsequently convened conferences on the Bertillon International List of Causes of Death in 1900, 1920, 1929 and 1938.[3] A truly International effort at standardizing and comparing public health needs was established prior to the First World War when in December 1907, at a convention in Rome, Italy, the United Kingdom, Belgium Brazil, Spain, USA, France, Italy, the Netherlands, Portugal, Russia, Switzerland, and Egypt established the International Office of Public Health. Eventually these standards were adopted by the Health Organization of the League of Nations – the forerunner to the United Nations.

The need for better systems for sharing public health issues was intensified by the large number of casualties stemming from World War I – a phenomenon that overtaxed most societies at the time, notably those further impoverished by the conflict. From this crisis emerged the League of Nations and its Health Organization. The effort now was to develop an expanded classification that would document injuries and diseases in addition to those resulting in death. This led to the development of a preliminary draft of a proposed *Statistical Classification of Diseases, Injuries and Causes of Death* in 1938. The end of the World War II saw the emergence of the United Nations (UN) in 1945 as a replacement for the League of Nations. Three years later, the World Health Organization (WHO) came into being replacing the League of Nations' Health Organization.[4]

A major work developed by the World Health Organization was the *International Classification of Diseases* (ICD). At the First World Health Assembly held in 1948, the WHO adopted the *Manual of the International Statistical Classification of Diseases, Injuries, and Causes of Death* as the ICD-6. Subsequence revision conferences in 1955, 1965 and 1975 led to the 7th, 8th and 9th editions of the ICD. The United States expanded on the ICD-9 creating the ICD-9-Clinical Modification (ICD-9-CM) where its codes (5 digit numerical classification) are the basis for Medicare and Medicaid claims. The ICD-9-CM also provides the codes for the American Psychiatric Associations, *Diagnostic and Statistical Manual of Mental Disorders* (DSM).[5]

The American Medical Association (AMA) and the American Psychiatric Association (APA) [not to be confused with the larger American Psychological Association, aka–APA] trace their origins to 1844 with the AMA eventually incorporating in 1897 and the APA in 1927. Both organizations rely on the WHO's International Classifications of Diseases for medical diagnoses. Similarly, the American Psychological Association was founded by G. Stanley Hall at Clark University in Massachusetts in 1892. Today it is the largest professional organization of psychologists in the world with over 152,000 members. Members of both the American Psychiatric Association (38,000 members) and the American Psychological Association rely heavily on the *Diagnostic and Statistical Manual of Mental Disorders* (DSM) in their clinical practice.[6]

     The DSM series are published by the American Psychiatric Association in conjunction with multi-disciplinary input from social work, psychology and other branches of the medical and clinical professions. Following the lead of the

Bertillon Classification conferences, the American Psychiatric Association saw the additional need for a statistical manual for clinical diagnoses. Toward this end, they convened a National Commission on Mental Hygiene in 1917. The outcome was the *Statistical Manual for the Use of Institutions for the Insane* which included 22 clinical diagnoses, an improvement on the existing 1880 classification of seven categories: mania, melancholia, monomania, paresis, dementia, dipsomania and epilepsy. The need for a new and improved manual came out of World War II and the unmet needs of hundreds of thousands of U.S. soldiers.[7]
     Now the focus was on the clinical process itself and not just the end result of a debilitating mental illness. William C. Menninger, a U.S. Army psychiatrist with the rank of brigadier general, paved the way in 1943 for a new clinical classification known initially as *Medical 203* which became prototype for the *Diagnostic and Statistical Manual* (DSM-I). By 1949, Menninger's classification system became the standard not only for the U.S. Armed Forces during World War II but for the Veterans Administration (VA) and VA and military hospitals as well. Menninger's Medical 302 also corresponded closely with the World Health Organization's ICD-6 which included mental disorders for the first time. The U.S Armed Forces and VA *Medical 203* officially became the *Diagnostic and Statistical Manual of Mental Disorders* (DSM-I) in 1951 and published a year later for general use offering 106 mental disorders classified and coded. The DSM-I soon became the clinical standard for psychiatrists and other clinicians in the United States. In 1968, the American Psychiatric Association published the DSM-II with 182 clinical disorders. This edition opened up the debate within the clinical fields, notably psychiatry, concerning the distinction being made between diagnoses that were classified as "neuroses" versus those labelled as "psychoses." [8]
     In 1974, an effort was underway to standardize the DSM and ICD classifications and codifications allowing both to reach a wider universal audience of practitioners. In 1980, the *Diagnostic and Statistical Manual of Mental Disorders* (DSM-III) was published with the new multi-axel format and a five-digit codification that was in concert with the World Health Organization's *International Classification of Diseases* (ICD-9). Here, Axis I was designated for major clinical diagnoses and conditions that, if left unattended, could result in a major clinical diagnosis (V-Codes). Axis II was reserved for Personality Disorders which were seen as reflecting socialization and character development rather than mental disorders, while Axis III was for the causes (etiology) of Axis I disorders and associated medical features. The DSM-III was considered a milestone in clinical classification, now with 265 diagnoses. This multi-axis format now allowed the DSM to be used as an assessment tool by citing criteria that needed to be met for reaching a definitive diagnosis.

Post-traumatic Stress Disorder (PTSD) first appeared in the DSM-III. In 1987, the DSM-III-R appeared as a revision of the 1980 version. This reorganization effort led to Mental Retardation being relegated from Axis I

(major clinical diagnoses and V-Codes) to Axis II along with Personality Disorders. This change came about due to a U.S. Supreme Court decision in 1985 (*City of Cleburne v. Cleburne Living Center, Inc.*) whereby the Court stated that a mental retardation diagnosis, in itself, did not qualify a person the protective class status associated with a major mental health diagnosis. Not only was a Mental Retardation (MR) diagnosis relegated to a lower status, it also verified the legal culpability of Axis II disorders – including Personality Disorder. This later became a major issue during the Gulf Wars – notably those actions following the terrorist attacks of September 11, 2001. In 1994, the current diagnostic classification system (DSM-IV) was introduced with 297 disorders. A "Text Revision" was issued in 2000 (DSM-IV-TR) but it is basically the same as the 1994 edition.15 A DSM-V is currently being developed along with a corresponding ICD-10-CM.[9]

Classifying War Trauma

Given that this study includes both Western and Islamic groups involved in both the Gulf and Balkan wars, it should be noted that early psychiatry is traced to medieval Islam as early as the 8th century in Bagdad, in what is now Iraq, and the 10th century in Persia, now Iran. Certainly, elements of these early holistic clinical techniques survived to the Ottoman age and beyond providing folk remedies both to contemporary Turkish Muslims residing within the former Yugoslavia. By the same token, asylums existed in England in the 13th century for *lunatics* but were mainly for the purpose of separating the seriously mentally ill from the general population. France is credited with providing the first treatment-oriented facilities, doing so in the late 18th century. The United States of America (USA) adopted the British and European model when the republic separated from Great Britain in the late 18th century. Even then, the awareness of war trauma as a clinical syndrome in the United States was associated with the establishment of "modern medicine" in the mid-1800s.[10]

In the United States of American, this awareness came to light during its most traumatic war – the War Between the States, also known as the U.S. Civil War (1861-65). This was the worst conflict in the history of the USA resulting in even more casualties (over 600,000) than the Second World War. Horrific battles waged between the Confederate and Union forces using muskets, bayonets, swords and cannons. Medical techniques were crude compared to today's standards and battle fatigue was common. At this time the phenomenon of battle fatigue was known as – *nonpsychotic nostalgia*. This category included battle fear as well as mental confusion following combat which was thought to be due to "homesickness." It was thought that these conditions were transitory without lasting effects. Those veterans with noticeable wounds, like amputees, and those whose health was seriously compromised by prison camp life, became the wards of their home state and communities. At the end of the 19th century and the beginning of the 20th century, colonial wars flared including the Spanish American War (1898) and the related Philippine-American War (1898-1913),

the Boxer Rebellion (1900-1901), the 2nd Boer War (1899-1902) and the Russo-Japanese War (1904-1906). Here combat fatigue was termed *traumatic war neurosis* drawing on the terminology emerging from the new discipline of psychiatry.[11]

Most advances in recognizing the psychological effects of war trauma came during and following the first and second world wars. The very nature of trench warfare during World War I led to the belief that war trauma was of a transient nature hence the diagnosis of *shell shock*. However, this was also the time when the Committee on Statistics (later the American Psychiatric Association) was attempting to clarify and expand upon the then (1880) seven categories of *idiocy and insanity:* mania, melancholia, monomania, paresis, dementia, dipsomania and epilepsy. It soon became apparent that some returning veterans did not readily recover from their shell shock resulting in more lasting mental health diagnoses. This phenomenon led to calls for the provision of care for these veterans at the federal level in the USA. Three agencies were caring for these World War I veterans: the newly created Veterans Bureau (1921), the Bureau of Pensions (Interior Department) and the National Home for Disabled Volunteer Soldiers.

In 1930, the U.S. Congress consolidated these three agencies into the Veterans Administration along with the 54 veteran's hospitals (VA) that existed at that time. Seriously mentally and/or physically impaired veterans resided in these facilities. World War II saw an even greater need for veteran's care if only due to the vast number of people drafted into the U.S. military. With the Korean War (1950-1953) following on the end of the Second World War, these veterans comprised a large cohort of disabled individuals with needs that taxed the existing veteran and civilian mental health systems. The generic term used for these veterans was *combat fatigue*. It was estimated that the system had to deal with over 750,000 wounded me returning from World War II and Korea - not counting those suffering from mental illnesses without physical injuries. As stated earlier, new inroads into mental health classifications was a by-product of the overwhelming treatment needs of war trauma survivors. General Menninger's *Medical 203* became the basis for the *Diagnostic and Statistical Manual* (DSM-I) while the newly created World Health Organization (WHO) became an important aspect of the United Nations especially with its improved versions of the *International Classification of Diseases* beginning with the ICD-6 in 1949.[12]

On another front, mega-studies were being conducted on the nature of group survival during war-time military service. In the USA, social psychology, notably at the University of Chicago (Chicago School) and Harvard University, led the way in group dynamics and attitudinal research. These techniques were employed by the Research Branch, Information and Education Division of the United States Army to measure the personal adjustment of draftees and volunteers into the regimented life of the military as well as noting special problems associated with combat and its aftermath. At the forefront of this research, was Samuel A. Stouffer, a sociologist with his Ph.D. from the

University of Chicago who also did post-doctoral work at the University of London as a Social Science Research Council Fellow. His last appointment was as the Director of the Laboratory of Social Relations at Harvard University where the post-war analysis of the data was conducted. Stouffer was also interested in race relations in the United States of America and worked with the Swedish sociologist, Gunnar Myrdal on his massive project – *An American Dilemma: The Negro Problem and Modern Democracy* – published in 1944. This relationship influenced Stouffer to survey the attitudes of African American soldiers during World War II which was included in the four volume set of the landmark work –*Studies in Social Psychology in World War II* of which the first two volumes were entitled: *The American Soldier.*[13]

A major outcome from the four-year study of American GIs was the emergence of social psychological concepts which have relevance to the analysis of shared group experiences especially in times of conflict: reference group; relative depravation; organizational justice; audience effect; attribution bias; risky-shift phenomenon and the like. These are the parameters necessary when looking at war trauma and its aftermath. They provide the basic tools for understanding how behaviours are influenced by, and compared with, those sharing the same or a similar experience. These are the concepts that are used to analyze both intra- and inter-group dynamics setting the stage for the more complex mix of U.S. military personnel that occurred during the Vietnam conflict where the military was now fully racially integrated, and the Gulf Wars which added gender integration to the veterans cohort from which the diagnosis of Post-Traumatic Stress Disorder (PTSD) emerged.

In a similar fashion, Leon Festinger's theories of cognitive dissonance and social comparison theory, along with the works of the German School of Gestalt Psychology (Max Wertheimer, Wolfgang Kohler, and Kurt Lewin...), also made valuable contributions to the growing field of social psychology in the area of the individual's response to group dynamics including group conflict. In all, these new dimensions of social psychology provided a conceptual model for inter-group relations, including the terms: tolerance (ability to understand the merits of other beliefs, cultures and social groups); ethnocentrism (judging other groups beliefs and culture through our cultural perspective – believing ours is superior); stereotype (the process of associating members of a particular group with negative traits); prejudice (negative feelings toward persons based solely on their group membership); discrimination (behaviour resulting from our prejudices); racism (discrimination based on a person's skin color or ethnic heritage); sexism (discrimination based on a person's gender); hate (intensely hostile aversion, compounded by anger, ignorance and fear); atrocities/massacres (the killing of a large number of humans indiscriminately and cruelly); and genocide (intent on destruction, in whole or part, of a national, ethnic, racial or religious group).[14]

The implication of these new inroads into understanding the nature of interpersonal relations aided in the care of returning veterans. The sheer number of personnel drafted into the U.S. military during World War II overwhelmed

the resources of the Department of Veterans Affairs. The VA had added responsibilities with passage of the World War II GI Bill (enacted in June, 1944) which impacted the availability of vocational and academic facilities leading to the creation of new technical institutes, colleges and universities to serve the multitude of returning veterans. There was a corresponding growth in VA hospitals, medical centers and nursing homes to accommodate the wounded. On the mental health front, group therapy was introduced as a cost-effective method for treating veterans with adjustment disorders and other mental health problems. A serendipitous discovery from the group therapy approach was the greater efficacy of this method vis-à-vis the traditional approach at that time of individual psychotherapy.

Group therapy was in response to the fact that there were not a sufficient number of psychiatrists available for the volume of clinical needs stemming from returning World War II and Korean War veterans. Moreover, the VA began to use other clinicians, notably psychologists, social workers, psychiatric nurses, addiction counsellors…to fill the void of available therapists. One of the most noted training center for these clinicians was Kurt Lewin's National Training Laboratories in Bethel, Maine. Today, the Veterans Administration is the second largest federal agency in the United States with over 170 hospitals and medical centers, some 350 outpatient, community, and outreach clinics, and 126 nursing home units. VA hospitals are also major research and training facilities for universities and medical programs.

These inroads into psychology, social psychology and psychiatry following World War II greatly influenced the medical/clinical perception of war trauma during the long Vietnam conflict (including military actions in Cambodia and Laos) where U.S. involvement began in November 1955 and not did end until the Mayaguez Incident on May 1975, two weeks following the fall of Saigon and the evacuation of U.S. personnel from Vietnam. This conflict resulted in over 58,000 U.S. casualties and some 150,000 physically injured veterans. The U.S. and allied forces (Australia, Canada, New Zealand, Philippines, South Korea, Thailand, Republic of China - Formosa) were the focus of clinical studies into the phenomenon of war trauma resulting in the codification and classification of Post-Traumatic Stress Disorder in the Diagnostic and Statistical Manual of Mental Disorders (DSM-III) in 1980.[15]

For the most part, millions of Vietnamese Laotians and Cambodian military and civilians caught up in this conflict were excluded from intensive PTSD research (it is estimated that three to four million Vietnamese and one to two million Laotians and Cambodians perished in this conflict alone) limiting these studies to military personnel serving with the U.S. and its allies. Like their counterparts in World War II and the Korean War, most Vietnam veterans were drafted into the U.S. military with the majority assigned to the U.S. Army. But unlike these former conflicts, the Vietnam War was, for the most part, very unpopular in the USA with returning veterans often scorned by anti-war groups. Clearly, the psychological level for stress associated with the Vietnam War

complicated the readjustment of these veterans returning back home following their tours of duty. It was from this cohort that the American Psychiatric Association, and its affiliate clinical/medical colleagues, studies the PTSD phenomenon.

The initial DSM-III (1980) PTSD diagnosis remains virtually unchanged in the current DSM-IV-TR (2000). The major criteria for a PTSD diagnosis are:

-A subjective sense of numbing, detachment, or absence of emotional responsiveness;

-A reduction in awareness of his/her surroundings (being in a daze);

-Derealisation (change in an individual's experience of the environment, where the world around him/her feels unreal and unfamiliar);

-Depersonalization (change in an individual's self-awareness with feelings of being detached from their own experience with self, body and mind seeming alien);

-Dissociative amnesia (inability to recall significant aspects of the trauma);

-Trauma-related seizures (non-epileptic psychogenic seizures).

Associated features include:

-Persistently re-experiencing the perceived source of the trauma in images, thoughts, dreams, illusions, flashbacks or a sense of being back in the traumatic environment;

-Marked avoidance of stimuli that arouses recollections of the traumatic environment;

-Marked symptoms of anxiety or increased arousal (difficulty with sleep, irritability, poor concentration, hyper-vigilance, exaggerated startle response, motor restlessness...) when reminded of the traumatic environment;

-Free-floating anxiety with no discernable stimuli present (panic attacks; agoraphobia...) resulting in avoidance.

Socio-cultural features include:

-Survivor guilt and self-imposed isolation;

-A sense of shaming family (even if the act was not your fault) and/or;

-Suicide ideations;

-Diminished capacity for emotional intimacy with significant others or;

-Impersonal sexual acting out as a means of evaluating one's questionable self-worth.[16]

Incidence of PTSD Worldwide

The incidence of Post-Traumatic Stress Disorder is now recorded worldwide by the World Health Organization. The WHO lists PTSD under its Disability-

Adjusted Life Years (DALY) rate based on 100,000 inhabitants. The latest data (2004) shows that the United States, along with Asia/Pacific nations, are the nations with the highest PTSD rates. A sampling of PTSD-DALY rates:

Country	PTSD-DALY overall rate	Female rate	Male rate
Thailand	59	86	30
Indonesia	30	58	86
Philippines	30	58	86
USA	30	58	86
Bangladesh	29	57	85
Egypt	30	56	83
India	29	56	85
Iran	30	56	83
Pakistan	29	56	85
Japan	31	55	80
Myanmar	30	55	81
Turkey	30	55	81
Vietnam	30	55	80
France	28	54	80
Germany	28	54	80
Italy	28	54	80
Russia	30	54	78
Britain	28	54	80
South Africa	28	52	76
China	28	51	76
Mexico	30	46	60
Brazil	30	45	60

These data includes all forms of traumatic responses and are not limited to war trauma per se.[17]

Interestingly, the incident of PTSD for females is at least twice that of males worldwide. Physical and sexual abuse likely plays a role in this discrepancy. The U.S. National Comorbidity Survey on the lifetime prevalence of PTSD confirms the differential sex ratio indicating that women are twice as likely to suffer PTSD at some point in their lives. However, regarding war trauma veterans the PTSD incidence ration is reversed with male having a higher rate for the Vietnam War cohort. The U.S. Department of Veterans Affairs estimates that 830,000 Vietnam Veterans suffered from symptoms of PTSD with males having a higher rate (15%) than their female counterparts (8.5%). This may be to the fact that females served mainly a supportive role during the Vietnam War – a situation that changed dramatically in the current Gulf War with the greater reliance on female National Guard personnel serving in combat zones as military police or in transportation. Females, for the first time, also serve as combat pilots.[18]

This study expands the war trauma response to include a continuum of social and clinical factors in addition to PTSD including associated features. All too often VA classifications were restricted to a narrow set of factors forcing an

"either-all-or-none" diagnosis with little consideration for other intervening variables including mitigating and aggravating circumstances. Chapter two addresses the continuum of socio-cultural adjustments to war trauma, from sublimation to suicide while chapter three presents the neuropsychological and neurophysiological mechanisms associated with trauma adjustment. Chapter four explores new dimensions of traumatic stress emerging from the Gulf Wars starting in 1991 and continuing to the present and Chapter five provides a comprehensive review of the Slavic-language clinical and medical journals relevant to the aftermath of the Balkan Wars of 1991-2002. Chapter six reviews the literature for current assessment and treatment tools for both the diagnoses of war trauma symptoms and the treatments available for these conditions. The last chapter (seven) is a comprehensive international bibliography relevant to both the English-language and Slavic-language journal articles and books addressing war trauma.

Chapter Two

Continuum of Socio-Cultural Adjustments to War Trauma:
From Sublimation to Suicide

Introduction

It has long been recognized that not everyone experiences trauma in the same way. Indeed, for some a traumatic event provides the catalysts for positive personal and professional growth. A number of scholars noticed this phenomenon including Sigmund Freud. In his attempt to explain the neurophysiology of impulsive behaviors emanating from the *Id* [greater limbic system] and conscious attempts to regulate these drives by the *Ego* [prefrontal lobe] according to our specific socialization of normative behaviors, the *Superego* [parietal lobe functioning], Freud came up with a list of mechanisms used to mediate these impulses. He called them *defense mechanisms.* Defense mechanisms, in turn, can be classified on a continuum with serious pathologies at one end and mature adjustments at the other.[1]

Many of these defense mechanisms have applications to individual adaptations relevant to the adjustment process associated with traumatic stress. The most severe defense mechanisms present themselves in the form of denial and extreme projections along with distortions and delusions. Also at this end of the adaptation continuum lies neurotic (varying degrees of anxiety) including immature reactions that border on serious mental illnesses such as displacement, dissociation, hypochondriasis, intellectualization, isolation, rationalization, reaction formation, repression and regression. On the other end of the continuum are more positive adaptations to life stressors including thought suppression, identification, introjection, altruism and sublimation. Sublimation, in this sense, is the process of diverting the energy of the biological impulse from its immediate source to one that is more acceptable in terms of social and cultural norms. Accordingly, sublimation is the transformation of negative emotions into positive actions or behaviors.

Eric Erikson, a disciple of Sigmund Freud and his daughter, Anna Freud, added to this process of traumatic adaptation by noting the impact on cultural and familial differences in the socialization/enculturation process. Erikson studied the lifestyle of reservation children in the USA – the Sioux of South

Dakota and the Yuron of northern California during the post-World War II era. Here, Erikson examining the cultural elements of tribal-specific socialization and the resulting developmental process of the children and youth residing in Indian Country. This research was inter-disciplinary in that Erikson collaborated with noted anthropologists such as Franz Boas, Ruth Benedict and Margaret Mead as well as with the cultural psychiatrist, Harry Stack Sullivan. From these efforts emerged a better awareness of sub-cultural differences in childhood and adolescent development especially in pluralistic societies such as the United States of America. This awareness has significant implications regarding the variability in adjustments to traumatic stress by military personnel, especially those who experienced the trauma during their adolescent and young adult years.[2]

What resulted from his psychoanalytic training and subsequent multi-cultural field research was perhaps Erik Erikson's greatest contribution – his *Eight-Stage Model of the Human Life Cycle*. In his paradigm, Erikson articulates the polar outcomes from human experiences at each of the eight states of life: (1) infancy; (2) early childhood; (3) play age; (4) school age; (5) adolescence; (6) young adulthood; (7) adulthood; and (8) later adulthood.

1. Infancy: Birth to 18 months. Ego development outcomes: Trust versus Mistrust. Desired outcome is a sense of motivation and hopefulness.
2. Early Childhood: 18 months to 3 years. Ego development outcomes: Autonomy versus Shame. Desired outcome is self-control.
3. Play Age: Age 3 to 5 years. Ego development outcomes: Initiative versus Guilt. Desired outcome is purpose in life.
4. School Age: Age 6 to 12 years. Ego development outcomes: Industry versus Inferiority. Desired outcome is adequacy.
5. Adolescence: Age 12 to 18-21. Ego development outcomes: Identity versus Role Confusion. Desired outcome is a sense of purpose and belonging.
6. Young Adulthood: Age 18-21 to 35-40 years. Ego development outcomes: Intimacy and Solidarity versus Isolation. Desired outcome is a sense of affiliation and love.
7. Middle Adulthood: Age 35-40 to 55-66. Ego development outcomes: Generativity versus Self Absorption or Stagnation. Desired outcome is a sense of being productive and significant in our community.
8. Late Adulthood: Age 55-66 to death. Ego development outcomes: Integrity versus Despair. Desired outcome is a sense of living a purposeful life.[3]

The developmental sequence is a critical variable in looking at how individuals experience traumatic events in their lives. Essentially these stages provide valuable insights into the nature of pre-morbid conditions likely to impact the intensity of post-traumatic features. Clearly, the most significant developmental stage for military personnel is that of "Young Adulthood" given that this represents the age cohort most widely represented within the military both historically and today. This is the case with both the Balkan and Gulf

Wars. Obviously the preceding "Adolescent" stage also represents a critical pre-morbid stage for young military personnel especially if they suffer from any degree of role confusion when entering the military.

Hans Selye also provided a stress adaptation continuum stemming from his research on the physiology of stress and resulting in his General Adaptation Syndrome (GAS) model. Born in Austria, Hans Selye received his MD and Ph.D. from the German University of Prague as well as a D.Sc. at McGill University in Montreal. He was on Director of the Institute of Experimental Medicine and Surgery at the University of Montreal from the end of World War II until 1976 when he founded the International Institute of Stress at the University of Montreal. Dr. Selye was also a Fellow of the Royal Society of Canada. An endocrinologist, Dr. Selye was a pioneer in the study of the physiological effects of stress decades prior to the technological advances that we currently have today which allows us to better examine both the structure and functioning of neuro-pathways of the central nervous system.[4]

Simply stated, the General Adaptation Syndrome is a conceptual model that attempts to explain the cumulative effects of stressful stimuli on the human body. This phenomenon can reflect the accumulation of numerous and frequent minor stressors, which taken as a whole, reflect a major insult to the central nervous system which in turn impacts the immune system leading to physiological problems. By the same token, the body can react to a continuous major stressor with similar results. Hence, the three stages of this process are (1) an alarm reaction to the stressor or perceived stressor [in the case of the saturation point for cumulative stressors] followed by (2) the resistance stage whereby the body attempts to replenish depleted hormones and neurotransmitters accompanying the startle alarm stage. The final, third stage of the GAS is that of exhaustion, and even death. This last stage reflects the body's inability to restore the needed ingredients necessary for the sympathetic response within the Autonomic Nervous System leading to a compromised metabolic system increasing the likelihood of illnesses. Even then, Selye was aware of the positive aspect of stress noting a distinction between negative adjustments to stress or trauma – a situation he termed "distress" and a more positive stress reaction which he called "eustress". Eustress is yet another term for sublimation.[5]

Erik Erikson's work with Native Americans also led him to conclude that entire groups could suffer from cultural marginality thereby perpetuating the *identity crisis,* common in stage 5 (adolescence) forever. He was speaking of the dramatic cultural shock associated with a sudden change in lifestyle such as occurred with American Indians who were forced on to reservations – some no better than concentration camps – where their cultural traditions were no longer allowed. Laurence French continued this study of social ills in Indian Country in the 1970s and 1980s coining the term *psychocultural marginality.* According to French, the term depicts the psychological phenomenon of being caught between the demands of two, often diametrically opposed, culturally-based normative expectations without being able to fully join either. In this instance, the stigma of being phenotypically American Indian, but without knowing the tribal language or traditions, while, at the same time, not being able, or even wanting to, fully assimilate into the larger dominant culture perpetuates the identity crisis among these individuals keeping them in a constant state of stress. This stress often manifests itself in the form of adaptations resulting in behaviors such as alcohol and/or drug use which can eventually lead to mental and physical health problems. Prolonged military tours of duty in an alien and unfriendly culture and/or being a prisoner of war or incarceration in a concentration camp during conflicts can have a similar affect. This phenomenon can also impact the children of deployed military given the disruption in their lives at critical developmental stages. An important consideration here is the availability of socially-acceptably avenues for returning veterans so as to aid in their re-entry back into society.[6]

A major tool for sublimation in the USA was the "G.I. Bill" during World War II. The first G.I. Bill was proposed and drafted by the American Legion – the Congressionally-recognized veterans' organization created following World War I. The American Legions' proposal led to creation of the *Servicemen's Readjustment Act of 1944*. The intent of the Act of 1944 was to provide economic and educational incentives to the millions of returning veterans in an effort to avoid the protests resulting from the seemingly abandoned World War I veterans. The first G.I. Bill provided six benefits: (1) education and training, (2) loan guaranty for a home, farm or business, (3) unemployment pay of $20 per week for up to a year, (4) job-finding assistance, (5) expansion of VA Hospitals and services, and (6) military review of dishonorable discharges.[7]

The education component led to the *democratization of higher education* in the USA. Those opposed to the G.I. Bill feared that college standards would drop if higher education was opened to the general public and not restricted, as it had long been, to society's elite. This was not the case. By opening higher education to veterans, the ranks of public school teachers added a new element of males from varying backgrounds. In all nearly eight million World War II veterans benefited from the original G.I. Bill including over 2.2 million taking advantage of the higher education benefit. An unintended consequence was the growth of existing colleges and universities as well as the emergence of new colleges to accommodate the large number of returning veterans taking advantage of this opportunity. The G.I. Bill was non-discriminatory in terms of race, class, religion and gender opening up avenues rarely available to people often excluded from the educational elite in the United States of America. This provided a clear avenue for sublimation as an adjustment to war for many veterans who may otherwise have had a more difficulty adjustment period. Veterans' organizations like the Veterans of Foreign Wars (VFW) and the American Legion also provided de facto support groups for veterans – a major factor with aging veterans as well, especially those entering the eighth stage of development – late adulthood.[8]

In the former Yugoslavia, the most dramatic examples of sublimation involved women given that this society was predominately male-dominated regardless of sectarian affiliation. Our examples include the portrayal of a Bosniak (Muslim) woman whose family helped her flee war-torn Sarajevo at age 12 only to come back and earn her doctorate degree and become a viable member of the Faculty of Criminology, Criminal Justice and Security Studies at the University of Sarajevo. The other example is of a young Orthodox Serbian woman who began her college education during the war years, traveling to the province of Kosovo from the province of Vojvodina in order to obtain her undergraduate degree and later joining the "Mothers against Milosevic" helping to topple the Serbian dictator.

Irma's Story

Irma represented one of the tens-of-thousands of children and youth caught up in the Bosnian war and the siege of Sarajevo. The siege of Sarajevo is noted as the longest in modern warfare lasting 44-months from May 1992 until February 1996, ending two months following the signing of the Dayton Accord and the subsequent exit of Serbian forces from the high ground surrounding the city. It was actually more of a partial blockade given that no one could survive a total siege for that long a period. Nonetheless, the uncertainty of being shot by a sniper or having an artillery round bursting in your neighborhood merely intensified the stress level among those trapped in Sarajevo. In a city of about five hundred thousand at the time of the siege, it is estimated that some 10,000 people were either killed or went missing including 1,500 children.

The city is in a valley created by the Miljacka River and surrounded by hills and mountains that were controlled by the Bosnian Serb Army (VRS) who also had control of Yugoslavian artillery pieces. The United Nations Protection Force (UNPROFOR) occupied the airport – the largest in Bosnia-Herzegovina – allowing for essential cargo to enter the city. However, snipers controlled the areas surrounding the airport making it deadly for those attempting to retrieve much needed supplies. Consequently, a tunnel was started under the tarmac connecting the neighborhoods surrounding the airport. The tunnel was completed that summer connecting the neighborhood of Dobrinja with that of Butmir allowing for much needed resources including small arms which were imported despite a UN arms embargo for all warring parties in the Balkan War. The tunnel had a rail system like that used in mines and was about 5 feet in height and about 3 feet wide with turn outs for in-coming and out-going traffic. It was over a half-mile in length and was used to bring in some 20 million tons of food and other essentials as well as allowing a million people to either exit or to re-enter the city during the siege.

Irma is one of the children parents sent away to relatives residing outside the former Yugoslavia in order to spare them the horrors of the ensuing sectarian conflict. Irma's relative resided in western Canada – a long way from Sarajevo. She left at age 12 while her parents stayed behind striving to survive in Sarajevo – a city under siege. While food was in short supply, her father was a baker who continued to work despite the war being able to provide some basic subsistence to him, his wife, and other relatives. Nonetheless, Irma constantly worried about her father and mother and other relatives and this stress peaked after not hearing anything from them for nearly a year. Her biggest worry was not knowing if her parents were dead or alive. This was a salient stressors here given the widely promulgated news of civilian casualties following the July 1993 mortar attack on people waiting in line for water and the February 5, 1994 attack on the Markale marketplace with 68 deaths and over 200 wounded. This was the market place where her parents went for their meager provisions during the siege. Worried sick and finally hearing from her parents following the Markele marketplace massacre, Irma notified her parents that she was returning despite the dangers involved. The trip back was a harrowing one compelling her to be smuggled through enemy territory with bullets hitting the vehicle in which she was concealed and finally having to traverse the Sarajevo tunnel to finally be re-joined with her family. Once back home in Sarajevo, Irma continued her education attending high school despite the constant shelling and sniper attacks, even on children and youth. Surviving all that, at the wars end she pursued her studies at the University of Sarajevo earning her undergraduate, master's and doctor-of-science degrees in the Faculty of Criminology, Criminal Justice and Security Studies and obtaining an assignment in the Faculty at the rank of Assistant Professor where she teaches social psychology and substance abuse courses with a focus on children, adolescent and family issues. She maintains close ties to her family while remaining single.[9]

Lidija's Story

Lidija was only 11 years old when Marshall Tito died but she has vivid memories of the panic throughout Serbia and the anticipation of a Soviet occupation of Yugoslavia. Included in this preparation was militia training for all able-bodied Serbs regardless of gender. Within the public school system, universal militia training was in the form of a classroom course in high school which also had a field training component which taught the use of firearms (M-48 rifle). This course was called "defense of the country." Lidija took this course at age 15 where she learned to qualify to fire a rifle at the military rifle range. Following her graduation from high school in Pancevo she embarked on a career as an *au pair* so as to better learn to speak English given that the major additional language taught in the public schools in Serbia at that time was Russian.

With the fall of the Soviet Union came the breakup of the Socialist Republic of Yugoslavia and the beginning of the ultra-nationalist movements in Slovenia, Croatia and Bosnia-Herzegovina in 1989 – all resulting in the expulsion of orthodox Serbs and the unraveling of the pluralistic society Marshall Tito forged under his leadership. The ultra-nationalist leader of Serbia at this time was Slobodan Milosevic who led the coalition of Orthodox Serbs in Bosnia-Herzegovina, Serbia, Montenegro and the hundreds-of-thousands of Serbs born and living in Croatia and Kosovo at this time. Lidija returned home from London in 1991 just as the Balkan Wars began. She abandoned the safety of England to return home to be with her family. Despite these hazards, she began attending college at the University of Pristina in Kosovo, in 1992, some 200 kilometers away from Belgrade. Her course work was interrupted in 1996, when she left to work as an au pair in Italy to earn money to continue her education because of the wide-spread hardships caused by the UN-enforced embargo which continued under NATO even after the December 1995 Dayton Accord.

Things were heating up in Kosovo during this time with attacks from the KLA (Kosovo Liberation Army) against Serbs. When she returned in 1996 she took a job teaching at a secondary school in Pancevo while, at the same time, taking the train to finish her exams in Kosovo despite the dangers involved in this endeavor. She graduated from the University of Pristina in February 1999 earning her undergraduate degree (BA with Honors) in English and literature-one month prior to the NATO bombing of Belgrade and Pancevo which lasted from March until June. Lidija was part of the *bulldozer revolt* of October 5th, 2000 when Milosevic attempted to void the recent election results which he loss. The bulldozer, actually a front –end loader on rubber tires, became the iconic symbol of the popular uprising against Milosevic which involved both men and women, young and old who wanted an end to the wars. U.S.-led sanctions ended with the removal of Milosevic from office and his subsequent arrest for crimes against humanity at The Hague and the installation of Vojislav Kostunica as the last President of the Federal Republic of Yugoslavia, and later Prime Minister of Serbia. Despite the hardships imposed in Serbia at this time, Lidija worked as an English teacher at the High School of Mechanical Engineering in Pancevo doing so from 1997-2008. She married a fellow teacher at the high school and had a son who was born just following Milosevic's downfall. With an addition to the family, Lidija also became a Teaching Assistant in the Department of Criminal Science and General Law at the International University of Novi Paza, Pancevo campus. In 2005 she enrolled in an interdisciplinary Master's program in the faculty of law, University of Novi Pazar at the Pancevo campus completing her thesis in 2010.[10]

Serious Trauma: Rape and Torture

Rape and torture during times of conflict only exacerbates any trauma associated with war trauma. It certainly would take an exceptional persona to overcome the stigma and stress associated with these acts. Even under these circumstances people have gotten beyond the psychological and physical pain associated with these brutal acts. For most, however, these acts leave a lasting and devastating scar on their psyche. Sexual acting out, including rape, has long been associated with military forces during both times of war and occupation. For some it is a vengeful and hateful act while for most it reflects a form of tension release from the uncertainly of wars as well as the isolation and stress from being in a strange land away from home. The latter is known as a "sex-stress situation."

A valuable resource on war-time rape is Susan Brownmiller's classic work, *Against Our Will: Men, Women and Rape* published in 1975. Looking at the history of war-related rape, Brownmiller posited that rape was often seen as part of the spoils of war especially for the winning side. In this sense rape is the act of conquest: "to the victor belong the spoils." Rape not only provided an immediate reward for the combatants but was also used to further humiliate the vanquished losers.　Brownmiller shows how rape later became part of propaganda campaigns beginning in World War I with German atrocities committed against Belgian women and girls. With the advent of the mass media during and following World War I, propaganda techniques became more sophisticated and widespread among the competing socio-political movements underway – Communism, Fascism, Capitalism…. What World War I did was raise propaganda to a new level in the promotion of out-group hatred with accusations of rape being one of the most significant emotional stimuli in this endeavor.

Rape was a major factor in World War II and its aftermath setting the stage for current military scenarios involving Western military forces.　An added factor here was the movement to enfranchise women with in Western societies hence challenging their long-held status as being subservient to male dominance and desires. The male-superiority elements of both the Germans and Japanese worldviews at this time further fuelled cries of massive rape – charges that were heard at the subsequent Nuremberg International Military Tribunal and the International Military Tribunal for the Far East. Indeed, both the Germans and Japanese had *rape camps* for the recreation of their soldiers. The most widely-spread media coverage of during this time was not the rape of death camp women run by the Nazi but rather the earlier atrocities during the Japanese occupation of the Chinese capital Nanking beginning in December 1937. This became known throughout the world as *The Rape of Nanking*.[11]

Interestingly, the Nuremberg Tribunals did not charge any Nazi war criminal with rape despite testimony from victims.　One theory for not doing so is because these proceedings would also subject Allied troops to similar charges, notably by US, French Moroccan (Goumiers) and Soviet soldiers. However, its counterpart, the International Military Tribunal for the Far East (IMTFE) did so mainly due to the publicity surrounding the rapes in Nanking.　General Iwane Matsui was tried and convicted by the IMTFE in 1948 for his command of Japanese troops in Nanking China in 1937.　His defense was that he issued orders not to rape and plunder but that this order had little effect among his commanders and troops resulting in some 20,000 women and girls being raped during the initial occupation.　Matsui was prosecuted even though he retired in 1938 and had little to do with World War II per se.　He was subsequently hanged on December 23, 1948, at age 70, along with six other Japanese leaders, including Hideki Tojo. Yet, no US military leaders were put on trial despite the fact that some 10,000 Japanese women were raped by American troops during the Okinawa campaign in 1945.　This selective application of justice regarding rape was corrected in 1949 with Article 27 of the Fourth Geneva Convention which now explicitly prohibits wartime rape and enforced prostitution.[12]

With an estimated 30% sexual assault incidents among the women currently serving in the US military and tens-of-thousands of rapes of both men and women in the Balkan Wars (1991-2002) coupled with the proliferation of prostitution for the benefit of peacekeeping troop stationed in the former Yugoslavia, sexual assault and sexual deviance are critical factors when looking at war trauma relevant to the Gulf and Balkan Wars and their aftermath. While there is no official classification of *war rape* per se, what is available is a clinical classification of sex offenses.

Sexual offenders general fall into two clinical categories – those *fixated* by their sexual deviance and those whose sexual offense is due to *regression*. *Regression* is considered to be a transitory reaction to a stress situation, including war stress. Regression is also known as a *sex-stress situation*. *Fixated* sexual offenders are those with a more pervasive clinical problem falling into the classification of *paraphilias*. The defining element of paraphilias is the autonomic involvement of recurrent, intense, sexually arousing fantasies; sexual urges, or specific ritualistic behaviors. The Diagnostic and Statistical Manual of Mental Disorders (DSM-IV-TM) provides the following description of paraphilias:

Exhibitionism: The exposure of one's genitals to an unsuspecting stranger.

Fetishism: The use of nonliving objects for sexual satisfaction (e.g., women's undergarments…).

Pedophilia: Sexual activity with a *prepubescent* child or children (this included infants and children who have not reached puberty).

Sexual Masochism: Actual acts of being humiliated, beaten, bound, or made to otherwise suffer.

Sexual Sadism: Real acts in which the psychological or physical suffering of the victim is sexually exciting to the person inflicting the pain (this is a dangerous category because it often results in the death of the victim). This classification is not to be confused with a hate sex crime perpetrated toward a known victim.

Transvestic Fetishism: Sexual satisfaction from cross-dressing (applies to heterosexual men and not to homosexuals who feel that they are caught up in the wrong body).

Voyeurism: The act of observing an unsuspecting person who is naked, in the process of disrobing, or engaging in sexual activity.

Paraphilia Not-Otherwise-Specified (NOS):

-Telephone scatologia (obscene phone calls);

-necrophilia (urge to have sexual contact with a corpse);

-partialis (exclusive focus on a part of the human body, e.g. foot…;

-zoophilia (morbid fondness of animals); and

-coprophilia (morbid sexual attractions to feces).

Again, the common theme of paraphilias is intense sexual arousing fantasies, sexual urges, or sexual behaviors. These innate urges, emanating from the limbic system, have a powerful control over one's affect, often overriding the cognitive constraints of the frontal lobe. A consequence of this clinical process and powerful sexual urges is the *depersonalization* or *objectification* of the victim.[13]

Currently there is no known universal biological factor that can explain the cause of sexual aberrations resulting in paraphilias. Life situations usually trigger critical stressors which, depending on our social-psychological and biological makeup, are idiosyncratic in nature and therefore unique to each person. In the late 1960s and early 1970s, a genetic etiology was offered for sexual deviance given that some dangerous sexual offenders were found to have the extra male sex chromosome. However, it was later found that the presence of the XYY profile, in itself, does not accurately predict deviant sexual behaviors as an expression of male aggressiveness. Socio-cultural factors provide some insights into promiscuity especially in those cultures where sexual acting out is considered to be normative (acceptable) behavior. In other, non-Western cultures, it is customary for older males to take as their brides girls who have just reached child-bearing age (puberty). These cultural differences often pose legal issues when these sub-cultural norms are pitted against the more restricted laws of the dominant society.

Familial and socialization factors provide mitigating circumstances for sex-stress situations. A theme common among many sexual offenders is a history of abuse and neglect during their formative years, including being sexually exploited. Early indicators of childhood stress often present themselves in the following behaviors: stuttering, bed-wetting, truancy and pyromania as well as other impulse control disorders. At puberty sexual expressions generally emerge for boys which may present as paraphilas, including voyeurism, hard-core pornography, inappropriate or excessive masturbation, exhibitionism and the theft of undergarments. For most adolescent boys these behaviors are generally reflective of a transitory stage of the maturation process. Moreover, these sexual expressions and fantasies are more prevalent among male youth who are members of social settings where sex is seen as being taboo.[14]

While none of these adolescent sexual expressions constitutes a clear indication of future sexual deviance, those individuals who fail to adequately transfer these early sexual expressions to acceptable norms do form the potential pool of dangerous sexual offenders. Incarceration during the formative years seems to exacerbate the intensity of sexual deviance in males. Here, the penal environment substitutes a hostile, uni-sexual atmosphere for the normative social milieu resulting in many youthful offenders emerging back into society with a confused sexual identity. The victim/offender syndrome is yet another early socialization factor. An intriguing element of the socialization process is the relationship between sexual offenders (both males and females) and their own role as adult victims of childhood sexual assault. It is estimated that about 30% of sexually abused children grow up to become sexual abusers themselves. Here, factors most likely to contribute to the cycle of child sexual abuse include: (1) persistent abuse by the same offender over time; (2) multiple abuses by numerous abusers; and (3) the occurrence of intense sexual trauma coupled with no means for adequate psychological processing. The mechanism of action for impulsive sexuality involves stimuli that trigger intense levels of excitability. Anger, revenge, paranoid ideations, a sense of entitlement to sex, are all indicative of *sex-stress situations.*

Paraphilics, on the other hand, attempt to satisfy innate sexual drives in a more impersonal fashion. They are dealing with a malfunctioning *hypothalamic-pituitary-adrenal-gonad axis.* Like other impulse-control dysregulations, collectively known as "the manias", the primary goal of this autonomic process is sexual gratification per se without any overriding social-cultural agenda. Part of this dysregulation involves testosterone. We know that the fetal brain is "masculinized" by testosterone and that post-pubertal males have up to 10 times as much testosterone as females. Testosterone receptors are found throughout the brain but are most highly concentrated in the hypothalamus. Females have the same proportion of testosterone as their pre-pubertal male counterparts but only one-tenth of that of males at the age of puberty. While females continue to have the same proportion of testosterone as pre-pubertal males of post-pubertal males, decreases in this level is associated with female sexual dysfunctions notable diminished sexual desire and arousal. Conversely, greater levels of testosterone in males are *not* directly associated with a greater sexual arousal or sexual behavior challenging a long-held assumption in both the clinical and legal realms of Western societies. Sex offenders have not been found to have increased serum testosterone. Indeed, marked levels of testosterone are more likely associated with irritability and aggression rather than sexual behavior. However, post-puberty males differ from their post-puberty female counterparts in that they:

-have more sexual fantasies;
-initiate sexual behavior more frequently;
-masturbate more often;
-have more lifetime sexual partners; and
-are more easily aroused by visual stimuli ("eye candy").

Yet, the marked reduction of testosterone due to surgical castration is associated with a corresponding decrease in sexual recidivism. Marked reductions in serum testosterone have similar effects of both men and women – that of a significant reduction in their libido.

So, if sex offenders do not have increased levels of serum testosterone why is there usually a marked decrease in sexual recidivism following surgical castration? The answer lies in the complexities associated with impulsive arousal. Here, the brain areas involved in the neurocircuitry associated with visual stimuli and sexual arousal are the limbic system and the frontal lobe which work in concert relative to the *hypothalamic-pituitary-adrenal-gonad axis.* It is now realized that certain clinical conditions, notably *dysthymia* reflect problems within this circuitry including sexual impulsivity and impaired social judgment (executive functioning). It now appears that the *luteinizing hormone* (LH) plays a more significant role than testosterone in activation of the hypothalamic-pituitary-adrenal-gonadic (HPAG) axis. The action of LH in males is that it stimulates the production of testosterone activating the autonomic response of the HPAG process.

The luteinizing hormone is associated with eliciting sexual fantasies and contributing to the impulsive sexual fantasies of the fixated paraphiliac. LH, which is secreted by the pituitary gland (pituitary component of the HPAG process), plays a crucial function during a woman's menstrual cycle causing the wall of the follicle within the ovary to separate and release the mature ovum. LH is also associated with the undesired effects of Premenstrual Syndrome (PMS). Chemical castration currently involves progesterone (Depo-Provera) which influences the sex-drive by decreasing the male libido through the suppression of both testosterone and luteinizing hormones. Also used is Depo-Lupron (Triptorelin). Triptorelin is a gonadotropin releasing hormone agonist whose action is in the hypothalamus leading to a decrease in the LH secretion and testicular testosterone production and secretion.

Serotonin (5-HT) also plays a role in impulsive sexual behaviors. Serotonin is a neuromodulator (a substance that modifies the function or effect of a neurotransmitter) which also acts independently as a neurotransmitter that affects mood, behavior and substance tolerance. The mechanism of action for serotonin is that it helps modulate CNS inhibitions within the limbic system and in the prefrontal cortex. Accordingly, mood, anxiety (including PTSD) and impulsive dysregulation are all associated with 5-HT imbalances with the CNS. Thus, serotonin enhancement is indicated for treating mood and anxiety disorders as well as impulsivity. Enhanced serotonin also serves to reduce testosterone's pro-sexual signal effect in the hypothalamus and the limbic nuclei. This relationship within the HPAG process helps answer the question which rose earlier regarding why do people who are physically castrated have a reduced sex drive? It is because castration increases hypothalamic serotonin receptions in males while serotonin depletion is associated with hypersexual behaviors. In this sense, 5-HT modulates the neurotransmitter Dopamine (D) regarding sexual activity. The recent advent of psychopharmacologic medications known as *Selective Serotonin Reuptake Inhibitors* (SSRI's) plays a crucial role in controlling mood and anxiety disorders as well as impulsivity (including hypersexuality) by enhancing 5-HT neurotransmission in the CNS. More of this process is presented in the next chapter on the neuropsychology and neurophysiology of trauma adjustment.[15]

Trauma and Suicide

Untreated neurochemical imbalances with the Central Nervous System secondary to trauma such as sexual abuse can lead to chronic depression, even difficult to treat refractory depression and suicide. In research on paternal health both premorbid schizophrenia and major depression are associated with pregnancy during times of stress or famine. Both factors foster maternal malnutrition thereby more likely to disrupt the neural development of the fetus. Moreover, post-trauma self-medication secondary to the often lacking clinical resources can lead to an increase of premature delivery, low birth weight and even Fetal Alcohol Syndrome (FAS) or fetal alcohol effect. While the effects of depression, PTSD and other mental disorders and the prevalence of suicide is discussed further in subsequent chapters the plight of women and girls in Afghanistan, where war has raged for decades, is a poignant example of this phenomenon. A study released in July 2010 indicated that some 2,300 Afghan women and girls, aged between 15 and 40, commit suicide subsequent to their untreated depression. It is estimated that nearly 30 percent of the women in Afghanistan suffer from depression, many of them within the child-bearing age. This scenario is further complicated by the strict patriarchal social structure in that country whereby women and girls have little choices regarding marriage and pregnancy. In this section we look at the complexities associated with suicide.[16]

Emile Durkheim, the noted French sociologist, devised a paradigm for the classification of suicides in the early 1900s – one that still holds true today. Simply stated, Durkheim associated suicide with social integration. Accordingly, the degree of our integration (socialization/enculturation) into the group with which we identify determines our ability to copy with crisis or sudden disruptions in our lives (anomie). Toward this end, Durkheim developed three types of suicide: Anomic suicide; egoistic suicide; and altruistic suicide.

Anomic Suicide: This represents the type of suicide which erupts from sudden social or personal disorganization. Anomie means normlessness - reflecting the inability of the individual's socialization to sustain them through the impending crisis.

Egoistic Suicide: On the other hand, egoistic represents a situation whereby over time the individual comes to feel more and more alienated from his/her social group losing the necessary connections to keep him/her tied to the social norms. The homeless and aging single males with weak family ties, especially those with poor health provide examples of those who elect to take their own lives in despair.

Altruistic Suicide: This type of suicide represents situations where the individual is so well integrated into his/her reference group that their individuation becomes secondary to the collective norm. Altruistic suicides can be spontaneous, during a crisis situation where a person takes on a heroic act to save other groups members or it can be a planned action targeted against the group's enemy. The former is illustrated by the soldier who jumps onto a grenade to save his buddies or the parent who gives their live to save a family member in a fire. The latter reflects planed suicide missions like those of the kamikaze pilots during World War II and by the Islamic suicide bombers in the current Gulf War in Iraq and Afghanistan.

Fatalistic Suicides: This type of suicide can be of the egoistic nature like the inmate who is deemed to live his/her life in prison without the possibility of parole. Herbert Hendin noted that this is also a phenomenon among impoverished blacks in American ghettoes where they are so enraged that they murder themselves. "Suicide by cop" is an example of fatalistic suicide. It can also be tied to altruistic suicides, especially when this act speaks of collective oppression for the person's group. Palestinian suicide bombers in Israel can fall into this category.[17]

According to Durkheim's suicide topology, the more a person's status is dependent upon their socialization, the greater the likelihood of them committing anomic suicide during a period of normlessness – situations where their social status no longer sustains them during times of crisis. The rationale for this behavior is a sense of *loss* of their social self. The suicides of prominent businessmen during the Great Depression of the early 1900s illustrates this phenomenon as does the suicide of high status individuals once indicted or suspected of criminal activities. This type of suicide is also more likely if one's cognitive capacity is diminished by alcohol or other substances.

In contrast, egoistic suicide occurs when an individual feels alienated or separated from society. These individuals never were, or are no longer (disengagement), dependent upon their social status and therefore are more prone toward making existential decisions, including ending their own life – often due to pain and suffering from health problems. For some, like the terminally ill, this choice better reflects a rational process, while for others, it reflects psychological marginality. French attributes the high rate of suicide among American Indians to their psychocultural marginality.[18]

At the other end of the social integration continuum lies, what Durkheim termed, altruistic suicide. This reflects the opposite of egoistic suicide. Here an individual is so enmeshed into his/her society that he/she cannot separate him/herself from the group. These individuals essentially have no status beyond that of the group at the time of their suicide. Their social status at the time of the suicide act reflects their total identity. Altruistic suicide differs from anomic suicide in that the latter reflects confusion regarding how they will be viewed by the public from which they draw their status. Durkheim noted three types of altruistic suicides: obligatory; optional; and acute. Historically, sacrifice victims illustrated obligatory suicides while Japanese kamikaze pilots during World War II represented a form of optional altruistic suicide. Acute altruistic suicide is best represented by the soldier who "jumps on a hand grenade" or single-handedly charges a machine gun nest devastating his outfit. As stated earlier, in on-going conflicts today, Western societies (Israel, USA, EU, NATO…) have a difficult time understanding the Islamic suicide bomber. Clearly, they represent a form of altruistic suicide, perhaps more likely a combination of the obligatory and optional forms with an element of fatalistic suicide.

Another dimension of suicide and socialization was put forth by Stuart Palmer in the late 1950s when he tested the *frustration/aggression theorem* devised at Yale University in the late 1930s in an attempt to better conceptualize Sigmund Freud's typology of anxiety. The frustration/aggression theorem states that aggression (notably violence) is a consequence of frustration (stress) and, conversely, all frustration (stress) leads to aggression (violence). Here, Palmer postulated that the degree of socialization determines the method of violence with highly socialized persons, those with dominant superegos, generally *internalize* their aggression. Internalized aggression, in turn, results in psychosomatic complaints and illnesses with the extreme form of self-aggression being suicide.

In contrast, externalized aggression, that directed toward others, presents itself in antisocial behaviors, conduct disorder, rape, aggravated assault/battery, and in its extreme form – homicide. Palmer also noted that trauma at the pre-verbal age exacerbated the intensity of aggression regardless if internalized or externalized. Variants of Palmer's model include "murder followed by suicide" and "suicide by cop". A common type of "murder followed by suicide" is when a family member, usually the father, is caught up in an acute stress situation which he feels is hopeless (anomic conditions) but also feels compelled to spare his family the perceived shame he thinks his situation will bring upon them – hence he kills them (obligatory altruism) and then himself (anomic suicide). Another form of "murder followed by suicide" involves egoistic suicide whereby the distraught individual kills the perceived source of his/her extreme stress (intimate partner) and them him/herself. Or, the distraught person destroys the product of the relationship (killing the children) as well as him/herself. Palmer conducted an empirical study on his theory resulting in a 1960 book entitled, *The Psychology of Murder.*[19]

Jack Gibbs, a contemporary of Palmer, also expanded on Durkheim's thesis by looking at suicide rates noting that the greater the incidence of disrupted social relations in a population, the higher the suicide rate of the population. Gibbs also noted that all suicide victims have experienced a set of disruptive social relations that is not found in the history of non-victims. French and Bryce later analyzed the influence of the " women's movement" in the USA during the 1960s and 1970s finding a significant increase in the level of aggression (gunshot, hangings…) among suicidal women as against the typical passive methods (pills, gas asphyxiation). This change in suicide method was attributed to the disruption of the traditional female role.[20]

An early research project, funded by the U.S. National Institute of Mental Health (NIMH) based on Palmer and Gibbs work involving psychological autopsies was conducted at the Neuropsychiatric Facility in New Hampshire by Niswander, Casey, Humphrey and French in 1968-1970. This research led to the sequential ordering of event (losses) that occurred in the lives of some 160 suicide victims. Female suicide victims had 12 significant losses compared to 20 for male suicide victims.

Top 20 losses in ascending order of significance:
1. Abandonment by parents;
2. Death of a parent;
3. Foster home placement;
4. Childhood institutionalization;
5. Loss of student role;
6. Death of a sibling;
7. Alcoholism;
8. Ill health;
9. Death of a close relative;

10. Arrest;
11. Incarceration;
12. Suicide attempt;
13. Sexual incompatibility;
14. Divorce;
15. Psychiatric hospitalization;
16. Loss of occupational role;
17. Violent assault;
18. Abandonment by spouse;
19. Death of a child;
20. Suicide threat.

It is important to note that not all twenty events are not necessary in order to predict neither the likelihood of a suicide attempt nor that these events necessarily need to occur in this order. It is interesting to note that fewer events precipitated female suicides – most notably abandonment by parents and foster home placement. Also important were disruptions in social relationships or less of social roles as well as the loss of expected roles during childhood and early adolescence. Or the loss of parents, home, siblings, close relatives and student role followed by chaotic marriages, poor work history and mental and physical health problems. All these factors are critical in predicting suicide risks.[21]

On another dimension is the consideration of mental health and biological factors contributing to suicide. Comorbidity of substance use disorders and other mental disorders are also strongly associated with suicide regardless of age cohort involved or race or cultural factors. Here, hopelessness or acute anomie associated with a mental disorder contributes to a sense of unresolved trauma leading to impulsive resolution. Essentially, these medical conditions contribute to a profound sense of helplessness and normlessness - the sense of being alienated from the social resources needed to carry them through their crisis. Clinical depression is the most common mental disorder associated with suicide. Bipolar disorder (manic-depression), panic disorder, post-traumatic stress disorder (PTSD), schizophrenia and borderline personality disorders are other mental disorders with a high prevalence of suicide especially when combined with substance abuse. Additionally, there is the neurodysregulation associated with acute substance abuse per se, notably substance-induced mood disorders; anxiety and/or psychosis – mental states conducive to suicide ideations. Jail suicides clearly reflect this phenomenon. The sobering guilt and shame associated with intoxication and arrest often leads to an acute stressful situation where suicide seems the only redemption for their actions.[22]

Another area of consideration when looking at the etiology of suicide is that of medical conditions, including conditions created by medication side effects. For instance, hypothyroidism is a common cause of medically-induced depression. Other medical disorders that can cause depression, and subsequent, suicide ideations are Addison's Disease, AIDS, anemia, asthma, chronic fatigue syndrome, chronic infection, chronic pain, congestive heart failure, Cushing's disease, diabetes, infectious hepatitis, influenza, malignancies, malnutrition, multiple sclerosis, porphyria, rheumatoid arthritis, and ulcerative colitis, among others. The medical profession has long known of the suicide potential (deliberate overdosing) of certain psychotropic medications notably the tricyclic antidepressants (TCSs), benzodiazepines and lithium. What has not been widely known is the neurodysregulation of critical neurotransmitters secondary to non-psychotropic medications such as those prescribed for hypertension.

Engelberg researched this problem when noting that longitudinal studies on the efficacy of drugs used to treat coronary heart disease (CHD) indicated significantly fewer deaths due to heart failure but no overall decrease in mortality from the overall study cohort per se. Interestingly, while a positive relationship appeared to exist between medications that lowered serum cholesterol concentrations and a decrease in frequency of coronary heart disease, an inverse relationship also appeared to exist with an increase in the number of deaths due to suicide or violence. In Muldoons's review of six randomized, controlled, primary prevention trials of middle-aged subjects on medications designed to lower serum cholesterol, his group found a significant increase in mortality due to suicides or violence compared with control groups. Indeed, the treated groups had 28 fewer deaths from CHD but 29 more deaths from suicide, homicide and accidents. Engelberg suggests that this problem involves the relationship between blood cholesterol and cerebral serotonin.

According to this theory, brain-cell membrane fluidity and micro-viscosity are critical to the maintenance of membrane lipids and blood proteins whereby a higher cholesterol content increases membrane lipid viscosity contributing to the increased of protein serotonin receptors on the membrane surface resulting in a better uptake of serotonin from the blood and hence into the Central Nervous System (CNS). Conversely, medications that reduce lipid micro-viscosity greatly decrease the availability of protein serotonin within the CNS, notably the frontal lobe where executive functioning occurs. This condition fits Spoont's thesis and other research regarding the role of decreased serotonin within the frontal lobe and the increased likelihood of impulsive aggression including homicide and suicide. Hence, this phenomenon represents a situation where biological factors provide strong indicators for impulsive behaviors, including suicide offering a cautionary note regarding the choice of medications used to treat traumatic stress.[23]

These models help us understand the high suicide rate in societies following conflict like that associated with the Balkan Wars within the former Yugoslavia from 1991 until 2002 as well as the high, yet differential, suicide rate among veterans serving in Iraq and Afghanistan.

Chapter Three

The Neurophysiology and Neuropsychology of Trauma
Adjustment

Introduction

We have learned more about the central nervous system (CNS) and related
systems within the past thirty years than what was previously recorded
throughout the history of neurophysiology. Thanks to the advent of new
computerized technologies such as the CT scan (computerized tomography) and
the MRI (magnetic resonance imaging) for the study of the structure of the
brain, the PET (positron emission tomography) and BEAM (brain electric area
mapping) for the study of the function of the brain, we can now study the human
central nervous system directly. In a 1996 article in the journal *General
Psychologists*, Posner noted that these advances in neurosciences have changed
the opportunity to study the human brain directly as it performs the tasks of
daily life. These advances certainly greatly aid in the advances within the
medical field including a better understanding of brain dysfunctions secondary
to physical injuries and mental disorders, or a combination of both, such as is
presented with traumatic stress and brain injuries.[1]

The Basis of Human Neurophysiology

Any discussion of neurophysiology requires a requisite knowledge of the
basis of the structure and function of human cell, including CNS cells – neurons
and glial cells. This knowledge base must include the study of cell structure and
its functioning, especially the role of ion pumps and the synthesis of vitamins
and minerals and their relationship to the development of carbohydrates (notably
glucose), proteins (notably lipoproteins), amino acids (notably nucleic acids),
enzymes (including coenzymes with proteins) and the structure of DNA
(deoxyribonucleic acid – a four base peptide combination) and RNA
(ribonucleic acid – a nucleotide comprised of ribose and a phosphate bridge) and
their role in protein conversion and genetic coding.

The basic knowledge needed here is that *transcription* involves the
conversion of genetic DNA to messenger RNA and that from this transfer, RNA
and the codes are passed on through the cells via the rough endoplasmic
reticulum. These processes are required for the production of cellular energy

and metabolism. The energy process focuses on ATP (adenosine tri-phosphate) and, simply stated, involves ion pumps and enzymes that convert amino acids so that they are useful for glucose metabolism within the mitochondrion. Critical to this energy generating process is the oxygenation of glucose or the conversion of pyruvate (PHD stage of glycolysis). This is known as the *citrate acid cycle* or as the *Krebs Cycle*.[2]

Another significant component of neurophysiology is an understanding of the brain, notably the neuronetwork, and the role of neurotransmitters and neurotransmission. This component involves an understanding of the endocrine system and the peripheral nervous system as well. An element of this process is an understanding of the vital organs involved in the endocrine and nervous systems. This includes the vascular system, liver, kidneys and intestinal tract as well as blood and other body fluids. Prior to the recent technological advances allowing for a more detailed view of both the structure and functioning of the human body, the human brain was presented as a rather simple organ thought to be comprised of only a few significant elements: the right and left hemispheres, neurons, the blood/brain barrier, the frontal lobe, temporal lobes, parietal lobe, occipital lobe, sensory/motor cortex and an oversimplified understanding of certain structures within the limbic system, notably the hypothalamus, thalamus and hippocampus.

The advent of computerized technology has provided new insights into both the structure and function of the human brain. Today we know that the brain consists of about one trillion cells of which 100 billion are neurons (gray matter) and 900 billion are glia cells (white matter). We now classify the brain into three major components: the forebrain, midbrain, and hindbrain, with four basic lobes – frontal, parietal, temporal and occipital. The once overlooked limbic system is often referred to as the *primitive* or *emotional* brain while the cerebral cortex is known as the *thinking* and *reasoning* brain. Our new understanding pertains both to the neurons and glia cells. Indeed, it was only recently discovered that a number, perhaps all, of the neurotransmitters reside in vesicles within the soma of the neuronal cell body. It was long believed that each neuron only addressed a single neurotransmitter. This recent finding indicates that the human brain is much more complex than previously thought.[3]

Another discovery pertains to the neuron's dendrites, or branches. Recent discoveries indicate the advent of rapid dendrite growth from the prenatal stage until the onset of puberty while, at puberty, the once latent frontal lobe neuronet begins its growth while unestablished dendrite neuro-networks are pruned. The dendrite growth spurt adds a new dimension to developmental psychology and the recent concept of brain stimulation and growth. Frontal lobe development has implications for both developmental and abnormal psychology in that it also explains the phenomena of adolescent risk taking as well as the neurophysiology of impulsive behaviors and disorders. Another recent finding pertains to the role of the corpus callosum relevant to neuronal compensation and information retrieval. We now know that, in general, females have a denser neural network within the corpus callosum, one that approximates that of the frontal lobe, than do males. This helps to explain why certain seizure disorders afflict females more than males and why females are more likely to recover faster from strokes and other insults to the brain. This same mechanism of action within the corpus callosum involves accessing both hemispheres of the brain with more rapid access in the female brain than that in males. This mechanism of action may also help to explain why females with bipolar disorder are more prone to type I hypermania than males.

Our understanding of the role of glia cells (white matter) has expanded tremendously as well. Once thought to merely provide insulation for the neurons (gray matter), we now realize that glia cells do much more than this. They are a major component of the meninges, membranes that encase the brain providing the nutrients to the brain as well as its protection with the dura and blood/brain barrier. Perhaps the most significant glial cell is the astrocyte which plays a significant role within the blood/brain barrier and throughout the glia cells. They are star-shaped cells that comprise most of the glial cells in the brain. Their role is to regulate the chemical content of the extracellular space and actively remove (scavenge) many neurotransmitters from the synaptic cleft. It is also felt that astrocytes play a role in glucose distribution (glutamate) to neurons and the redirection of blood flow during neuronal up-regulation. Another important role for glia cells is in the development of the myelin sheath, a compact wrapping material that surrounds and insulates axons of some neurons. Insult (damage) to the myelin sheath is seen as one cause of seizure activity.

Clearly, a better understanding of the subcortical limbic system and its interaction with the cerebral cortex represents one of the areas of most significant discovery. Many of the structures of the limbic system were not fully understood until recently including that of the thalamus, hypothalamus, amygdale, hippocampus, septum and basal ganglia, especially their role in emotions, memory and certain aspects of movement. The thalamus plays an important role in relaying sensory information coming in and going out of the forebrain. It is the connector between the neocortex, where interpretations, or meaning, are conferred to our sensations, and the limbic system – the emotional/primitive portion of the brain. We now realize that the pituitary gland is not the *master gland* regulating the endocrine system and the secretion of hormones and certain neurotransmitters. Instead, it is the hypothalamus that regulates these functions via the pituitary gland. Briefly stated, the hypothalamus is involved with maintaining homeostasis by reading blood levels and providing neurocompensation whenever dysregulation occurs. The amygdale (shaped like a almond nut, hence its Greek name) is now seen as playing a major role in emotions notably those pertaining to sex, hunger and aggressive behaviors and fear reactions. The hippocampus (shaped like a couple of sea horses, hence its Greek name) plays a role in learning, memory retrieval and with alcohol withdrawal seizures.[4]

The septum (Greek for a partition) forms the wall between the fluid-filled lateral ventricles and is associated with rage. It also plays a role in neurotransmission between the hippocampus and the hypothalamus. The basal ganglia,of which the amygdale is a part, is a set of subcortical forebrain structures that play an important role in motor systems and neurotransmissions. It is part of the neuronal network that assists the thalamus in processing sensory motor activity to the neocortex for interpretation and meaning. Greater limbic structures relevant to impulsive behaviors include the substantia nigra (black area) which provides the major neurotransmitter, dopamine (D). Dysregulation in this network contributes to the motor disorders like Parkinson's disease. Another significant associated structure is the locus coeruleus, or blue area, located within the pons whose function is associated with the secretion of the major neurotransmitter, norepinephrine (NE). The reticular formation is yet another greater limbic structure. It provides a communication neuro network stemming from the medulla near the brain stem to the higher brain areas with the role of bridging the limbic system with the neocortex. The reticular formation is also seen as an important structure related to human emotions. It activates selective behavioral arousal such as a mother hearing her baby's cry over louder sounds and stimuli.

An understanding of the peripheral nervous system (PNS) is yet another critical area of concern when looking at human emotions and impulsive behaviors. The PNS is a division of the nervous system consisting of all the nerves not part of the CNS – that is the brain or spinal cord. It includes the autonomic nervous system (ANS) and its diametrically opposite components: the sympathetic and the parasympathetic nervous system. The sympathetic nervous system is the component of the ANS responsible for mobilizing the body's energy and resources during times of stress and arousal. This mechanism of action involves activation of the adrenal medulla to secrete norepinephrine (NE) and epinephrine (E or adrenalin), two excitatory catecholoamines whose actions influence the bronchi in the lungs, heart, veins, and arteries in order to increase blood flow to the muscles, the heart and the brain for quick response to the stress situation.[5]

The parasympathetic nervous system, the other branch of the autonomic nervous system, is associated with the conservation of the body's energy and resources during relaxed states and following sympathetic nervous system activation. A failure of the body to be able to enter the parasympathetic state following an autonomic stress reaction can lead to the General Adaptation Syndrome (GAS), a process articulated by the late Hans Selye who recognized the effects of excessive stress when the sympathetic mode of the ANS is not allowed to enter the parasympathetic mode in order to replenish the body of depleted glucose, lipids and neurotransmitters. As stated earlier, GAS has three phases: (1) alarm and activation of the sympathetic mode of the ANS, (2) resistance to parasympathetic input, and (3) exhaustion which can ultimately lead to death.[6]

The activation of the ANS involves the endocrine system and its relationship to the major neurotransmitters. Involved in this process are the pituitary anterior and posterior lobes, gonads, thyroid, parathyroid, adrenal cortex, adrenal medulla, pancreatic islets, and the intestinal mucosa. The major neurotransmitters relevant to human behavior include: (1) amino acid transmitters, the most common neurotransmitters in the brain, including glutamate and aspartate which are excitatory, along with gamma-aminobutyric acid (GABA) which has an inhibitory action; (2) acetycloline (Ach) a regulatory neurotransmitter found both in the brain and in the peripheral nervous system (PNS) that is involve in memory and the actins of skeletal and smooth muscles; (3) adenosine triphosphate (ATP), the energy source of cells which also acts as a neurotransmitter; (4) the catecholamines excitatory neurotransmitters, notable dopamine (D), epinephrine (E), and norepinephrine (NE), transmitters that function both in the brain and in the sympathetic nervous system (SNS); (5) serotonin (5-HT), a major regulatory neurotransmitter that acts in conjunction with other neurotransmitters either to up or down regulate neuronal actions; (6) peptides, chains of amino acids that function as neurotransmitters, neuromodulators, or hormones which are also known as neuropeptides.

The mechanism of action for neural transmission occurs at the cell level and involves the sodium-potassium pump where changes on the surface of the neuron (cellular membrane) initiate changes in the cell's "resting potential." This process of depolarization changes the resting potential charge from negative to positive, an action known as the "excitatory postsynaptic potential" (EPSP). When this action exceeds the internal resistance, known as the "threshold of excitation (TOE)," it sends an electrical current of about 65 to 70 millivolts down the axon activating the appropriate vesicle in the button of the soma hence releasing the appropriate neurotransmitter(s) into the synaptic gap. The myelin sheath enhances the action potential making for faster conductivity. Hyperpolarization, on the other hand, involves resistance to firing. Here, the "inhibitory postsynaptic potential (IPSP)" reinforces the neuron by slightly increasing the interior negative charge thereby inhibiting the cell from firing. This process is associated with the GABA and benzo anxioletic effect whereby GABA inhibits the firing of neurons by opening the chloride channels of the neuronal membrane causing a hyperpolarization that requires a greater depolarization to trigger an action potential.[7]

The role of the locus coeruleus (LC) is central in understanding the nature of traumatic stress and its associated feature notably panic attacks. The noradrenergic hypothesis holds that intense, recurring anxiety attacks are caused either by hypersensitive neurons in the locus coeruleus or by a dysfunction in the natural braking mechanism (hyperpolarization process), or both. This process occurs with the release of norepinephrine (NE) back upon itself in the same cell that released it in the first place. Once stimulated, the LC cell continues to fire alerting signals in the limbic system, uninhibited by the normal braking mechanism. Antipanic agents are thought to have their effect by normalizing the cells self-stimulation. Benzodiazepines (GABA agonist) serve to reinforce the braking effect but may not stop the LC from firing NE back on itself. Consequently malfunctioning within the CNS and PNS are increasingly addressed by the introduction of agents (medications) into the blood stream with the intent of modifying or normalizing the body's attempt to maintain homeostasis. Toward this end, medications/agents used to regulate these functions are of four basic types: (1) those that block postsynaptic receptors; (2) those that stimulate postsynaptic receptors; (3) those that block the neurotransmitter re-uptake pump; and (4) those agents that inhibit the neurotransmitter deactivating enzyme.[8]

The Neuropsychology of Human Behaviors

The American Psychiatric *Association's Diagnostic and Statistical Manual on Mental Disorders* (DSM) is an excellent source of psychological diagnoses associated with dementias, psychoses, depression, anxiety, sexual dysfunction, impulse control and substance abuse, as well as personality disorders. DSM disorders associated with impulsive behaviors include: dementias with delusions and depressed mood; schizophreniform disorder; schizoaffective disorder; delusional disorder, notably those of the erotomanic, grandiose, jealous and/or persecutory types; the hypermanic stage of bipolar I disorder; panic disorder; post-traumatic stress disorder; obsessive-compulsive disorder; dissociative identity disorder; the paraphilias; impulse-control disorders, including intermittent explosive type and pyromania; adjustment disorders with disturbance of conduct; and certain personality disorders, mainly paranoid, schizotypal, antisocial and borderline types.

Of these classifications, the ones most relevant to traumatic stress include the following disorders. The most significant classification is the anxiety disorders.

Agoraphobia: This is anxiety about, or avoidance of, places or situations from which escape might be difficulty, or embarrassing, or in which help is not perceived to be readily available. This condition is often linked to a Panic Disorder or other disorders where avoidance is a symptom.

Panic Disorder: Sudden recurrent unexpected attacks about which there is persistent concern.   This disorder can occur in conjunction with Agoraphobia. Symptoms include at least four of the following: (1) palpitations, pounding heart, or accelerated heart rate; (2) sweating; (3) trembling or shaking; (4) sensations of shortness of breath or smothering; (5) feeling of choking; (6) chest pain or discomfort; (7) nausea or abdominal distress; (8) dizziness or light headedness, feeling faint; (9) derealization or depersonalization; (10) fear of losing control or going crazy; (11) fear of dying; (12) paresthesias – a numbness or tingling sensation; (13) chills or hot flushes.

Specific Phobias: Significant anxiety provoked by exposure to a specific feared object or situation, often leading to avoidance behavior. The subtype of social phobias most relevant to traumatic stress is the "situational type" whereby fear is cued by a specific situation. This subtype is similar to Panic Disorder with Agoraphobia.

Social Phobia: Significant anxiety provoked by exposure to certain types of social or performance situations, often leading to avoidance behavior.

Obsessive-Compulsive Disorder (OCD): Obsession which causes marked anxiety or distress and/or compulsions which serve to neutralize the anxiety. This disorder generally begins in childhood and has a strong familial pattern and needs to be discerned from a OCD personality disorder.

Posttraumatic Stress Disorder (PTSD): The reexperiencing of an extremely traumatic event accompanied by symptoms of increased arousal and by avoidance of stimuli associated with the trauma. For a definitive PTSD diagnosis, the person needs to have been exposed to a traumatic event where: (1) the person experienced, witnessed, or was confronted with an event or events that involved actual or threatened death or serious injury, or a threat to the physical integrity of self or others; and (2) the person's response involved intense fear, helplessness, or horror. PTSD has three major classes of symptoms: (1) reexperiencing the traumatic event; (2) persistent avoidance of stimuli associated with the trauma and numbing of general responsiveness; and (3) persistent symptoms of increased arousal such as sleep difficulties, irritability or angry outburst, difficulty concentrating, hypervigilance and exaggerated startle response. PTSD is considered to be acute if the duration of symptoms are less than three months and chronic if the duration of symptoms are longer. Delayed onset is when the symptoms of PTSD occur at least six months following the traumatic event. Risk factors for PTSD include: pre-existing emotional disorders, notably depression and a family history of anxiety disorders; alcohol and drug abuse; a history of abuse and neglect within the family; an early separation from parents; and the lack of a strong social support network.

Acute Stress Disorder: These are symptoms similar to those of PTSD that occur immediately in the aftermath of an extremely traumatic event. If adequately treated, Acute Stress Disorder does not necessarily lead to PTSD. Conversely, if not treated, Acute Stress Disorder most likely will result in PTSD.

General Anxiety Disorder (GAD): Persistent and excessive anxiety and worry of at least six months duration. Females are more likely to suffer from GADs.

Anxiety Disorder due to a General Medical Condition: Prominent symptoms of anxiety that result from psychology consequences of a general medical condition such the loss of limbs due to a traumatic event.

Substance-Induced Anxiety Disorder: Prominent symptoms of anxiety resulting from a drug, a medication, or toxin exposure. Panic attacks, obsessions or compulsions, generalized anxiety and phobic symptoms are various manifestation of Substance-Induced Anxiety Disorder. These symptoms can occur during intoxication or withdrawal.

Other conditions related to anxiety include the following diagnoses:

Adjustment Disorders: Adjustment Disorders involve psychological responses to an identifiable stressor and generally reflects the autonomic neurological recompensation process which is initiated at the onset of the stressor and lasts approximately for six month duration. If not resolved during this period of neurocompensation, then the symptoms of anxiety and/or depression can result in a more pervasive problem that then needs to be reclassified based upon these persistent symptoms. Adjustments Disorders are: (1) with Depressed Mood associated with tearfulness or feelings of hopelessness; (2) with Anxiety where the predominant symptoms are nervousness, worry or jitteriness; (3) with Mixed Anxiety and Depressed Mood; (4) with Disturbances of Conduct where there is violation of rights of others or of major age-appropriate societal norms and rules; and (5) with Mixed Disturbances of Emotions and Conduct.

Conversion Disorder: This is when there is a sensory overload that overwhelms the CNS so that a diversionary voluntary motor or sensory function becomes the substitute target. These symptoms are not intentionally produced or feigned as in Factitious Disorders or Malingering and the symptom or deficit cannot be fully explained by a general medical condition. These types of symptoms can include motor deficits, sensory deficits, seizures or convulsions, or mixed presentations. Moreover, these conditions cause clinically significant distress or impairment in social, occupational, or other important areas of functioning.

Dissociative Amnesia: This reflects the inability to recall important personal information associated with a traumatic stressful nature. The disorder involves reversible memory impairment. The acute form of Dissociative Amnesia is more likely to occur during combat situations, natural disasters or other forms of severe trauma.

Depersonalization Disorder: The essential features of this disorder are persistent or recurrent episodes of feeling of detachment or estrangement from one's self- such as transcending one's body and observing it from without. Derealization, the sense that the external world is strange or unreal, may also be present. It is important to discern Depersonalization Disorder from similar symptoms that may be associated features of another anxiety disorder, including PTSD.

Mood Disorders are another classification of mental disorders associated with traumatic experiences, including war trauma. These disorders include both uni-polar and bipolar depressions. Depression is listed, along with Panic Attacks, as being among the most frequently diagnosed problems among those suffering from traumatic stress. Depression can be the result of a number of factors including being an enduring feature of an Adjustment Disorder or it may be due to premorbid or comorbid conditions. Mood disorders can also be associated features of substance abuse. The neurotransmitters Serotonin (5-HT), Norepinephrine (NE) and Dopamine (D) are associated with uni-polar depressive disorders although dysregulation in the hypothalamic-pituitary-adrenal axis apparently plays a role in the neuro-endocrine response to stress resulting in increased levels of the hormone cortisol.

Major Depression: This condition is characterized by one or more serious episodes where the conditions last at least two weeks. This condition significantly impairs one's personal life and social interactions and is manifested by a very low mood and an inability to experience pleasure at levels previously realized. Symptoms of major depression can include a sense of worthlessness, inappropriate guilt, shame or regret; a sense of helplessness, hopelessness, and despair, including suicidal ideations. Agitation and fatigue are other common elements of Major Depression. Sleep disturbances are common during the depressive episode. Major Depression is classified as being mild, moderate, or severe, with or without psychotic features. Major Depression has a higher prevalence among females.

Dysthymic Disorder: This condition is less severe than Major Depression but is more chronic in nature (at least two years duration). It has a pervasive melancholic feature with a strong familial pattern. The person usually can function adequately without major impairments or disruptions but feel that they are not enjoying life at the same level as others in within their social circle Double Depression is a term used to describe the incident of a Major Depressive episode experienced by someone already suffering from Dysthymia.

Bipolar I Disorder: This condition reflects the existence of both a Major Depression and Manic Episodes. In Bipolar I Disorders, the manic episode is major (hypermania) with significant psychological and behavioral consequences. There is a strong familial pattern with this disorder as well - with early onset associated with those with first-degree biological relatives also suffering from this disorder. When the Major Episode and Manic Episodes co-exist, the Manic Episode is treated first and then the depression otherwise the anti-depressive medications may exacerbate the manic episode. Bipolar Disorders occur about equally among females and males but with different outcomes and sequences. Behavioral disturbances associated with hypermanic episodes include impulsive behaviors and, in many cases, hypersexuality (from their normal baseline).

Bipolar II Disorder: Bipolar II Disorders do not manifest the extreme range of either depression or manic episodes. In fact, many with this diagnosis decline treatment since the euphoria experienced during the hypomanic episodes are pleasurable and endogenous, hence a legal "high". Many Bipolar II candidates find that they can work longer hours with less sleep and be more productive. The downside is that the endocrine system needs to replenish itself following the hypomanic episode generally resulting in a period of lethargy or melancholia. Besides, the chances for the onset of a hypermanic episode increases as the neuronal network and body organs become less plastic with age.

Cyclothymic Disorder: This condition reflects Bipolar II Disorders but to a lesser extent.

Mood Disorder due to a General Medical Condition: This condition is characterized by a prominent and persistent mood disturbance that appears to be a direct physiological consequence of a general medical condition.

Psychotic disorders include a class of diagnoses that involve serious thought disorders that are devoid of reality namely hallucinations, delusions and disorganized speech. War trauma and other significant stressors can exacerbate premorbid conditions that were latent up to that time. Moreover, extreme stress can push a person beyond his or her psychotic threshold causing a transitory condition that is reversible if treated effectively.

Schizophrenia: This thought disorder involves delusions, hallucinations, disorganized speech, grossly disorganized behaviors with Paranoid, Disorganized, Catatonic, Undifferentiated and Residual subtypes. The disorder has to have lasted at least six months for this diagnosis.

Schizophreniform Disorder: This diagnosis is used when the symptoms for Schizophrenia are manifested but have not been present for at least six months duration.

Schizoaffective Disorder: This diagnosis involves a comorbid mood disorder with Schizophrenic symptoms.

Delusional Disorder: This classification differs from Schizophrenic-type disorders in that it is characterized by nonbizarre delusions whereby the person otherwise looks and acts normal. Moreover, the delusional set is usually consistent overtime presenting in one of the following themes: erotomatic type, grandiose type, jealous type, persecutory type and/or somatic type.

Brief Psychotic Disorder: Often know in lay terms as a "nervous breakdown", a Brief Psychotic Disorder involves the sudden onset of at least one of the following thought disorders – delusions, hallucinations or disorganized speech. It is felt that persons already suffering from a Personality Disorder are at greater risk of a Brief Psychotic Disorder when encountering extremely stressful situations or events. This diagnosis would be the most likely form of psychotic disorder afflicting those suffering from war trauma. This condition can be effectively treated by a combination of medications and psychotherapy.

Shared Psychotic Disorder: An essential feature of this disorder is a delusion that develops in a person who is involved in a close relationship with another person who is susceptible to a delusional disorder. This condition can manifest itself in war stress situations among those with premorbid susceptibilities sharing an extremely stressful environment including rape and torture situations.

Substance-Induced Psychotic Disorder: This condition is usually transitory and is caused by the use of or withdrawal from substances including alcohol and other drugs that are likely to cause hallucinations, delusions or disorganized speech.

Psychotic Disorder due to a General Medical Condition: Here clinical symptoms such as hallucinations and delusions are associated features of a medical condition resulting in insults to the brain including head injuries or brain tumors. When associated with dementia this condition is often termed paraphrenia or organic hallucination. Traumatic Brain Injuries can result in either transitory or pervasive psychotic features.

Impulse-Control Disorders, notably the Intermittent Explosive Disorder is yet another potential diagnosis associated with untreated traumatic stress. The DSM states the essential features of the Intermittent Explosive Disorder as the occurrence of discrete episodes of the failure to resist aggressive impulses that result in serious verbal and/or physical outbursts of aggression directed toward others or to property. This disorder is not to be confused with a single explosive episode often termed, *running amok,* or better explained by an associated feature of another major mental disorder. It is also not to be confused with a premeditated criminal act of aggression attempting to be masked by a mental disorder.[9]

Another area of concern are the Personality Disorders (PD) which are not considered to be major mental disorders per se, but rather are the result of a person's socialization reflecting the development of one's character. The International Classification of Diseases (ICD-10) sees the behaviors that deviate from the culturally expected and accepted range as manifesting themselves in the areas of cognition, affectivity, control over impulses and the gratification of needs and in the manner of relating to others and in the handling of interpersonal situations. Both the ICD and DSM state that these behaviors cannot be better explained by other mental disorders, including organic brain injury or brain injury. The DSM series lists Personality Disorders as Axis II classifications exempting them from the same legal protection afforded Axis I, major clinical disorders. Personality Disorders are disruptive behaviors resulting from enduring patterns of inner experiences and behaviors that deviate markedly from their cultural and social norms. Personality Disorders fall into three clusters.

Cluster A: These are commonly known as odd behaviors and include Paranoid (irrational suspicions and mistrust), Schizoid (a-social, introspective, loner) and Schizotypal (odd behaviors and thinking) PDs.

Cluster B: These are seen as dramatic behaviors and include Antisocial (disregard for law and rights of others), Borderline (instability in relationships, impulsivity), Histrionic (pervasive attention-seeking including sexual behaviors) and Narcissistic (sense of grandiosity, need for admiration, self-centered without empathy for feelings of others) PDs.

Cluster C: These are the anxious behaviors and include Avoidant (social inhibition, extremely sensitive to criticism of self), Dependent (pervasive psychological attachment on others), and Obsessive-Compulsive (rigid conformity to rules and morality, excessive orderliness) PDs.[10]

A common theme among those with mental disorders associated with traumatic stress is the susceptibility of impulsive outbursts. Common to these impulsive-prone disorders is a dysregulation in the neurotransmission between the neocortex and the greater limbic system. Some these malfunctions are due to genetic factors while others are self-induced by such actions as substance abuse. Nonetheless, the new computerized brain scanning technologies have allowed for better insights into the mechanism of these behaviors hence leading to new advances in clinical psychopharmacology in order to better treat these conditions. Neuronal malfunction at the synapse is indicative of a number of problems. The initial synthesis and production of the neurotransmitter may be inhibited not allowing for a sufficient amount of the neurotransmitter to be released into the synaptic cleft. Certain biological and genetic based disorders may also play a role here resulting in either the facilitation or inhibition of the release of certain neurotransmitters from the presynaptic vesicles – a phenomenon associated with bipolar I disorders, obsessive-compulsive disorder, paraphilias, and post-traumatic stress disorder.   On the other hand, these conditions may involve problems at the postsynaptic receptors contributing to disorders like schizophrenia.   The neuron may overly conserve the neurotransmitter via premature reabsorption of the agent back into the presynaptic vesicles, a process known as re-uptake.   Presynaptic and postsynaptic surface inhibitory receptors may inhibit nerve electrical impulses acting as braking function.   This process can lead to either up-regulation and decreased neuronal excitability or down-regulation resulting in increased sensitivity.   Another dysfunction, one similar to the re-uptake malfunction, is when the astrocytes treat the neurotransmitters within the synaptic cleft as waste material and dissolve them before they can make the appropriate connection with their designated postsynaptic receptors.

The major neurotransmitters associated with impulse control are norepinephrine (NE), dopamine (D), and serotonin (5-HT).   Norepinephrine and dopamine are major excitatory neurotransmitters while serotonin is a regulatory neurotransmitter augmenting the action of other neurotransmitters.   The major NE pathways are located in the frontal lobe of the neocortex locus coeruleus with linkage to the hippocampus and thalamus.   As stated earlier, norepinephrine plays a significant role in arousal and a lack of NE is associated with certain forms of depression.   A better understanding of the dopamine pathways has led to the development of effective medications that are also more tolerable due to fewer side effects.   Five types of dopamine receptors are now recognized.   D1's action pathway is postsynaptic in the striatum while D2's action pathway is both presynaptic and postsynaptic in the striatum and limbic areas.   D3's action pathway is in the limbic system while D4's action pathway is in the frontal lobe, mid-brain and amygdale and D5's action pathway is in the hypothalamus and hippocampus.

Serotonin, due to its regulatory nature, can act either in an excitatory or inhibitory capacity in conjunction with other neurotransmitters.   Seven serotonin receptor sites have been identified.   5-HT1A's action pathway is located in the hippocampus and in the raphe nuclei and is associated with anxiety, depression, appetite and sexual arousal. 5-HT1B's action pathway is located in the basal ganglia and is associated with anxiety.   5–HT1C's action pathway is located in the striatum, limbic areas and the choroid plexus and is associated with appetite while 5-HT1D's action pathway is located in the nigra and pallidum and is also associated with appetite. 5-HT2's action pathway is located in the cerebral cortex and is associated with cognitive functioning and hallucinogenesis while 5–HT3's action pathway is located in the cortex, limbic areas and the hindbrain and is associated with anxiety, memory and cognitive functions.   The 5-HT4's action pathway is located in the hippocampus and the cerebral cortex and its association with behaviors has not yet been fully determined.[11]

Recent research has articulated the psychobiological mechanisms of traumatic stress.   One such study by Dennis Charney was published in February

2004 in *The American Journal of Psychiatry*. The article expanded on the relationship of psychological and physiological process related to extreme stress – a process known as the *allostatic load*. Charney notes that a number of neurotransmitters, neuropeptides and hormones are linked to the acute psychobiological response to stress as well as to the long-term psychiatric outcomes: Cortisol; CRH and its role in activating the hypothalamic-pituitary-adrenal axis and hypothalamic-pituitary-adrenal-gonadic axis; Locus Coeruleus-Norepinephrine System; Neuropeptide Y; Galanin; Dopamine; Serotonin; Benzodiazepine Receptors; Gonadal Steroids. The response of these agents and their functional interactions during extreme stress, the allostatic load, is contingent upon the balance among multiple inhibitory and excitatory neurochemical inputs. Of importance to traumatic stress, notably war stress, is the neural mechanism of anxiety and fear. Charney states that fear conditioning is a common element of PTSD and major depression and can activate vivid recall of memories of traumatic events, autonomic hyperarousal and even flashbacks. Untreated, these psychobiological processes lead to dysfunctional social behaviors including social isolation and avoidance – even suicide ideations.[12] Another study in *The American Journal of Psychiatry* (2009) linked the serotonin transporter gene (SLC6A4) promoter polymorphisms to the susceptibility to post-traumatic stress. On-going research shows promise in providing a clearer picture of the role of major neurotransmitters, like serotonin, play in traumatic stress. A promising area for treating specific symptoms of traumatic stress lies in new advances in psychopharmacology.[13]

Neurodysregulation has been greatly advanced through new medications beginning with the SSRI's (selective serotonin reuptake inhibitors) which started with Prozac (fluoxetine) and continued with Zoloft (setraline), Paxil (paroxetine), Celexa (citalopram), and Luvox (fluvoxomine), and others; and continued with NDRI's (norepinephrine and dopamine reuptake inhibitors) like Wellbutrin (bupropion); SNRI's (serotonin and norepinephrine reuptake inhibitors) like Effexor (venlafaxine); SARI's (serotonin antagonist reuptake inhibitors) like Serzone (nefazodone) and Desyrel (trazodone); SND's (serotonin and norepinephrine dishibibitors) such as Remeron (mirtazepine); and new grade neurolipics such as Orap (primozide), Risperdal (risperidone), Zyprexa (olanzapine) and Serlect (sertindole). These medications have a more direct approach replacing the "shotgun" approach of older psychotropic medications like the tricyclics: imipramine (Tofranil), desipramine (Norpramin), amitriptyline (Elavil) and nortiptyline (Avenlyl, Pamelor) which are associated with a higher incidence of unwanted side effects and could also lead to suicide when overdosed.

The newer neurolipics also have a more direct mechanism of action than those used in the past – chlorpromazine (Thorazine), thioridazine (Mellaril), trifluoperazine (Stelazine), fluphenazine (Prolixin) and even haloperidol (Haldol). Again, the newer neurolipics also have few side effects including sedation. Even then, certain medications are being used for multiple diagnoses such as the mood stabilizers with lithium carbonate widely used to augment the efficacy of other psychotropic medications. Other medications in this class, such as carbamazine (Tegretol), divalproex (Depakote), gabapenin (Neurontin), lamatrigine (Lamictal) and topiramate (Topamax) are being used not only for seizure activity but as alternative medications for bipolar and impulse control disorder as well. And rapid benzodiazepines like alprazolam (Xanax) and lorazepam (Ativan) work well for panic attacks if taken responsibly and only as needed (PRN). Buspirone (BuSpar), a non-addictive agent that acts like a benzodiazepine, is also indicated for long-term use for low-grade depression (Dysthymic Disorder), adjustment disorders and Generalized Anxiety Disorder. New atypical benzodiazepines for sleep disorders have also surfaced such as zolpidem (Ambien) but need to be closely monitored for long-term use especially among clients who are likely to abuse alcohol.[14]

Generally speaking, impulse control disorders involve dopamine and, to a lesser extent, norepinephrine, with action within the greater subcortical limbic region and serotonin within the frontal lobe in the neocortex. With this understanding of impulsive behaviors, treatments now indicate medications (mood stabilizers) that control the impulses emitted from the subcortical greater limbic system as well as SSRI's for regulation within the frontal lobe. The understanding here is that the limbic dysregulation needs to be controlled first and then serotonal regulation is required to mediate frontal lobe activity relevant to executive functioning. However, medications themselves may also be the cause of impulsive behaviors. Studies conducted on the role of lipid reducing medications for the purpose of reducing the chances of heart attacks also showed that by lowering lipids this had the unintended effect of increasing impulsivity. These studies showed that anti-lipid agents designed to treat coronary heart disease have a tendency to restrict serotonin production at the cellular level thereby increasing the chance for impulsive behaviors including homicide and suicide.[15]

The first challenge to determining the presence of a mental disturbance among war victims, whether they be military veterans or civilians, is to attempt to discern between transitory and pervasive disorders. It is also important to attempt to separate personality disorders from clinical diagnoses, although this is not always an easy task especially when pre-war baselines are not readily available. A third differential needs to be made concerning substance-related disorders since this often complicates determining which diagnoses are primary and which are associated or co-morbid features of the presenting mental problem.

Transitory mental disorders include the adjustment disorders which are quite common for returning veterans or refugees. A serious consequence of untreated transitory disorders is anomic suicide. These disorders, along with the V-Codes (Z-Codes in some European versions of the DSM), reflect conditions if left untreated could manifest as a major clinical disorder. Fortunately transitory mental conditions often lend themselves to effective treatments namely psychopharmacology and cognitive behavioral therapies. The pervasive mental illnesses, notably those that are prone to be of a genetic or organic origin, such as major depression, bipolar depression, schizophrenia, delusional disorders, obsessive-compulsive disorder and impulse control disorders, including paraphilia, are more complex to treat and often require a long-term treatment protocol. Included here are psychological outcomes from traumatic brain injuries (TBIs). Often diffuse (closed) head injuries are more difficult to identify than those injuries with a focal injury. Symptoms are associated with not only the type of TBI (diffuse of local) but are specific to the region of the brain insult.

With mild TBIs, the person may remain conscious or only lose consciousness for a few seconds or minutes. These are often concussions and present with headache, vomiting, nausea, poor motor control, dizziness and balance problems, lightheadedness, blurred vision, ringing in the ears, fatigue/lethargy and somatic difficulties. Behavioral problems include mood changes, confusion, memory problems and difficulty concentrating or thinking. Moderate or severe TBIs, while more obvious, also present with a host of physiological and psychological problems including persistent headaches, vomiting/nausea, convulsions, slurred speech, aphasia, weakness or numbness of limbs, poor motor coordination, confusion, and agitation or impulsive outbursts. Behavioral problems can include deficits in social judgment, inappropriate social interactions and cognitive problems associated with memory, attention and executive functioning. The treatment and rehabilitation needs of TBI patients include protocols that address: improving memory and problem solving skills; managing stress and emotional problems, including temper and impulsive outbursts; and providing social and occupational skills. Support groups are also highly recommended if only to let the traumatized victim realize that he or she is not suffering alone.[16]

Chapter Glossary

Acetylcholine (ACh): A prevalent neurotransmitter in both the brain, where it helps regulate memory, and in the peripheral nervous system (PNS) where it controls the actions of skeletal and smooth muscles. Its action is both excitatory and inhibitory.

Action Potential: A nerve impulse; temporary reversal of the interior membrane's electrical state from negative to positive relevant to the action of the sodium/potassium pump (ion exchange). Also termed – *depolarization.*

Agonist: A substance or agent that activates a receptor.

Allostatic Load: The process of the body and brain reacting to extreme stress: the protective and survival reactions and responses to acute stress.

Amino Acids: The building blocks of proteins; an acid containing an amine group (NH2); one of the components of peptides.

Amino Acid Transmitters: The most prevalent transmitter within the brain. These neurotransmitters include glutamate and aspartate, which are excitatory, and glycine and gamma-aminobutkyric acid (GABA), that are inhibitory.

   Amnesia: Dysregulation of the hippocampus due to some insult. Anterograde
Amnesia involves new memory while Retrograde Amnesia involves past

memory. Anterograde Amnesia usually results in permanent memory loss while
Retrograde Amnesia can be recovered.
   Post-traumatic amnesia: due to heal injuries, closed or open;
   Dissociative amnesia: due to severe sensory traumatic input that the
   CNS cannot process;
   Blackouts: anterograde amnesia due to bout drinking;
   Drug-induced amnesia: intentionally induced amnesia in order for the
   patient to forget medical procedure or for the purpose of improving
   one's chance for recovery from some intrusive event;
   ECT therapy: induced seizures that cause mimic amnesia derived from
   seizures.
Amygdale: A forebrain structure (temporal lobe) and important component of
the limbic system regarding emotions.
Anabuse: Trade name for disulfiram, a drug that prevents the breakdown of
acetaldehyde into acetic acid, and which therefore causes people to get sick if
they come into contact with alcohol.
Antagonists: A substance or agent that inhibits or blocks the action of an
agonist.
Aphasia: The loss of the ability to use or understand words – often associated
with traumatic head injuries.
ARASA (Ascending Reticular Activating System): System of heavily
interconnected neurons extending from the medulla into the forebrain that plays
a significant role in autonomic nervous system (ANS) responses.
Aspartate: An amino acid, used as a neurotransmitter.
Astrocyte: Large, star-shaped cell which makes up most of the glial cells (white
matter) in the human brain.   They regulate the chemical content of the
extracellular space and actively remove (scavage) many neurotransmitters from
the synaptic cleft. They also play a role in the distribution of glucose to very
active neurons and redirect blood flow to active regions of the brain.
ATP (Adenosine Triphosphate): A chemical the body uses as its main way of
delivering energy; also used as a neurotransmitter.
Basal Ganglia: Set of subcortical forebrain structures including the caudate
nucleus, putamen, and globus pallidus: four masses of gray matter located deep
in the cerebral hemispheres – the caudate, lentiform, the amygdaloin nuclei and
the claustrum.   It plays an important part in motor systems and
neurotransmission.
BBB (Blood/Brain Barrier): Diffusional barrier created by astrocytes and cells
in the walls of the blood vessels within the brain; prevents most blood-borne
substances from passing from the blood-stream into the brain.
Biogenic Amine: Neurotransmitter containing an amine group (NH2), such as
acetylcholine (Ach), serotonin (5-HT), epinephrine (E), norepinephrine (NE),
and dopamine (D).

Brain: Part of the Central Nervous System (CNS) that consists of one trillion cells (100 billion neurons and 900 billion glia cells). The human brain weights about 3 pounds with three major components – forebrain, midbrain and

hindbrain and four basic lobes – frontal, parietal, temporal and occipital. The limbic system is referred to as the primitive or emotional component while the cerebral cortex is known as the thinking or reasoning component.

Cholinergic: Pertaining to the actions of the neurotransmitter acetylcholine (Ach).

Catecholamines: Excitatory neurotransmitters – dopamine (D), epinephrine (E), and norepinephrine (NE) that function in both the brain and in the sympathetic nervous system (SNS).

Central Nervous System (CNS): The brain and the spinal cord.

Cingulate gyrus: A component of the limbic system; encircling the hippocampus and other limbic structures.

Citric Acid Cycle: A complex process of actions involving the oxidative metabolism of pyruvic acid in creating energy within the body. It is the main pathway of terminal oxidation for carbohydrates as well as fats and proteins.

Comorbidity: The occurrence of more than one disease at the same time in the same person. This can include a mental disorder and an independent physical disorder or multiple mental and/or physical disorders.

Confabulation: Attempts to fill in the gaps due to memory loss from other cues often involving inappropriate words.

Corpus Callosum: Compact neuronal network connecting the cerebral hemispheres of the brain: the great commissure of the brain between the cerebral hemispheres.

Cortisol: A glucocorticold released by the adrenal gland that helps maintain homeostatis by regulating certain enzymes. During stress, cortisol plays a significant role in increasing blood glucose levels and elevating blood pressure: it mobilizes and replenishes energy stores; it increases arousal, vigilance, focused attention and memory formation; it inhibits the growth and reproductive system; and contains the immune system.

Dendrite: Tree-like protrusions from the soma (body) of a neuron; along with the soma, constitutes the receiving zone for messages from other cells.

Diencephalon (between-brain): Section of the forebrain that includes the thalamus and hypothalamus – major components of the limbic system.

Dopamine (D): A major neurotransmitter, one of the catecholamines. Synthesized by the adrenal gland. Associated with psychosis and movement disorders like Parkinson.

Downregulation: A decrease in the number of sensitivity of receptors as a regulatory mechanism to compensate for increased activation of the receptors.

Epinephrine (E): Chemical that acts as an excitatory neurotransmitter, one of the catecholamines. Adrenalin is a symptom of epinephrine and plays a major role in activation of the sympathetic nervous system (SNS).

Endocrine System: Organs that secrete a substance (hormone) directly into the bloodstream in order to regulate the cellular activity of certain other organs know as glands.

Electroencephalograph (EEG): Device that measures electric impulses and neuronal activity in the brain.

Encephalitis: Inflammation of the brain.

Endogenous: Self-produced, produced from within.

Endogenous Depression: Depression that originates within the body and not as a reaction to outside events.

Endorphins: Category of neurotransmitters that stimulate the same receptors as opiates (endogenous morphine).

Enzyme: Protein that controls the rate of chemical reactions in the body.

Focal Lesions (Hematomas): Blood injuries in or around the brain. An intracerebral hemorrhage is bleeding in the brain tissue while extraaxial lesions include: epidural hematomas, subdural hematomas, subarachnoid hematomas, and intraventricular hemorrhaging.

Gamma-Aminobutyric Acid (GABA): The major inhibitory neurotransmitter (amino acid) in the brain whose primary function is to inhibit the firing of neurons.

Ganglion/Ganglia: Small encapsulated clusters of neuronal cells that direct internal muscles and glands – usually located entirely outside the CNS – in the sympathetic nervous system (SNS). GABA is associated with Anxiety Disorders, notably Panic Disorders.

General Adaptation Syndrome (GAS): Hans Selyes's description of the cycle of excessive stress that does not allow the sympathetic mode of the Autonomous Nervous System (ANS) to replenish itself by accessing the parapsympathetic mode. GAS has three phases: (1) Alarm, (2) resistance, and (3) exhaustion.

Galanin: A peptide containing 30 amino acids that is involved in learning and memory, pain control, food intake, neuroendocrine control and cardiovascular regulation – processes associated with anxiety.

Glia (brain glue): White matter in the brain that insulates and nurtures the brain neurons: the non-nervous or supporting tissue of the brain and spinal cord.

Glucocorticoids: A major adrenal stress hormone which includes cortisol.

Glucose (brain fuel): A simple sugar that is the main fuel of vertebrate neurons: considered to be a significant carbohydrate in body metabolism.

Glutamate: Chemical that acts as a neurotransmitter, generally as an excitatory neurotransmitter – the most common neurotransmitter yet discovered in the mammalian brain.

Gray Matter (brain neurons): Areas of the nervous system with a high density of cell bodies and dendrites, some myelinated.

Hepatic: Pertaining to the liver.

Hippocampus: Region of the limbic system that is thought to play a role in learning and memory retrieval as well as in alcohol withdrawal seizures.

Histamine: Chemical with numerous functions in the body, including that of a neurotransmitter.

Homeostasis: The body's self-regulatory mechanisms that maintains stability and equilibrium.

Hormone: Chemical secreted by a gland and conveyed by the blood to other organs whose activity it influences; some act both as hormones and as neurotransmitters.

Hypothalamus: Region of the brain (limbic system) that is involved with basic behavioral and physiological functions. It assesses blood-levels and maintains homeostasis.

Korsakoff's Syndrome: Brain damage with resulting amnesia due to the effects of long term alcoholism and malnutrition (B12 deficiency).

Limbic System: A group of brain structures, including the amygdale, hippocampus, septum and basal ganglia that work in alliance to help regulate emotions, memory and certain aspects of movement.

Locus Coeruleus (LC): Located within the pons, a concentrated set of neural cell bodies whose axons secrete the excitatory neurotransmitter – norepinephrine (NE).

Long-Term Memory (everyday memory): This memory is long lasting with unlimited capacity. This is the final phase of memory in which information storage may last for hours to lifetime.

Luteinizing Hormone (LH): Hormone secreted by the anterior lobe of the hypophysis that stimulates development of the corpus luteum.

Luteinizing Hormone release Hormone: A hormone produced in the hypothalamus that controls the release and synthesis of the luteinizing hormone.

Melatonin: A hormone, converted from serotonin (5-HT) in the pineal gland that when released into the bloodstream effects physiological changes related to time and lighting cycles – the circadian rhythm.

Myelin Sheath: Compact wrapping material (glia cells) that surrounds and insulated axons of some neurons, notably in the frontal lobe and corpus callosum.

Neuroleptics: Anti-psychotic agents/medications.

Neuropeptide Y: A neuropeptide consisting of 36 amino acids – one of the most abundant peptide found in the brain and which is involved with the amygdale relevant to anxiety.

Neuron: CNS and PNS cells that receive information via neurotransmission (chemical messengers) by conducting electrochemical impulses through a neuronal network (neuronet).

Neurotransmitter(NT): Chemical released by nerve cells (neurons) at a synapse for the purpose of relaying information (electrical impulses activate these chemical messengers that either excite, inhibit or regulate).

Neurofibrillary Tangles: Skeins of microtubules that have proliferated inside a brain neuron and eventually replaces the neuron, making the cell nonfunctional, contributing to a form of Dementia know as Alzheimer's Disease.

Neuromodulator: A substance that modifies the function or effects of a neurotransmitter.

Norepinephrine (NE): A catecholamine, produced both in the brain (locus coeruleus) and in the peripheral nervous system (PSN) -(sympathetic division of the autonomic nervous system (ANS). Associated with depression and anxiety disorders.

Parasympathetic Nervous System: A branch of the autonomic nervous system (ANS) concerned with the conservation of the body's energy and resources

during relaxed states following sympathetic nervous system activation. A failure of the body to activate the parasympathetic response following extreme stress can lead to what Selye termed the General Adaptation Syndrome (GAS).

Peptides: Chains of amino acids functioning as neurotransmitters, neuromodulators, or hormones, also know as neuropeptides.

Peripheral Nervous System (PNS): A division of the nervous system consisting of all the nerves not part of the brain or spinal cord. The PNS includes the sympathetic nervous system and the parasympathetic system.

Pituitary Gland: Endocrine gland attached to the hypothalamus; its secretions regulate the activity of many other hormonal glands.

Receptor: Neuron specialized to be highly sensitive to a specific neurotransmitter whose point of contact is referred to as the receptor site.

Reticular Formation: Network of neurons in the medulla and higher brain areas that are important for select behavior arousal such as mother hearing her baby's cry over louder sounds.

Renal: Pertaining to the kidney.

Septum: A structure of the telecephalon – the part of the limbic system that forms the wall between the fluid-filled lateral ventricles.

Serotonin (5–HT): 5-hydroxytryptamine – the major regulatory neurotransmitter. A tryptophan derivative with locations in the basal ganglia, limbic system, brain stem, spinal cord, cortex, gut, platelets and the cardiovascular system. 5-HT is associated with depression, sleep and perception.

Short-Term Memory (immediate memory): This input lasts less than a minute but can be retained longer with continual rehearsal. It has a limited capacity of about 5 to 9 items.

State-Dependent Memory (Flashback Memory): Recall of information stored under a particular state of emotion or arousal that will be readily retrieved when again subject to these stimuli.

Substantia Nigra: A concentrated set of neural cells, located in the midbrain, that secrete the neurotransmitter – Dopamine (D).

Sympathetic Nervous System (SNS): A branch of the autonomic nervous system responsible for mobilizing the body's energy and resources during times of stress and arousal.

Synapse: The area of contact between the axon of a presynaptic neuron and the dendrites or soma (body) of a postsynaptic neuron – the site of information transfer between nerve cells.

Telecephalon: The portion of the forebrain containing the cerebral cortex.

Thalamus: The portion of the diencephalon, serving as a relay station for almost all sensory information coming in and out of the forebrain whose role is to interpret and give meaning to incoming stimuli.

Traumatic Brain Injury: An injury incurred when an external force injuries the brain resulting in either a closed or open (penetrating) injury or insult. Also known as intracranial injuries.

Upregulation: An increase in the number of sensitivity of receptors as a method of compensation for situations resulting in a decreased activation of receptors.

White Matter: The bulk of the brain consisting of some 900 billion glia cells.

Chapter Four

Dimensions of Gulf War Trauma

Introduction

Armed conflicts have led to medical innovations as a response to the changing nature of the combat situations resulting in lifesaving measures that greatly enhanced the survival rate among the wounded. One such innovation was the establishment of Mobile Army Surgical Hospitals (MASH units), an idea that was conceived at the end of World War II but not implemented until the Korean War. These were fully staffed, portable, mobile medical units brought to forward combat areas just outside of enemy artillery range. The use of helicopters during the Korean War allowed for quicker battlefield evacuations to these MASH units. Seven MASH units were deployed during the Korean War. MASH units continued to be used in Vietnam and in the Gulf Wars. Indeed, the MASH model became the norm for military and civilian trauma care in the United States and the rest of the developed world. MASH units have evolved along with the ever changing combat situations with the current adaptations made in 2005 to Combat Support Hospitals (CSH) which are even smaller than the original MASH units and are designed to better facilitate the needs of brigade combat teams. The medical demands of these units went beyond surgical interventions to include treatment for toxic poisoning such as Agent Orange during Vietnam and the mysterious Gulf War Syndrome from the First Gulf War. With the Second Gulf War, traumatic head injuries, sexual assaults and suicide ideations have joined the mix of immediate medical/clinical care.[1]

Another dramatic change between the two major *Cold War* conflicts, Korea and Vietnam, is the changing nature of the U.S. military and its transformation from a mix of volunteers and draftees to an "all-voluntary" military force. The "draft" was discontinued in 1973, at the conclusion of the major ground operations in Vietnam. However, this did not do away with the Selective Service System and all males between ages 18 and 25 are still compelled to register so as to provide a readily available force if needed. During the colonial era, conscription was a local matter with each of the Thirteen Colonies creating its own militia. This system remained following the creation of the Republic and into the U.S. Civil War with both the Union and Confederacy instituting a draft. However, the draft was now administered by either the Union or the

Confederacy instead of the states within these entities. A major problem with this system was that draftees could provide substitutes, or buy out of their service obligation.

The prototype for the modern draft began with World War I when President Woodrow Wilson got Congress to pass the Selective Service Act of 1917. This Act eliminated the shortfalls of the previous system by prohibiting substitutions or the purchase of exemptions. Still, the selection was administered by local boards and every male, regardless of race or ethnicity; between ages 20 and 31 were required to register for the draft. Even then the draft was selective along class lines. The continuation of the draft following World War I provided the United States with a readily available, if not adequately trained, force at the time of its entry into World War II. This was due to passage of the Selective Training and Service Act of 1940 (STSA). The STSA required that all males between ages 21 and 45 enter the draft pool. Another change was that the selection for active duty from the registered draft pool was now done at the national level by lottery. During this draft period, 1940 to 1947, some 11 million men were inducted into military service. Those who served in combat areas were conscripted for the "duration" of the conflict.[2]

The second peacetime draft was instituted in 1948 with the Selective Service Act of 1948 (SSA) that now compelled all males between the ages of 18 and 26 to register. It also allowed for the drafting of medical personnel, a condition known as the "Doctor Draft", an important element in the care of wounded troops and the staffing of MASH units. The draft provided over a million and a half men during the Korean Conflict (1950-1953). The demands during the UN Korean police action led to passage of the Universal Military Training and Service Act in 1951 which now lowered the age requirement for the draft to 18 and extended the service commitment to two years. In 1955, in anticipation of future Cold War engagements, Congress passed the Reserve Forces Act which was designed to improve the National Guard and reserve systems now requiring a six-year service commitment for volunteers and draftees alike. This service would be a combination of active duty (two years for draftees; three or four years for enlisted volunteers; 6 months with active reserve for reserve personnel) with the remaining time being served in either an active or standby reserve status. This was the situation during the Vietnam War in which the U.S. was involved in from 1959 until 1975. While there was considerable anti-draft and anti-war protests in all the U.S. conflicts from the Revolutionary War to the Korean War, Vietnam was different due mainly to the universal media coverage of these protests coupled with the social unrest associated with racial and class biases inherent in American society at that time. Richard Nixon promised an end to the unpopular draft as part of his 1968 presidential campaign seeing this as a means for diminishing the anti-Vietnam War protests. The draft effectively ended in 1973 with the advent of the "All Volunteer Military Force." The National Guard now became the reserve force to augment deficiencies in volunteers into active duty units of the Army and Air Force. Both the U.S.

Marine Corps and U.S. Navy would have to draw on their reserve units to augment their regular force levels.[3]

The U.S. National Guard

A consequence of both the Reserve Forces Act and the unpopularity of the Vietnam War led to an increased membership within the National Guard. Given that the National Guard was seldom used during the long Vietnam conflict joining the Army National Guard or Air Force National Guard became popular legal means for avoiding the draft and, consequently, service in Vietnam or anywhere else outside of their state or territory. The National Guard is an outgrowth of the Colonial Militia tracing their origin the creation of the Massachusetts Bay Colony militia regiment created in December 1648. The new Republic formalized the state militias with the Militia Act of 1792 that recognized the President's authority to activate the militia for federal use in times of national interest such as wars and insurrections. The first use of this federal authority was during the War of 1812. Then in 1862, during the U.S. Civil War, the Militia Act was expanded to include blacks within their ranks (free blacks and emancipated slaves). The post Civil War Reconstruction era witnessed yet another modification under Title 18 of the U.S. Code (Section 1385) with the Posse Comitatus Act of June 1878. The intention of this Act was to restrict the role of the occupying Union army in the former Confederate states especially in those areas deemed more appropriate under state's right, including domestic law enforcement. This restricted use of federal or federalized military or militias allowed for the emergence of the *Jim Crow* laws governing segregation in the South, a process that was not adequately addressed until the Civil Rights Acts of the mid-1960s.[4]

The Militia Act of 1903 made the armed state and territorial militias the primary organized reserve forces in the U.S. military. This Act also changed the name of these militias to that of the Army National Guard (ARNG). In 1916, as war raged in Europe and Mexico, the National Defense Act of 1916 merged the National Guard and the Army Reserve along with the Regular Army into a composite whole deemed the Army of the United States, thus allowing for quick mobility without the cost of maintaining a large permanent military force. This new organizational structure prepared the National Guard for action during the Mexican Revolution of 1910-1920, notably the Punitive Expedition against Mexican General Poncho Villa in 1916-1917, hence preparing it for the ensuing fight in France during World War I where the National Guard made up 40 percent of the combat divisions serving in France. President Harry S. Truman was a National Guard artillery officer during World War I. The proven success of the National Guard as a ready reserve force led to the establishment of a federal chief of the National Guard under the 1920 amendments to the National Defense Act. The National Guard provided 19 Army Divisions during World War II and over 140, 000 Guardsmen were mobilized during the Korean Conflict. The creation of the U.S. Air Force from the Army Air Corps in 1947 also led to the creation of the Air National Guard as a reserve unit of the U.S. Air Force. President George W. Bush joined the Texas Air National Guard during the Vietnam era. Only the 113th Light Maintenance Company of the Army National Guard was mobilized from Texas during the Vietnam War. The U.S. Navy and U.S. Marine Corps do not have National Guard or militia affiliates.[5]

Following the Korean War, the National Guard resorted back to it main function of a state militia serving one week-end a month with a two-week annual training. All 50 states have a National Guard component. The Governor appoints the Adjutant General who heads the National Guard. The rank of the Adjutant General, even in the smallest states, was that of a Brigade General but this was elevated to that of Major General in the early 21st century with the increased use of the National Guard in the Second Gulf War. The federally-appointed Chief of the National Guard Bureau, essentially the Commanding General of the National Guard, was subsequently elevated to that of a four-star general. The state governors are the Commander-in-Chief of their respective Guard units unless elements of the Guard are called up for federal duty. Only Guard units, and not individual Guard members, can be federalized. Federalized guard units then fall under the U.S. Department of Defense where the President is the Command-in-Chief. At the state level, governors can activate the Guard for domestic emergencies, including riots, and disasters like hurricanes, earthquakes, forest fires, and floods, and for rescue operations. The 1987 Montgomery Amendment to the National Defense Authorization Act states that a governor cannot withhold consent to the federalization the state's Guard unit for duty outside the United States. This law was upheld by the United States Supreme Court in 1990 allowing for the federal call-up of Guard units for peace-keeping duties in addition to combat duties. Only about 7,000 National Guard personnel served during the Vietnam War out of the over 12,000 mobilized in May 1968. This represented the lowest percentage of Guard combatants in any major conflict involving U.S. troops since the Guards formal inception in 1903. Some 63,000 National Guard personnel were involved in the First Gulf War in 1990 while others served in UN and NATO peacekeeping missions in the Balkans, notably Bosnia and Kosovo. However, the number of federally deployed National Guard units rose considerably following the terrorists attacks on the United States on September 11, 2001. The ensuing demands for national security and the corresponding War on Terrorism saw a marked increase in the deployment of National Guard units at both the state and federal levels. As of April 2006, 139,733 Guard personnel had served in Iraq out of the more than 248,000 federally mobilized following the terrorists attacks of 9/11/01.[6]

The First Gulf War – Kuwait and Iraq

The First Gulf War began when Iraqi leader, Saddam Hussein invaded Kuwait on August 2, 1990. The primary reason for the invasion of Kuwait was most likely economical given that Iraq just ended a long, brutal and costly war with its invasion of Iran in 1980, a conflict that lasted until the fall of 1988, and needed Kuwait's oil resources to build up its nearly bankrupt economy. Besides, Kuwait, along with Saudi Arabia, declined Iraq's request for debt forgiveness from its neighbors. Saudi Arabia supported Iraq in its war with Iran lending them some 26 billion dollars which Saddam Hussein thought should be forgiven since he felt that the war also saved Saudi Arabia from potential conflict with the Shia-Muslim dominant Iran. The United States also sided with Iraq during its eight year war with Iran, especially in light of the 1979 hostage situation, and was in the process of establishing full diplomatic relations with the Hussein regime at the time of Kuwait invasion. Iraq also claimed Kuwait as one of its historical providences dating back to the Ottoman Empire when it was part of Basra. With the defeat of the Ottoman Empire during World War I, Great Britain gained this region as one of its colonial spoils-of-war. Britain then carved out Kuwait as a separate protectorate separating it from Iraq hence greatly restricting Iraq's access to the Persian Gulf. Iraq continued to claim Kuwait as its territory when it declared independence from Great Britain in 1932, holding that stance until 1963.[7]

The Kuwait military was no match for Iraq's Republican Guard and the country was occupied within two days of the invasion. United States and Kuwaiti delegations immediately called for a meeting of the UN Security Council while, at the same time, the Arab League sought to handle the conflict within the league nations and without outside interventions. However, the threat to Saudi Arabia and its oil supply quickly led to passage of UN Resolution 661 placing economic sanctions of Iraq. This was soon followed with UN Security Resolution 66 which authorized a naval blockade to enforce the economic sanctions. The United States response was for a buildup of U.S. military personnel in neighboring Saudi Arabia. This was coined *Operation Desert Shield* and lasted from August 2, 1990 until January 16, 1991.[8]

It was during this stage that Saddam Hussein called for conditions for the withdrawal of Iraqi occupation of Kuwait, including Israel's withdrawal from occupied territories in Palestine, Syria, and Lebanon and Syria's withdrawal from Lebanon. He also called for all U.S. troops in Saudi Arabia to be replaced with an Arab Force with the exception of components from Egypt. This proposal was not taken seriously and on November 9, 1990, the UN Security Council passed Resolution 678 giving Iraq until January 15, 1991 to withdraw from Kuwait. Talks between the U.S. and Iraq in Geneva went nowhere and as the deadline approached, France proposed for a rapid and massive withdrawal from Kuwait with the proviso that the UN would look into the Arab-Israeli conflict. The French proposal was supported by Belgium, Germany, Spain, Italy, Algeria, Morocco, and Tunisia among others but was flatly rejected by the United States, Great Britain and Russia.

Operation Desert Shield began on August 7, 1990 with the deployment of U.S. troops to Saudi Arabia ostensibly at the request of King Fahd to protect its oil fields. A major concern here was that if Iraq attacked Saudi Arabia it would then have control of the Saudi oil fields in addition to its own oil reserves as well as those of Kuwaiti hence having control over the majority of the world's known oil reserves at the time. This is why some considered the First Gulf War to be a resource war with Western powers interfering into a regional conflict for the purpose of safeguarding their oil supply. President George H.W. Bush felt he had the constitutional authority to use U.S. troops in supporting the UN resolutions against Iraq. Nonetheless, he did request Congressional authorization resulting in a four-day debate with Senator Joseph Biden of Delaware (later Vice President under President Obama) and Senator George Mitchell of Maine leading the opposition. President Bush prevailed with a 52 to 47 Senate vote in support of the military buildup and Operation Desert Shield commenced on August 7, 1990.[9]

While the United States and Great Britain were the main players in the First Gulf War, U.S. President George H.W. Bush forged together a 34-nations "coalition" in order to give the impression of a world-wide support for these actions. Saddam Hussein, in turn, attempted to gain Arab support by attacking Israel with long-range missiles. However, Israel's restraint during the conflict served to calm the Arab sentiments leaving Iraq alone in its fight with the "coalition" forces. The coalition forces consisted of: Argentina, Australia, Bahrain, Bangladesh, Belgium, Canada, Czechoslovakia, Denmark, Egypt, France, Greece, Italy, Kuwait, Morocco, Netherlands, New Zealand, Niger, Norway, Oman, Pakistan, Poland, Portugal, Qatar, South Korea, Spain Saudi Arabia, Senegal, Sierra Leone, Singapore, Spain, Syria, the United Arab Emirates, Great Britain and the United States. Although impressive on paper, the U.S. provided the bulk of the military forces (695,000) followed by Great Britain (43,000) and France (18,000) while Canada provided ships for the blockade and a squadron of CF 18 Hornet fighter planes. Turkey assisted by deploying a readiness force of 100,000 along its border with Iraq.

Operation Desert Storm began on January 17, 1991 with coalition air and cruise missile attacks. Ground forces entered Kuwait on January 22 with Bradley Fighting Vehicles. The costliest battle was that for Khafji which took place from January 29 until February 1st. In all, the First Gulf War involved 43 days of air sorties and 100 hours of ground combat resulting in 379 coalition deaths (190 during combat) of which 294 were US military personnel (114 by enemy fire, 145 in accidents, and 35 due to friendly fire). Great Britain forces had 47 deaths (38 in combat and 9 due to friendly fire) with the next highest coalition casualty being Saudi Arabia with 18 deaths. It is estimated that up to 50,000 Iraqis died in the conflict. Short as it was, the First Gulf War was not without controversy. On February 26th and 27th a long column of Iraqi troops and vehicles (estimated to be some 1,400) were attacked while withdrawing from Kuwait back into Iraq. U.S., British and French air forces indiscriminately attacked these retreating forces even though they were back in Iraqi territory causing heavy casualties and the virtue destruction of all the vehicles. This was known as the *Highway of Death*. The withdrawing Iraqi forces, in turn, were responsible for eco-terrorism setting some 737 Kuwaiti oil wells on fire contributing to the most significant post-war problem – that of the Gulf War

Illness.   Other controversies involve the use of anti-mine plows attached to Bradley Fighting Vehicles in burying alive Iraqi soldiers in trenches along the "Saddam Hussein Line" and the alleged killing of surrendering Iraqi soldiers under a "take no prisoners" order.   Another coalition controversy was the collateral damage of civilian casualties during the bombing of Iraq's civilian infrastructure – a criticism level against NATO years later in its attacks in the Balkan War.

The interim between the First and Second Gulf Wars, along with the continuous coalition monitoring of the "no fly zones" in both southern and northern Iraq, had flare ups in both 1993 and 1998.   In 1993, U.S. warships fired 23 cruise missiles at Iraqi secret service headquarters in response to a Center Intelligence Agency (CIA) report that Saddam Hussein had plans to assassinate former U.S. president George H. W. Bush. Many felt that this is one of the main reasons that his son, George W. Bush, started the second Gulf War once he became president. The second incident occurred when Saddam Hussein evicted the UN inspectors, as agreed upon in the 1991 cease fire, leading to a four-day bombing campaign by U.S. and British planes in what was called operation *Desert Fox.*[10]

The burning oil fields, pesticides, anthrax vaccines, possible exposure to sarin and the use of depleted uranium (DU) by coalition forces contributed to the mysterious *Gulf War Illness* which afflicted many more veterans than the ensuing 100 hours of combat. The depleted uranium was widely used in cannon ordnance by the coalition forces.   It is a known pyrophoric, genotoxic an teratogenic heavy metal and is suspected as being a major factor in the Gulf War Illness especially given that the symptoms afflicted coalition and Iraqi forces as well as civilians. The January 2011 issues of the *VFW Magazine – Persian Gulf War Special 20th Anniversary Issue* states that of the 700,000 service members participating in the First Gulf War between August 1990 and July 1991, some 250,000 veterans show symptoms of the Gulf War Illness. The article goes on to state that while the specific etiology of the Gulf War Illness is not clearly understood, a review by the U.S. National Academy of Science's Institute of Medicine concluded that the only illness clearly caused by the Gulf War is post-traumatic stress disorder which it estimates was present in 2 to 15 percent of the coalition forces. Nonetheless, in March 2010, the U.S. Veterans Administration agreed to look again at disability claims related to the Gulf War Illness relevant to a diagnosis of the following conditions: Brucellosis; Campylobacter jejuni; Chronic fatigue syndrome; Coxiella burnetii (Q fever); Fibromyalgia; Irritable bowel syndrome; Malaria; Mycobacterium tuberculosis; Non-typhoid Salmonella; Shigella; Visceral leishmaniasis; and West Nile virus. Among the 629,778 First Gulf War veterans still alive in 2011, 277,171 have filed VA disability claims with the VA granting service-connected disability for 165,840 and with another 40,67 claims still pending.[11]

The Second Gulf War – Iraq and Afghanistan

Ostensibly, the Second Gulf War was directly linked to the terrorist attacks on the United States on September 11, 2001- an event that galvanized public support for retribution. We now know that the events leading to *Operation Enduring Freedom* and *Operation Iraqi Freedom* actually began before the 9/11 attacks especially the invasion of Iraq. It now appears that attacking Iraq and toppling Saddam Hussein was a priority of George W. Bush as soon as he took over as President of the United States. According to sources linked to former U.S. Treasury Secretary Paul O'Neill, President Bush initiated his revenge against Saddam Hussein in January 2001, just days after taking office. These secret initiatives were known as the "Plan for Post-Saddam Iraq" and "Foreign Suitors for Iraqi Oilfield contracts." However, these plans were not feasible until the events of September 11, 2001 which not only solidified U.S. public opinion against Islamic terrorists but gained considerable sympathy worldwide as well providing the Bush administration carte blanch authority to initiate the Second Gulf Wars.[12]

Operation Enduring Freedom

The attacks on the Twin Towers in New York City and the Pentagon in Washington, DC by al Qaeda initiated the U.S. response on October 7, 2001 with Operation Enduring Freedom (OEF). The action taken at this time was to provide air and missile attacks by U.S. and British forces on Taliban and al-Qaeda targets while, at the same time, landing a small contingency of U.S. military personnel, known as Special Operation Forces (SOF), to provide assistance to local Afghan tribal units, notably the Northern Alliance, in fighting the Taliban. President Bush outlined the objectives for this operation as the destruction of terrorist training camps and infrastructure within Afghanistan as well as the capture of al-Qaeda leaders. On January 16, 2002, the UN Security Council unanimously approved an arms embargo and the freezing of al-Qaeda assets. The combination of the air/missile strikes and the use of the SOF military contingency resulted in the overthrow of the Taliban government by mid-December 2001.

The use of U.S. military personnel as advisors and forward observers for air strikes coupled with a simultaneous humanitarian relief effort led to the installation of a new transitional Afghan government. Hamid Karzai was elected president on October 9, 2004 following elections. Parliamentary elections followed in 2005. With a friendly government in Afghanistan the U.S. and coalition partners now provided a ground stabilization force of some 15,000 to 20,000 military personnel. Coalition forces included U.S., British, Norwegian Canadian, German, Australian and New Zealand forces. In January 2006, a NATO International Security Assistance Force (ISAF), made up mainly of British, Canadian and Dutch forces, took over the combat duties of Operation Enduring Freedom in southern Afghanistan while the U.S. continued combat operations elsewhere in the country notably Kandahar, Bagram, and Kabul. To some Operation Enduring Freedom represented a anti-Islamic crusade especially since similar OEF initiatives were conducted in other Muslim strongholds like the Philippines and the Horn of Africa. A review of Operation Enduring Freedom by the Pentagon concluded that the conflict contributed to the legitimacy of warlords and opium production in Afghanistan.

The war in Afghanistan continues to the present (2011) as an ongoing part of the Global War on Terrorism. Eventually NATO troops included German, French, Italian, Polish, Turkish, Romanian, Australian, Spanish, Georgian and Danish military components as well. Other countries have also provided security assistance. Indeed, 42 countries have contributed to the International Security Assistance Force since its initial involvement in 2006 with the United States making up half of the 119,819 force. U.S. President Barack Obama authorized a troop surge in 2010 bringing U.S. force levels to 30,000 with the expectation that these troops can stabilize the situation until sufficient Afghan military and police personnel can be trained and deployed to take over the major defense and public safety of Afghanistan. President Obama then plans a gradual withdrawal of U.S. troops beginning in July of 2011.[13]

Operation Iraqi Freedom

The Bush administration began a troop buildup for the invasion of Iraq as a second prong on the Global War on Terrorism in late 2002. Here the U.S. and British governments linked Saddam Hussein with al-Qaeda insisting that Iraq planned on deploying weapons of mass destruction (WMD) at the U.S. despite UN evidence contrary to this assertion. Nonetheless, Operation Iraqi Freedom was launched on March 20, 2003 by joint U.S. and British forces. Actual preparations began with an increase in air attacks throughout 2002 by U.S. and British planes over the "no-fly" zones in Iraq reaching a full-air offensive by August. In October 2002, the Bush administration convinced the U.S. Senate that Iraq had the capacity to attack the east coast of the United States leading to the October 11 passage of the "Joint Resolution to Authorize the Use of United States Armed Forces against Iraq." And on February 3, 2003, Secretary of State Colin Powell presented the U.S. case before the UN Security Council. At this time NATO members France, Germany and Canada, along with Russia, promoted disarmament through diplomacy policy over armed intervention. Former U.S. President Bill Clinton also warned about the dangers of a pre-emptive military strike against Saddam Hussein.

Initially, Operation Iraqi Freedom seemed to be a repeat of the First Gulf War – quick war with few coalition causalities. Beginning with heavy bombardment, known as "Shock and Awe" the invasion of Iraq began on March 20, 2003 with a coalition force led by U.S. Army General Tommy Franks. The coalition force consisted of 248,000 U.S. military personnel, 45,000 British soldiers, 2,000 Australian soldiers, and 194 Polish troops in addition to some 70,000 Iraqi Kurdish fighters. The initial battle was short much like the First Gulf War with the fall of Bagdad on April 9th and Tikrit, Saddam Hussein's home town, on April 15th and most major fighting over within three weeks. Only 139 coalition forces were reported KIA (killed in action) and fewer than 500 wounded. These events led a jubilant President George W. Bush to declare the combat operation completed and "mission accomplished" in May while aboard the Air Force carrier, Abraham Lincoln.

What was not anticipated by the Bush administration was the severity of the sectarian civil war that emerged once the Saddam Hussein regime was toppled. Certainly, the ensuing sectarian violence in the Balkans and in Northern Ireland should have been clear indicators of what was likely to occur in a post-Saddam Iraq. Besides the "no-fly" zones, maintained by U.S. and British forces, were a condition resulting from the First Gulf War with the intent of fostering sectarian revolt against Saddam Hussein from the Kurds in the northern no-fly section and from the Shiites in the southern no-fly zone. The idea that coalition forces would now simply be relegated to a mere security presence following the overthrow of Saddam Hussein was quickly rebuffed with the ensuing Sunni/Shiite/Kurdish civil war and encroachment of outside Islamic revolutionaries, including al-Qaeda, in the spring offenses of 2004. Indications of the battles ahead was brought to the public's attention with the March 31, 2004 assault on a *Blackwater USA* convoy resulting in the display of the mutilated bodies of the private military contractors. The First Battle of Fallujah in April soon followed as well as worldwide disclosure of the prisoner abuse by U.S. military personnel at the Abu Ghraib prison. The civil war intensified following the 2005 elections and installation of a transitional government eventually resulting in the U.S. troop surge beginning in early 2007.[14]

By 2008, pressure was building at home for the pull-out of coalition forces culminating with the loss of the United States strongest ally in the Gulf Wars – Britain. With a change in government, Prime Minister Gordon Brown ended British combat operations in Iraq on April 30, 2009 and newly elected U.S. President, Obama announced the end of active U.S. combat operations in Iraq in 2010. As of September 1st, 2010, Operation Iraqi Freedom ended and was replaced with Operation New Dawn. On August 19, 2010, the last U.S. combat brigades departed Iraq for Kuwait leaving a force of 50,000 U.S. military personnel to provide assistance to Iraqi forces. These troops are slated to leave no later than December 31, 2011. Many of these U.S. military personnel were transferred to the Afghanistan operation including the surge initiated in 2010 by President Obama in an effort to combat the renewed al-Qaeda insurgency operating from both Afghanistan and within the tribal border areas of Pakistan.[15]

Dimensions of Combat Stress

For the United States the Gulf Wars differed from previous major conflicts, including the Second World War, the Korean Conflict and the Vietnam War, in that the Gulf Wars did not rely on the draft and instead were fought using the "all-volunteer" military. While this was not a problem during the short First

Gulf War, it did place a considerable strain on the Second Gulf Wars being fought in Iraq and Afghanistan. The greater reliance on the National Guard and Reserve units coupled with multiple deployments and extensions led to a host of social and psychological problems. Added to this mix is the vague distinction between "combat" and "peacekeeping" roles, especially with National Guard personnel, which, for the first time, saw the largest deployment of female military personnel into a war zone. The use of suicide bombers and improvised explosive devices (IEDs) brought the potential for attacks and death and injuries to all coalition forces regardless of their role as infantry, transportation, trainers or military police. Collectively, these circumstances led to a heightened level of hypervigilance, and, consequently, stress among all those deployed to either Iraq or Afghanistan.

Invisible Wounds of War

Terri Tanielian and Lisa H. Jaycox compiled a report sponsored by the California Community Foundation entitled *Invisible Wounds of War: Psychological and Cognitive Injuries, Their Consequences, and Services to Assist Recover* that was published by the RAND Corporation in 2008 as part of a joint endeavor of RAND health and the RAND National Security Research Division. The Preface provides an overview of these problems facing U.S. military personnel deployed in either Iraq or Afghanistan:

> Since October 2001, approximately 1.64 million U.S .troops have been deployed for Operation Enduring Freedom and Iraqi Freedom (OEF/OIF) in Afghanistan and Iraq. Early evidence suggests that the psychological toll of these deployments – many involving prolonged exposure to combat-related stress over multiple rotations – may be disproportionately high compared with the physical injuries of combat. ...Concerns have been most recently centered on two combat-related injuries in particular: post-traumatic stress disorder and traumatic brain injury. Many recent reports have referred to these as the signature wounds of the Afghanistan and Iraq conflicts. With an increasing incidence of suicide and suicide attempts among returning veterans, concern about depression is also on the rise. ...(U)nlike the physical wounds of war, these conditions are often invisible to the eye, remaining invisible to other servicemembers, family members, and society in general. All three conditions affect mood, thoughts, and behavior; yet these wounds often go unrecognized and unacknowledged. The effects of traumatic brain injury is still poorly understood, leaving a large gap in knowledge related to how extensive the problem is or how to address it. ...Data collection for this study began in April 2007 and concluded in January 2008.16

The 2008 RAND report goes on to state that post-traumatic stress (PTSD) and traumatic brain injuries (TBI) are the *signature wounds* of the Second Gulf War due mainly to the injuries, both mentally and physically, from improvised explosive devices (IED). In addition to the thousands of direct injuries caused by TBIs, a greater number (up to 30 percent) of coalition troops engaged in combat in either Iraq or Afghanistan are subject to subtle, not readily discernable brain trauma secondary to IED, and suicide bomber, blast waves. Furthermore, the constant worry concerning these blasts throughout these countries, regardless of the intensity of active combat, lends itself to states of psychological hypervigilance – a condition that leads to a heightened stress level and, subsequently, a compromised immune system needed to cope within this environment. This combination of factors links PTSD and TBI as a critical comorbid dimension of the wars in Iraq and Afghanistan.

Another dimension of the Gulf Wars, notably the Second Gulf War, is the high rate of survivability of wounded veterans. According to a 2007 President's Commission on Care for America's Returning Wounded Warriors, the advances in combat medicine and body armor has resulted in the highest wounded to kill ratio of any combat action in U.S. history. A January 2008 Department of Defense report shows a total of 3,453 hostile deaths in relation to 30,721 wounded in action in Afghanistan and Iraq. However, many wounded veterans return with severe injuries, illnesses and disabilities including amputations, serious burns, spinal cord injuries, blindness and traumatic brain injuries, and PTSD leaving the potential for long-term physical, emotional and cognitive impairments and the need for significant rehabilitation services.

Social and Cultural Factors of the U.S. Military

Social factors also come into play here. The military, regardless of country, has its own caste-like culture along with its unique rank and unit status. The United States military follows this trend with a clearly divided caste system demarking commissioned officers from enlisted personnel, each with its own internal status hierarchy. Field grade versus junior grade officers; staff NCO (non-commissioned officers) versus junior NCOs and non-NCOs; warrant officers, etc, make up the internal pecking order within the coalition forces. Alleged unit superiority is also part of the U.S. military subculture with active duty U.S. Marine Corps and the Army Airborne and joint-military Special Forces claiming the top combat status, followed by their reserve units, and last on this hierarchy is the National Guard. U.S. military personnel, like those throughout the world, wear their resume on their right breast in the form of medals, ribbons and badges. This form of individual recognition is for a specific audience – fellow veterans. In order of significance are medals and/or ribbons depicting valor, meritorious service, commendations, achievement and conduct followed by campaign and service medals and ribbons. Badges usually indicate pilot or airborne status as well as weapons qualifications. Within this mix of relative status is the veteran's MOS (military occupational specialty). Infantry and artillery reflect the MOSs most likely to be engaged in direct ground combat. Army National Guard units are generally trained in artillery or transportation while the Air National Guard provides medical support. However, many Army National Guard units deployed during the Second Gulf Wars (Iraq and Afghanistan) were retrained as military police working in peace keeping and corrections.

Status is an important psychological factor within all military forces. The significance of the relative status, or relative deprivation, of a member of the military speaks to the audience effect which determines the veteran's standing vis-à-vis others sharing the same environment. Active duty Army airborne and FMF (Fleet Marine Force) Marines claim to be the "toughest" hence claim top status regardless if they are within the enlisted or commissioned ranks. Interestingly, the sense of being a cohesive group within the enlisted ranks, especially within the Marines, often tops that of their commissioned counterparts. Additional status is afforded those with direct combat experience and campaign medals take precedence over those who have not earned a combat action badge or ribbon. The Second Gulf War, like the Vietnam War before it, was divided between occupational/support personnel and combat troops while the entire country (Iraq/Afghanistan or Vietnam) was considered to be a potential combat arena. Only those military personnel directly engaged in a combat operation were considered active combat troops. A direct attack, such as a road side bomb, suicide bomber or a mortar attacks, was needed in non-combat areas for the training, security and transportation military personnel to qualify for combat status. This scenario accounts for the vast numbers of National Guard deaths and injuries, including those of female military personnel.

Unfortunately, sexism is also a strong component of military bias with females generally being looked down upon within the military caste system – a status once held by African American soldiers. National Guard units, regardless of MOS or gender, are generally seen as being on the bottom of the military status hierarchy. This pecking order plays a major role in how members of the military perceive themselves and often plays a role in post-release social problems and mental health issues. Ironically, the public unwittingly plays into the status role-confusion by treating all returning military personnel either with praise, like that which happened with the Gulf Wars, or scorn like during the Vietnam War. The labels of "hero" and "warrior" do not help minimize the status differential especially when these labels are assigned indiscriminately to all units returning from deployment in the Gulf Wars.

The deployment rate for the U.S. military during the Second Gulf War was 36 percent of the total combined active, reserve and National Guard force. This compares to 31 percent for the Korean War; 39 percent for the Vietnam War and 26 percent for the First Gulf War. The federal activation and deployment of National Guard Units under the current Global War on Terrorism (GWOT) has depleted the State National Guard Armories of personnel and equipment placing many Army and Air National Guard units on a "not ready" status. The May 2006 deployment of an additional 6,000 National Guard personnel to the U.S./Mexico border to interdict illegal aliens and another 2,736 in January 2008 in Operation Jump Start has also drained State National Guard resources. At the end of 2007, 254,894 National Guard personnel have been deployed to Iraq or

Afghanistan. The 2008 RAND report, it stated that reserve components (including the National Guard) tend to be older than their active duty counterparts with five times the number of personnel age 45 or older. Regarding race and ethnicity, the active and reserve Army had the highest percentage of black service personnel (23%/24%) while the U.S. Marine Corps had the fewest (12% active; 9% reserves). However, the Marine Corps had the highest percentage of Hispanics (14% active and reserve status). Overall, 14 percent of the U.S. armed forces comprised of women at this time.[17]

Women nursed troops during the U.S. Civil War as civilians and became an official part of the U.S. Army during the Spanish-American/Philippine War when the Nurse Corps was created in 1901. The Navy followed with its Nurse Corps in 1908. During World War I the role of women enlistees was expanded beyond the role of nurses with some 30,000 women serving at this time, a third of them overseas. However, this was not a career option for women and they were discharged once the war ended. Women were allowed to join the U.S. Military during World War II serving in many MOSs including nursing, parachute riggers, mechanics, amp-makers, translators, welders and transport pilots. Over 400 women were killed during the war out of the 400,000 that served. In 1948, the U.S. allowed women to serve during peacetime as part of the regular military forces with the provision that they could not make up more than two percent of the total armed forces. Even then women were not allowed to serve in combat and there was a cap placed on officer's rank limiting it to 06 status (colonel in the Army, Air Force or Marine Corps and captain in the Navy or Coast Guard). This happened a year following President Harry S. Truman's integration of the U.S. military. Women officers served in the MASH units during the Korean War from 1950 to 1953 as well in additional capacities. Another 7,500 women, mainly nurses, served close to the front lines in Vietnam as well often entering the combat zone to helivac wounded troops.[18]

The First Gulf War witnessed the largest deployment of women to a combat zone with some 40,000 including female pilots. Thirteen were killed in the line of duty and two were taken as prisoners of war (POW). Here women demonstrated their ability to effectively fly in a combat zone resulting in Congress lifting the ban on women flying in a combat role. Two years later in 1993, women military personnel were allowed to serve on Navy ships operating in combat zones. Nonetheless, women still are not allowed to serve in direct ground combat excluding them from infantry, armored and artillery units and Special Forces. They also cannot serve on Navy submarines although these restrictions are being debated in the U.S. Congress in 2011. The Second Gulf War witnessed the largest deployment of women to a combat zone with many being part of the National Guard which deploys entire units when federalized and authorized to deploy to Iraq or Afghanistan. In 2005, Sergeant Leigh Ann Hester became the first women to receive the Silver Star decoration (the third highest decoration for Valor) since World War II cited for killing three enemy combatants in a March attack on her support group stationed in Iraq. The Gulf Wars also saw the restrictions of rank lifted for women service personnel resulting in female generals and admirals in the U.S. Military. Major General Maggie Woodward was the first woman to command a combat air operation doing so during the 2011 Operation Odyssey Dawn – the coalition forces attack on Colonel Gaddafi's forces during the Libyan civil war.[19]

The democratization of the U.S. Military also has a downside especially when joining during difficult economic times or during an unpopular war. The draft took care of the deficient ranks within the army during World War II and the Korean and Vietnam wars but this is not a readily available option during the current "all volunteer" force. The military option, rather it be active, reserve or National Guard, is often most enticing for those from the lower social strata with poor educational or occupational opportunities. In order to fill the ranks of the military forces, age, educational, criminal background, mental and physical health requirements were reduced. A combination of these social and psychological factors plays a significant role in pre-deployment susceptibility to combat stress. The 2008 RAND report addressed this phenomenon using the *Stress-Diathesis Model.*

According to this model, diathesis refers to those aspects of our lives that are likely to increase our vulnerability to stress. These pre-existing conditions and circumstances, known as diathesis, including individual and/or family mental health issues, lack of education, criminal behavior, substance abuse, poverty, social isolation, unemployment, relational difficulties and the like. This list is similar to the "loss" categories listed earlier regarding the New Hampshire Hospital study on suicides. The RAND study purports that the presence of diathesis, in itself, is not sufficient to result in a significant mental disorder but that the presence of diathesis in combination with prolonged or significant stressors can result in a serious debilitating mental illness. The role a diathesis plays in this formula is it reflects a deficiency in the person's resilience to stressful situations. In the RAND study, major depressive disorder (MDD), post-traumatic stress disorder (PTSD) and traumatic brain injuries (TBI) are considered a diathesis. Accordingly, the stress of one disorder increases the risk of comorbid conditions. Studies show that U.S. service personnel deployed to Iraq and Afghanistan have higher rates of PTSD than their counterparts serving elsewhere. From this population, 88 percent of the men and 79 percent of the women suffering with PTSD experience other major disorders with half having three or more comorbid diagnoses with the number of comorbid disorders increasing with the severity of the PTSD. With stress comes the need for stress release. This is difficult in a stressful milieu and the absence of legitimate outlets often fostering impulse control dysregulation resulting in violent outbursts, sexual assaults and suicide.[20]

The Unintended Consequences of War Trauma

A number of factors regarding war trauma have emerged during the post-Vietnam era including the role of age, shame, anger, aggression, including self aggression (suicide), cognitive impairments and secondary PTSD. Studies have found that age, race and gender all influence trauma outcomes. These studies show that minority members of the military, particularly blacks and Hispanics, experience a greater level of difficulty in their readjustment back into society. This is also the case with female military personnel in general. Sexual assault victims, especially those whose cases go unresolved, are also prone to alterations in their self-perception leading to intense emotional shame and associated features such as impulsive aggressive outbursts including self-harm. Similarly, many veterans suffer from survival guilt – questioning why their life was spared while others in their outfit were killed or seriously maimed during a road side explosion or suicide bombing attack.

Emotional and cognitive impairments are generally associated with the three major elements of post-traumatic stress: the reliving of selective traumatic memories; attempts at avoiding reminders of these traumatic events; and a pattern of increased arousal. The constant exposure to olfactory, auditory, visual and atmospheric sensory input initiates autonomic neurological responses that, in effect, activate responses from the autonomic nervous system. The result of this process is extreme physiological states of hyper- (sympathetic) or hypo- (parasympathetic) arousal resulting in uncontrollable sadness, rage, fear, confusion, trembling, or paralysis that in effect lead to a confused self-image and poor interpersonal interactions and eventually to greater alienation from one's primary and secondary support groups within their cultural milieu. A natural response to these intrusive memories is an attempt at avoidance of anything that is linked to, or perceived to be associated, with these memories leading to an inability to enjoy the basic pleasures of life and further eroding interpersonal relationships. The avoidance behaviors fuel increased arousal manifested by hypervigilance, irritability, memory and concentration problems, sleep disturbances and an exaggerated startle response.

Secondary post-traumatic stress is yet another new dimension of war trauma that has received greater attention since the initial Vietnam War studies. Interestingly, the Gulf Wars have had the effect of exacerbating war-related stressors that were apparently dormant among aging Vietnam War veterans resulting in an influx of these veterans at VA facilities in the USA. Another group likely to suffer from secondary post-traumatic stress is medical personnel who are constantly exposed to injured veterans. Studies have shown that prolonged exposure to seriously injured veterans can impair their ability to care for these patients. This population includes Navy Corpsmen serving with the U.S. Marines and Army Medics as well as field surgical unit nurses and doctors. Another secondary aspect of war trauma is those changes resulting in cultural separation from the military milieu. Adjustment to an alien environment, especially a war zone, fosters a greater dependence on the unit creating an emotional bond among those members of the group. This in-group cohesion is based on a mutual interdependence and trust forged under these potentially hostile and dangerous circumstances often resulting in subtle personality changes and behaviors. This modified persona is what the veteran arrives home with and for many a quick readjustment to the prevailing status quo is difficult, if not impossible making for a difficult transition. This is an especially complicated process for married veterans given that their spouse (husband, wife, or partner) has also undergone a major adaptive transformation in that they had to take on many responsibilities that were once shared by both parties. Many are reluctant to then relinquish these recently acquired prerogatives to the returning veteran further complicating the veteran's adjustment to the home environment.

Readjustment stressors merely compound war trauma increasing the likelihood of physical and mental health symptoms. A study of Canadian coalition forces serving in Iraq and Afghanistan showed that untreated war trauma led to major depression which, in turn, aggravated physical health problems. A study of British soldiers serving in Afghanistan showed an increased prevalence of deafness among its veterans. While hearing defects are a consequence of heavy combat, left untreated may also contribute to mental stress if this condition is not addressed properly. Studies of aging U.S. veterans from World War II and the Korean and Vietnam wars indicate an increased rate of heart disease among those also suffering from PTSD. Contributing to the high prevalence of untreated symptoms of war trauma is the military culture itself. Inherent in this culture is the shame and embarrassment of admitting psychological distress. These admissions are contrary to the military code of silence. A soldier is seen as being weak if they "cry" about emotional or psychological problems. There is a fear of peer rejection and of being ostracized or even "drummed out" of the service thus losing membership in a significant reference group. For many troubled veterans, it is better to "suck it up" and take care of the problem themselves, such as self-medicating with alcohol and other mind-altering substances.[21]

Untreated stressors lead to a difficult adjustment back into the "home world" environment. The 2008 RAND study noted that this often affects marriages and parenting. Untreated symptoms of war trauma inhibit a veteran's ability to reestablish the level of emotional intimacy that once sustained the pre-deployment relationship often resulting in failed relationships. Intense war trauma, such as PTSD, can lead to secondary PTSD among the spouse and the children within the family. In a 2009 issue of *Current Opinion in Psychiatry,* the authors noted that over a million U.S. children and their families have experienced the stress of the deployment of a family member during the Second Gulf Wars in either Iraq or Afghanistan. The returning veteran often seems a stranger to their spouse and children manifesting role ambiguity regarding their expected and traditional roles. Other studies show that the children in the occupied countries also suffer higher rates of violence, suffering and mental health issues. In a study of 11 to 16 years old children in Afghanistan, the researchers found that two-thirds of the children reported traumatic experiences. The war environment in Afghanistan exposes children and youth to violence that are not confined to acts of war. It is because of the overall unsettled and violent nature of the war environment that produces a high percentage of mental health problems among the adult population as well. In this mix, children and youth suffer from both primary and secondary traumatic stress.[22]

Failed relationships often lead to homelessness for many veterans. Every major conflict has produced its cohort of homeless veterans and the wars in Iraq and Afghanistan are no different. Homelessness is often the result of a failure to readjust back into society. The 2008 RAND report puts the homeless rate for returning veterans at four times higher than that for non-veterans, and this during a severe economic downturn in the United States with an exceptionally high number of home foreclosures resulting in an above-average rate of homelessness overall. The RAND report states that while veterans represent about 11 percent of the U.S. civilian population, they are disproportionately represented among the homeless with 26 percent of that population. Studies on homeless veterans from the Vietnam War showed that these veterans suffered from readjustment problems including PTSD and substance abuse along with interpersonal difficulties and high unemployment. The current population of Gulf War homeless veterans includes those suffering from mental illness, substance use disorders, those suffering from PTSD and traumatic brain injuries. Moreover, the homeless veteran is likely to be suffering from serious mental disorders including schizophrenia, chronic major depression, and bipolar depression than their non-homeless counterparts. For some the mental illnesses, especially depression, contributed to their homelessness while for others it became a consequence of their homelessness. The risk factors contributing to homelessness for veterans include untreated mental illnesses, substance use, poor physical health, extreme poverty, underutilization of support programs, less social support and greater encounters with the legal system. Homelessness merely exacerbates mental illnesses, which in turn leads to more physical health disorders. Even then, homeless women are at greater risk for violence directed against them. Victimization is also greater among the homeless veterans suffering from traumatic brain injury due mainly to their diminished cognitive capabilities. The longer a veteran remains homeless, the greater the spiraling into hopelessness and the more difficult is the road to recovery. Substance abuse, sexual abuse and violence, including suicide are other significant unintended consequences of war trauma.[23]

Substance Abuse

Substance abuse has long been associated with the U.S. military with *slop shouts* provided at all major military bases. Enlisted men, NCO and Officer's clubs abound often with a 1600 (4:00 PM) *happy hour* for anyone old enough to serve in the military. Alcohol is a tradition within many military organizations; a ritual that continues after discharge in canteens affiliated with the two major U.S. veterans' organizations- the Veterans of Foreign Wars (VFW) and the American Legion. Efforts to address drinking in the military has only recently been seriously considered especially the ritual of binge drinking – the process of consuming large amounts of alcohol within a limited time period. Past efforts to limit the alcohol content of beer served (3.2 beer) on military bases did not address the ritual of binge drinking itself; a behavior that often was initiated during military service and then carried into civilian life.

The drinking problem is compounded in the Gulf Wars by the prohibition of alcohol use within these Islamic societies. The 2008 RAND report cites evidence that alcohol misuse has actually increased among active-duty personnel within the past ten years; the period of the Second Gulf War. One study showed that the rate of alcohol abuse in the Army increased by 30 percent between 2002 and 2005 with junior service members at a higher risk of alcohol abuse than their senior counterparts. Another study found similar findings when focusing specifically on Gulf War veterans serving in either Iraq or Afghanistan. Here, the rate of alcohol abuse was 33 percent; a third of those deployed.[24]

Reasons stated for the potential of alcohol abuse among deployed military personnel, regardless of where they are stationed, include the anxiety associated with the adjustment to an alien culture; one where they are separated from their primary support networks. Self-medication is yet another factor where alcohol becomes the anxioletic of choice for taking the edge off the stressors associated with being in an alien environment, especially one where the potential for violence looms constantly in their minds. Drinking is also a social norm within the military milieu and often a requisite for acceptance within the peer cohort. A new dimension of military drinking, however, can be linked to the availability of new internet technologies; gadgets not available to veterans in previous wars. This included e-mails and Skype – the ability to have instant visual and auditory contact with family and friends in the states. This, in itself, can intensify the ambivalence of separation and stress associated with a foreign deployment.

When alcohol is not readily available, military personnel will substitute another more easily accessible drug agent. Sometimes these other agents are used even when alcohol is readily available due mainly to their more rapid mechanism of action in providing psychoactive relief. During the Vietnam War, U.S. service personnel often used heroin and marijuana which were both inexpensive and readily available on the black market. Some studies estimate that over a third of Army personnel deployed to Vietnam used heroin alone. Longitudinal studies showed that most Army veterans ceased using heroin once back into the states but those that continued to use heroin became addicts with devastating social and health consequences. Among those who stopped using heroin altogether, many merely substituted alcohol as the agent of choice for curbing anxiety and depression associated with readjustment or unresolved psychological issues. This problem is a serious one for coalition forces deployed in Afghanistan given that it is now ranked to be the major opium producer in the world.[25]

The Boston University, School of Public Health provides research summaries for current research on alcohol and drug policy, prevention and treatment in its *Join Together* bulletins. Recent bulletins addressed the issue of substance abuse within the U.S. military. A May 2007 issue noted that the U.S. Marine Corps

allows service members ages 18 and older to drink at its facilities; this despite a nationwide age-21 drinking law.   A January 25, 2011 United Press International
(UPI) item, noted that alcohol abuse is a serious problem with the U.S. Marine Corps despite efforts to promote treatment. The report cited Pentagon reports noting that the years 2009 and 2010 recorded the highest alcohol-related injuries among Marines since 2005 including nine Marine deaths due to alcohol-related vehicle accidents.[26]

A May 2007 *Join Together* bulletin, noted that substance use among young military personnel differs from their civilian counterparts according to data from the Survey of Health Related Behaviors among Active Duty Military Personnel. In this study, one-fourth of reported heavy alcohol use compared to 17 percent among civilians of a similar age. In contrast, the percentage of military personnel ages 18 to 25 reported using illicit drugs at a rate half of that of their civilian counterparts. The study noted that this last comparison may be questionable in that military personnel are less likely to report illegal drug use in a survey given that it could be grounds for dismissal.[27]

This cautionary note was again reinforced in the April 2008 *Join Together* bulletin where it was reported that many veterans suffering from PTSD and other combat-related traumas self-medicate with alcohol and other drugs and this fact compromises treatment efforts. It is estimated that 40 percent of military personnel serving in either Iraq or Afghanistan suffer from some form of mental health problem and, of those, 60 percent will have a comorbid substance use disorder. Two months later in June 2008, the U.S. Senate passed a bill that addresses both addiction and mental health treatment for veterans. The bill called for pilot treatment program to be initiated in certain states to address these problems. However, discretionary funding for those operational pilot programs are currently being challenged in 2011 with the U.S. Congress bent on drastic cuts in domestic programs which these programs fall under given that they deal mainly with returning veterans.[28]

Similar issues plague other members of the coalition forces, notably British and Canadian forces. One study in the May 2010 *Join Together* bulletin highlighted the fact that drinking is a major problem for British troops who were stationed in either Iraq or Afghanistan. Indeed, while PTSD appears to be problematic with U.S. and Canadian troops, this is not so much the case with British military personnel where the biggest problem seems to be alcohol abuse. According to a King's College London study published in *Lancet* alcohol abuse, anxiety and depression were the leading mental health problems among British troops with the alcohol rate among those who served in Iraq and/or Afghanistan being nearly double (22%) that of the rate (13%) for the military in general. The prevalence of PTSD for British troops, on the other hand, was only four percent and 20 percent for less severe mental disorders. Another study published in 2007 in the *British Medical Journal of* showed that candidates for PTSD within the British forces were associated with a deployment of 13 months or more within a three-year period and that the PTSD was generally comorbid with multiply physical symptoms. Even then, severe alcohol problems were more prevalent than PTSD among this class of soldiers serving in the Second Gulf War.[29]

The relationship between PTSD and substance use among deployed military personnel is interesting in that current studies indicate that alcohol and PTSD symptoms tend to increase at similar rates in that as PTSD symptoms worsen so does substance use. This direct relationship most commonly thought to be due to the use of alcohol and other substances for the purpose of self-medication. However, when PTSD symptoms are effectively treated or reduced, a corresponding decrease in substance use does not always follow leading to a plausible conclusion that the substance abuse takes on a life of its own and is more difficult to treat than many of the symptoms associated with the PTSD diagnosis. Hence, while substance use may have begun as an associated feature of PTSD in the long run it had the tendency to become a disorder independent of the PTSD.

The relationship of substance use and violence in the military is common knowledge. The 2008 RAND report notes that rising rates of substance abuse has also led to an increase in the number of alcohol- and drug- related crimes perpetrated by U.S. troops serving in Iraq and Afghanistan. The RAND report claims that over a third of all Army criminal prosecutions, including murder, rape, armed robbery and assault, for military personnel serving in the Second Gulf War involved alcohol or drugs. It is interesting to note that these offenses occur despite an official prohibition against alcohol among coalition troops serving in Iraq or Afghanistan. The relationship of substance use and violence is especially relevant to the next sections of sex abuse and violence and suicide.[30]

Sex Abuse within the Military

Rape has always been an unfortunate, if not unintended, consequence of war and the Gulf Wars are no exception. The association between rape and war was discussed earlier in chapter two. and the U.S. military has long been complicit in getting host countries, notably those occupied by U.S. forces, to provide prostitution for its service personnel. This was the case in Japan at the end of World War II where the vanquished Japanese were expected to provide *comfort stations* staffed with Japanese women for the benefit of the U.S. occupation force. This practice continued officially in Okinawa until its occupation ended in 1972 and it was given back to Japan. Similarly, prostitutes were provided for U.S. troops during and following the Korean War. A 2007 article in the journal *Violence Against Women* by Hughes, Chon and Ellerman, exposed the "modern-day comfort women" in South Korea and their role in the transnational trafficking of women. These authors found that U.S. military bases in South Korea, established to prevent attacks from North Korea in the on-going Korean War, serve as hubs for the transnational trafficking of women from Asia, Pacific, and Eurasia to South Korean and the United States. They estimate that 1 million Korean women have served as comfort women for U.S. military personnel since the Korean War began in 1950. Korean women who come back to the United States as wives of U.S. servicemen also contribute to the pool of prostitutes found in bars and massage parlors located near military bases in the U.S.[31]

A new dimension of rape in the Gulf Wars, especially among U.S. troops, is the increased proportion of females in the military including those deployed to either Iraq or Afghanistan, mostly with National Guard units. We also mentioned earlier that rape is often used as a powerful propaganda tool used to incite out-group hostility directed toward the enemy. Men throughout history feel that it is their role to protect women adding to the sense that men are superior to women especially in the realm of physical assertiveness and aggression. Here lies another problem, that of male disapproval of women in the military. In one respect men in the military feel that they are safeguarding the "women at home" while at the time harboring hostilities toward women serving in the military who they feel threaten their masculine role. Added to this mix is the sex-stress situation whereby women become available as an outlet for this frustration. Within this scenario any female outlet will do; prostitutes or civilian or military rape victims. Often underreported and ignored is the issue of male rape victims. This phenomenon was common within the concentration camps by all sides during the Balkan Wars but only recently acknowledged among coalition troops, especially those serving in Iraq and Afghanistan. The April 11, 2011 issue of *Newsweek* addresses the issue under the title, "The Military's Secret Shame." Men are reluctant to report being sexually assaulted not only due to the shame associated with rape, but also due to the response from the military staff which tends to blame the victim for the offense.32

Early in the Second Gulf War in Iraq the United States Defense Department attempted to stir up American emotions by publicizing the death of the first U.S. female combat casualty, Lori Piestewa (first female of American Indian descent killed in action) and the alleged capture and rape of one of her comrade, Jessica Lynch, both serving with a the U.S. Army's 507th Maintenance Company providing combat support for the 2003 invasion of Iraq. Private First Class Jessica Lynch MOS was that of a supply clerk. The supply-convey made a wrong turn that inadvertently brought them into an enemy sector. The convoy's wrong turn and subsequent firefight was termed as an *ambush* by the Department of Defense press. Then, obviously playing on the sentiments of Western chivalry, the Pentagon's press release had Private Lynch fighting heroically only to be overwhelmed by the Iraqis resulting in her being shot, stabbed, sexually abused and tortured. Her rescue was then presented as a daring nighttime rescue conducted under heavy enemy fire. In fact none of this occurred. Private Lynch did not fire her weapon and she was not shot, stabbed, sexually abused or tortured. In fact, she was taken to a local hospital by concerned Iraqi citizens and treated for injuries sustained when her vehicle crashed during the altercation. Moreover, her rescue was an uneventful operation made possible by an Iraqi informant whose wife worked as a nurse at the hospital where Private Lynch was being treated. When the real facts emerged, later substantiated following a Congressional inquiry, there were no corrections made by the military press and Private Lynch was held incommunicado by the military until her release from active duty. Private Lynch received a medical honorable discharge and was awarded the Bronze Star Medal (Meritorious), Purple Heart Medal, the Prisoner-of-War Medal and the Army Service Ribbon. Eight of her colleagues died in the incident including her best friend, Lori Piestewa. On a similar note, the Marine captain in charge of Lynch's rescue also received the Bronze Star thus greatly enhancing his status and opportunities for promotion.[33]

While the Pentagon was quick to exploit Private Lynch for its propaganda effort, little was being done to address the increasing incidents of sexual assault within the U.S. military. Many see the military culture as rape conducive especially with the military cast system. A 2010 Department of Defense report indicated an 11 percent increase in reported sexual assault in the military over the past year with a 16 percent increase among those U.S. troops serving in Iraq and Afghanistan. In 2004, the Care for Victims of Sexual Assault Task Force was established by the Department of Defense resulting in the creation of the Sexual Assault Response and Prevention Office (SAPRO) with the specific task of providing training and education programs; treatment and support for victims; and system accountability. SAPRO is now the authority for sexual assault policies within the Department of Defense. Many veterans still feel that the Department of Defense is not doing enough to combat this problem and in February 2011, over a dozen U.S. veterans 15 women and two men, filed a class action suit against the Pentagon in federal court claiming that they were sexually assaulted while serving in the military and that their superiors ignored their complaints at the time often forcing them to continue serving under abusive superiors. The suit names both the current Secretary of Defense, Robert Gates and his predecessor, Donald Rumsfeld. The plaintiffs want to force a change in existing reporting structure where individual commanders have too much discretion in handling this allegations.[34]

Nonetheless, efforts are being made at the Veterans Administration (VA) to address the issue. The VA put forth a handout in September 2008 articulating the treatment for MST (Military Sexual Trauma). According to this publication, MST includes any sexual activity where someone is involved against his or her will including being pressured into sexual activity by superiors. Also included under MST is unwanted sexual touching or grabbing; threatening offensive remarks about a person's body or sexual activities; and/or threatening and unwelcome sexual advances.

The components of Military Sexual Trauma are similar to that of PTSD and can affect a person's mental and physical health, even many years later. The symptoms of MST include:

> -Strong emotions: feeling depressed; having intense, sudden emotional reactions to things; feeling angry or irritable all the time.
> -Feelings of numbness: feeling emotionally 'flat'; difficulty experiencing emotions like love or happiness.

-Trouble sleeping: trouble falling or staying asleep; disturbing nightmares.

-Difficulties with attention, concentration, and memory.

-Problems with alcohol or other drugs.

-Difficulty with things that remind them of their experiences of sexual trauma: feeling on edge or 'jumpy' all the time; difficulty feeling safe; going out of the way to avoid reminders of their experiences; difficulty trusting others.

-Difficulties in relationships: feeling isolated or disconnected from others; abusive relationships; trouble with employers or authority figures.

-Physical health problems: sexual difficulties; chronic pain; weight or eating problems; gastrointestinal problems.[35]

Since 2008, the VA provides free, confidential counseling and treatment to both male and female veterans for mental health and physical conditions related to experiences of MST. These services will likely increase with the recent (2011) advent of the United States finally repealing the "Don't Ask – Don't Tell" military protocol that will allow gays to openly serve in the military as well as the initiative to end the ban on women in combat.

Recent high profile cases illustrated the prevalence of sexual abuse within the military continues to make the news. In January 2011, Chief Master Sergeant William Gurney, the highest ranking enlisted man at the Air Force Materiel Command at Wright Patterson Air Force Base outside Dayton, Ohio, plead guilty to sexual misconduct and adultery for a number of affairs he initiated with subordinate female personnel.[36] In July 2010, the former head of Canadian Forces in Afghanistan, Brigadier General Daniel Menard, was charged with two counts of conduct to the prejudice of good order and discipline for having an affair with Master Corporal Bianka Langlois while both were stationed in Afghanistan with coalition forces. Langlois was charged with one count of conduct to the prejudice of good order and discipline related to military fraternization regulations.[37] These public charges of sexual misconduct within the Canadian military was highlighted by the sexual sadism and murder convictions leveled against Colonel Russell Williams, the Commanding Officer of the largest Air Force base in Canada, CFB Trenton, in October 2011.

This case is interesting in that it illustrates how difficult it is to readily recognize a paraphilic sexual-sadist. The popular, handsome, affable, married, and well respected 47 years old Air Force pilot was a veteran of the Afghanistan War who was entrusted with flying both the Canadian Prime Minister and the British Royal family. His wife did not know about his dangerous sexual behaviors that apparently began with breaking into homes near his country retreat and stealing women's undergarments. He would then video tape himself wearing these garments. He even had a photo of himself masturbating in the bedroom of a 12-year old girl wearing one of her skirts. This was in the home of a supposed family friend. His behaviors escalated to actual encounters with his victims beating and humiliating them. Then in November 2009, he stalked a member of his unit, 37-year-old Corporal Marie-France Comeau, beating and sexually assaulting her for hours and then murdering her. Following her murder, Colonel Williams, in his capacity of the Commanding Officer of the base where she was stationed, wrote an official letter of condolence for her death. In January 2010 he abducted a neighbor, 27-year-old Jessica Lloyd, from her home and took her to his retreat where he repeatedly raped her. He then strangled her with a piece of rope and left her body in the woods off a rural road. Both of these victims begged Williams to spare their lives. Williams only became a suspect after two men driving by early on the morning that he dumped Jessica's body noticed a vehicle with its parking lights in a remote area. They later contacted the police who then took tire prints from the scene and later traced them to Colonel Williams' vehicle in a road block. The main detective asked Williams to come for a routine interview on a Sunday wearing the same shoes that matched the prints were found at the scene of Jessica Lloyd's home. Confronted with the evidence, Williams confessed only to spare his wife the embarrassment of a prolonged trial. Williams plead guilty to two counts of first degree murder, two counts each of sexual assault and forcible confinement and 82 fetish break and enters. He was sentenced to the maximum allowed under Canadian law, two concurrent life-sentences where he had to serve at least 25 years. Canada abolished the death sentence in 1976 but is considering allowing for consecutive sentencing for cases such as this. He is serving his sentence in segregation at Kingston Penitentiary. On October 2010, the Canadian military stripped Williams of his rank, revoked his commission and took back his military decorations, the Canadian Forces Decoration Medal for good service and the Southwest Asia Service Medal for his service in Afghanistan. This case illustrates how a paraphilic can treat his victims as mere stimuli, objects to be discarded after their use, doing so seemingly devoid of humanity while, at the same time, feeling guilt, shame and compassion for his wife with whom he maintains a "normal" interpersonal relationship. Such is the complicity and magnitude of impulse control dysregulations.[38]

War Related Violence and Suicide

War stress, immediate or delayed, can manifest itself in violence directed toward oneself or toward others. Palmer's research on the *frustration-aggression theorem* provides vivid evidence of this phenomenon. Outward-directed violence can involve homicide while the worst form of inwardly-directed violence is suicide. Both forms of stress-related consequences are closely related to unresolved war trauma. Self-medication, notably by alcohol, merely fuels these events. A March 2007 *Join Together* item noted that alcohol problems among U.S. soldiers in Iraq are tied to violence. Coalition forces, especially those from Western cultures, serving in Iraq and Afghanistan have the additional burden of secret or illicit consumption given the de jure prohibition against the consumption of alcohol in these Islamic societies. Iraqi moonshine however is easily available like it was in the U.S. when and where alcohol was prohibited. While U.S. soldiers are barred from drinking alcohol while stationed in Iraq or Afghanistan, alcohol and other drugs were involved in 240 of 665 Army criminal prosecutions within these two war zones. These offenses included murder, rape, armed robbery and assault. The bulletin goes on to say that drinking rates are rising among those Army and Marine Corps personnel directly involved in combat operations. Another contributing factor to the substance abuse problem among the U.S. troops is the lowering of recruiting standards where convictions for alcohol and/or drug abuse were waived hence enhancing the susceptibility of these soldiers to using under stress. An April 2008 article by Lolita Baldor for the Associated Press noted that both the U.S. Army and Marine Corps have allowed entry into their ranks more recruits with felony convictions including some with manslaughter and sex crimes convictions. These represent only a fraction of the overall number of active duty recruits but, nonetheless, highlight a trend that is troublesome for those serving under combat stress situations.[39]

The point of stress-related impulsive rage was brought to the attention of the world media with the March 2005 rape and murder of a 14-year-old girl, Abeer Hamza, by troops from the 502 Infantry Regiment of the 101st Airborne Division where they were manning a checkpoint in Mahmudiya, Iraq. The incident apparently followed a drinking bout of locally distilled alcohol. Miss Hamza was gang-raped and murdered in her home by five U.S. soldiers who also killed her six-year-old sister and her parents. They then set Abeer's body on fire to destroy any evidence of the gang rape. Five out of the six-man team participated in the atrocity. Two younger brothers, aged 11 and nine, were spared because they were away at the time. Neighbors reported the fire to another checkpoint guarded by Iraqi soldiers. They, in turn, reported to the same group that perpetrated the rape-murder blaming it on Sunni insurgents.

The matter was laid to rest until June 2006 when the sixth man at the checkpoint revealed the U.S. involvement while undergoing a psychological evaluation subsequent to the revenge killings of two U.S. soldiers from the same platoon, Private First Class Thomas L. Tucker and Private First Class Justin Watt, by Iraqi insurgents – the Mujahideen Shura Council. The main perpetrator, Steven Dale Green, had already been discharged from the Army when the identification of the real killers came to light and therefore was tried within the U.S. Federal District system. Green had been honorably discharged that May due to an "antisocial personality disorder." Green was found guilty but was spared the death sentence. He is serving a life sentence without parole at a U.S. penitentiary but is challenging his conviction claiming that the Military Extraterritorial Jurisdiction Act is unconstitutional and that he should have to face a military trial like the other four involved in the incident. The sixth member of the team, the one who did not participate but who later reported the crime was medically discharged from the Army.[40]

A similar case was being processed in 2010 involving a "kill team" led by a Staff Sergeant that was charged with randomly killing Afghan civilians in Kandahar province. Twelve U.S. soldiers serving with the 5th Stryker Brigade have been charged. Staff Sergeant Calvin Gibbs and four subordinates are charged with murder and "killing for sport." The other seven soldiers are charged with lesser offenses including conspiracy. All twelve are being tried under military justice. Data compiled in 2008 indicates that 349 known murders occurred within the U.S. military in the first six years of the Second Gulf War (2001-2007) representing an 89% increase over the previous six years. Three-quarters of these murders involved Gulf War veterans and at least 121 Iraq and Afghanistan war veterans have committed murder, or have been charged with murder, in the United States following their return home from combat.[41]

These cases of assault and murder wane in comparison to suicides. Like rape and murder, suicides do not discriminate according to military rank. In May 1996, the highest ranking naval officer, Admiral Jeremy Michael Boorda, committed suicide shooting himself in the chest following a controversy over his military awards. He was the first enlisted sailor in U.S. history to rise to the top position in this branch of the military – that of Chief of Naval Operations with a seat on the Joint Chiefs of Staff. He was the first top Navy commander to rise to this position without graduating from the Naval Academy. In fact Boorda was a high school dropout who lied about his age to enlist in the Navy at age 17. He attended Officer Candidate School (OCS) and received his commission in August 1962. He later earned his bachelor-of-arts (BA) degree from the University of Rhode Island in 1971. Admiral Boorda was also responsible for opening up assignments for women to serve on combat vessels. He earned his fourth star in December 1991 and became Commander-in-Chief, U.S. Naval Forces Southern Europe where he became involved in the Balkan Wars serving as commander of NATO forces in southern Europe authorizing air strikes for alliance forces, the first such action in NATO's 44-year history. In 1993, in his capacity as Commander-in-Chief of Allied Forces Europe, he coordinated humanitarian relief airdrops to Bosnia-Herzegovina. The immediate issue surrounding his suicide was his wearing a combat "V" on two of his decorations, the Navy Commendation and the Navy Meritorious Service awards which he included the combat "V" for his service during the Vietnam War. He was to meet with the Washington bureau chief of Newsweek magazine concerning this issue when he killed himself. Following his death the Secretary of the Navy later authorized the combat "V" for Admiral Boorda.[42]

The 2008 RAND reports analysis of suicides among U.S. military personnel and veterans noted that the overall rate 10 to 13 per 100,000 troops is similar to the suicide rate across the United States in general. However, when controlling for gender, male veterans have twice the suicide rate than their civilian counterparts. Studies based on Vietnam War veterans showed that the highest suicide risk is within 5 years of discharge from active duty. Depression, PTSD and TBI all increase the likelihood of suicide and suicide attempts. A recent analysis of VA medical centers showed that 30% of suicides among their clients indicated a comorbidity with affective disorders while 40% of the patients attempting suicide had a comorbid anxiety disorder with PTSD being the strongest anxiety disorder linked to suicide attempts. Veterans with comorbid

PTSD and depression are more likely to commit suicide than person with only depressive symptoms.

The demographics of suicides and suicide attempts among veterans clearly show that males are more likely to commit suicide. Males comprise 85% of the Army population but 95% of Army suicides. Whites are also more likely to commit suicide than other races. Whites make up 59% of the total Army population and 71% of all Army suicides. Moreover, white veterans are three-times more likely to die from suicide than non-white veterans. About half of Army suicides occurred among men between ages 17 to 21 while 40% of discharged male veterans die by suicide after age 65.[43]

A 2008 report by the Associated Press points out evidence that the Department of Veterans Affairs has downplayed both the number of successful suicides and suicide attempts, much of this due to domestic problems with returning veterans, especially those who have been involved in numerous deployments to Iraq and/or Afghanistan. The suicide rate among U.S. Army personnel in 2006 rose to over 17 per 100,000 troops, the highest rate in the 26 years that records have been kept. A 2008 report stated that 53 percent of these suicides occurred among National Guard and Reserve troops returning from having served in the Second Gulf War. The suicide rate among Canadian soldiers has also climbed since their involvement in the Second Gulf War. One study shows the suicide rate among Canadian soldiers doubling from 2006 to 2007 to a rate that is triple that of the general population. The 2007 suicide rate for regular and reserve Canadian troops in 2007 was over 41 per 100,000. These suicides mostly involve the some 2,500 Canadian soldiers who served in Afghanistan's Kandahar region. In 2011, Canadian military personnel have been withdrawn from active combat status and will instead serve in a support capacity much like the U.S. National Guard units.[44]

Chapter Five

Dimensions of Balkan War Trauma

Introduction: The First and Second Balkan Wars

The Balkans have long been a region of intrigue and conflict extending back to the conflicts leading to the dissolution of the Ottoman Empire in the late 19th and early 20th centuries. A brief overview of these events is necessary in order to better understand the current situation especially given that it is generally understood that the Balkan Wars of 1912 and 1913 precipitated the First World War. The *First Balkan War* was instigated by Russia, whose earlier actions set into play events leading to the dismantling of the Ottoman Empire during the Russo-Turkish War (1877-1878). The outcome of this conflict also resulted in an enlarged Orthodox Serbian territory. While the Ottomans were preoccupied with a conflict with Italy, a Balkan coalition was formed in 1912 to fight the Ottomans in order to gain territory in the region known as Rumelia which included Macedonia and Albanian territory. The Balkan League, comprised of Serbia, Bulgaria, Greece and Montenegro, intended on taking Macedonia and Albanian territory from Turkey. The war began with Montenegro declaring war on Turkey in October 1912 with the rest of the Balkan League soon following its lead.

The success of the Balkan League was so great that Turkey agreed to an armistice in December of 1912 – essentially ending 500 years of colonization. However, disagreements over how Macedonia was to be divided led to Bulgaria turning on its former allies leading to the *Second Balkan War* in June 1913 which now involved Romania as well. This event was coupled with the coup d'état by the Young Turks in Constantinople. The outcome of this conflict was Bulgaria losing most of its gains from the First Balkan War to Romania with the Turks regaining some of their lost territory in the region. This war ended with the Treaty of Bucharest. Albania used these conflicts to declare its independence from the Ottoman Empire, on November 28, 1912 during the First Balkan War.[1]

With the diminished influence of the Islamic Ottoman Empire, efforts were underway by the Southern Slavic provinces to minimize the encroaching influence of the Austro-Hungarian Empire. The Austro-Hungarian Empire, at that time, extended to Bosnia which had long represented the de facto line of influence between the Austro-Hungarian and Ottoman Empires in the region. The goal was for a Greater Serbia, or Yugoslavia, independent of both the Roman Catholic and Muslim influences. The plan of action was the assassination of the Archduke of Austria during his visit to Sarajevo in June 1914. A group of Bosnian Serb assassins, led by Danilo Ilic, were able to complete this task on June 28, 1914 when they killed both the Archduke Franz Ferdinand and his wife, Sophie, the Duchess of Hohenberg. This act led to World War I which ultimately saw the disintegration of both the Austro-Hungarian and Ottoman Empires. At the end of the world war, Albania became an Islamic republic and the newly created Yugoslavia (*land of the South Slavs*) became a Kingdom under King Alexander. The boundaries for Yugoslavia now comprised of Slovenia, Croatia, Bosnia-Herzegovina, Serbia, Montenegro and Macedonia – a region representing numerous sectarian and ethnic groups.[2]

Antecedents to the Third Balkan War

World War II provided the circumstances leading to the *Third Balkan War of 1991-2002*. Ethnic cleansing was rampant in Yugoslavia during World War II with Orthodox Serbs, Jews and Roma (Gypsies) targeted by the Nazi followers in Slovenia, Croatia and Bosnia-Herzegovina (Bosniaks). It took the leader of the partisan, Josip Broz (Marshal) Tito, to unify the six-provinces (Slovenia, Croatia, Bosnia-Herzegovina, Serbia, Montenegro and Macedonia), into the *Socialist Federal Republic of Yugoslavia*, a republic that severed ties with the Soviet Union subsequently initiating a group of not-aligned socialists states. Marshal Tito, in his effort to ensure that none of the six Yugoslav republics would dominate the others, granted semi-autonomy to two-provinces in Serbia the largest of the six republics. These were Vojvodina in the North and Kosovo in the South. Tito became a leader of the Non-aligned Nations during the Cold War gaining favors from both the West and the Soviet Union. He was also able to hold Yugoslavia together despite its marked sectarian divides – Orthodox Serbs, Roman Catholics in Slovenia, Croatia and Herzegovina and Muslims Slavs in Bosnia (Bosniaks) by allowing a relative high degree of cultural, if not religious, autonomy during his reign. The Constitution of the Socialists Federal Republic of Yugoslavia provided protection for ethnic enclaves throughout the nation allowing for a tolerable co-existence, even inter-marriage, among the various sectarian and ethnic groups. This is illustrated by the Roma population which often took on the language and religion of the larger sectarian group.. The Jewish population that once was a significant element of many of these sectarian communities was virtually eliminated during the Nazi-sponsored purges of World War II.3

Things began to unravel with Tito's death on May 4th, 1980 and further intensify with the collapse of the Soviet Union in the late 1980s. After Tito's death Yugoslavia was governed by a rotating presidency selected from the six republics. And with the fall of Communism, many of the former communist leaders now became heads of ultra-nationalist groups claiming to represent the majority of their sectarian members. Each group promoted their own interest through propaganda and fear tactics forcing even reluctant members of their group to view their neighbors as the enemy resulting in reciprocal antagonism. Naming the "out-group" as the enemy tended to increase the "in-group's" cohesion. This split within the former Yugoslavia was further fueled by economic reasons as well as the fact that the lid on sectarianism, maintained under Tito, brewed under the surface for a hard-core segment of the society for centuries. The outside influence of both the Roman Catholic Church and international Islam did not help matters. Serbian ultra-nationalists, on the other hand, drew their support from radicals within neighboring Orthodox communities notably, Russian, Greece and Romania. Nonetheless, all three major sectarian groups within all six republics were represented, to varying degrees, in this civil war. To the ultra-nationals leaders *ethnic cleansing* was deemed the only solution toward a pure state.

The Third Balkan Wars began with allegations of anti-Serb discrimination in the ethnic Albanian semi-autonomous Kosovo province in Serbia. Slobodan Milosevic, serving his term in the rotating Yugoslavian leadership partnership that emerged following Tito's death, used his influence to get changes to the Yugoslav constitution to terminate the autonomous status of both Vojvodina and Kosovo essentially bringing them under strict Serbian control. One outcome was dramatically minimizing the role of the ethnic Albanian majority in Kosovo. This action stirred ethnic sectarianism throughout Yugoslavia setting the stage for the breakup of the Socialist Federal Republic of Yugoslavia which eventually led to the dissolution of the former Yugoslavia over the next fifteen years with all six of the constituent states breaking away by 2006 resulting in two major battle fronts – the Croatian-Bosnian/Herzegovina-Serbian conflict from 1991 until the implementation of the Dayton Peace Accords in December 1995; and the Kosovo War (1996-2002) that led to the NATO bombings of Serbia in 1999 eventually resulting in Kosovo, a province of Serbia, declaring its independence in 2008.[4]

The Balkan War of 1991-1995
The chronology of events leading to the unraveling of Yugoslavia began in 1990 at the 14th Congress of the Communist Party with Slovenia and Croatia delegates leaving in protest. Then on June 25, 1991, Slovenia, after voting the Communists out of office, began the secession process resulting in their *Ten-Day War*. Their neighbors to the south, Croatia, also declared their independence from Yugoslavia. The standoff between the Yugoslav People's Army (JNA) and the Slovenian police and territorial defense resulted in several dozen deaths but no major battles. A tentative peace was established on July 9, 1991 and Milosevic withdrew the JNA from Slovenia on October 26, 1991. This minor scrimmage fueled the ultra-nationalism that fanned the flames of the ensuing Third Balkan War.[5]

The main battle leading to a full-fledged war was associated with Croatia's bid for independence. The problem here was that Franco Tudman, on December 22, 1990, got the Croatian parliament, to adopt a new constitution that eliminated the protective elements of the 1965 and 1974 Yugoslav Constitution that provided equal treatment for Serbian enclaves residing within Croatia. This action gave superior status to Croatian Catholics while discriminating against the indigenous Serb minority. This action led the Serbs in the Krajina (Military Frontier) region to demand its own independence within an independent Croatia. Serbs lived for generations in the Krajina region, brought there by the Austrian-Hungarian Empire in the mid-16th century to serve as a buffer against the Ottoman Empire. Indeed, the Serbs in this region constituted about 12 percent of the Croatian population at the time of its declaration of independence in 1991. The ensuing Croatian civil war pitted Tudman's ultra-nationalists against the *Serbian Autonomous Oblast of Krajina* (SAO) which now proclaimed themselves the *Republic of Serbian Krajina* (RSK). When this element of the Balkan War ended in 1995, tens-of-thousands of indigenous Croatian Serbs were forced into exile, mainly into Serbia, while those who remained were subjected to torture and murder. Likewise, the RSK attempted to cleanse its territory (a third of Croatia) of Croatian Catholics also resulting in mass displacements of people, the murder of civilians and the destruction of cultural artifacts. This action resulted in the introduction of the *United Nations Protection Force* (UNPROFOR) into the Balkan War and the establishment of *United Nations Protected Areas* (UNPAs).

In 1991, Macedonia also declared its independence with little resistance from its parent – the Federal Republic of Yugoslavia. The second major battle front in the 3rd Balkan War erupted when Bosnia-Herzegovina (BiH) declared its independence in April 1992. This conflict involved all three sectarian groups with extreme violence initiated by all parties – much of it directed toward civilians. Initially the fighting involved the Bosnian Serbs and the Bosniaks whereby the indigenous Serbs feared a Bosnia ruled by Islamic Slavs and a situation where they would again be labeled as second-class citizens. In 1993 the conflict now included Bosnian Croats, supported by Croatia, battling the Bosniaks. Some of the heaviest fighting in this theater was in the Herzegovina section of Bosnia. As early as March 1991, the ultra-nationalists leaders of Serbia (Slobodan Milosevic, also the leader of what remained of the Federal Republic of Yugoslavia) and Croatia (Franjo Tudman) conspired to partition BiH between their respective countries. This was known as the Karadordevo Agreement which essentially promoted both a *Greater Croatia* and a *Greater Serbia* out of the remaining Yugoslavia. The United Nations Security Council, in anticipation of growing conflicts in the region, passed Resolution 713 imposing an arms embargo throughout the former Yugoslavia.

Tudman's ultra-nationalist party, the Croatian Democratic Union (HDZ) attempted to do the same thing in Bosnia-Herzegovina that the Croat Serbs attempted in Krajina – taking over a segment of BiH and naming it the *Croatian*

Republic of Herzeg-Bosnia. This action occurred on November 18, 1991, when the HDZ branch leaders in Bosnia-Herzegovina declared their independence. In a similar fashion, the Bosnian Serbs, on October 24, 1991, abandoned the tri-ethnic coalition that governed BiH since 1990, creating their own Assembly of the Serb People of Bosnia and Herzegovina. On January 9, 1992, the assembly established the Serbian Republic of Bosnian and Herzegovina which late was changed to the *Republika Srpska* in August 1992. The stage was now set for the battle of Bosnia-Herzegovina, a conflict that engulfed the entire country until late December 1995 with the signing of the Dayton Accord.

There was the possibility for peace with the Cutileiro-Carrington Plan (Lisbon Agreement) forged by the European Economic Community (EEC) on March 18, 1992. This agreement proposed ethnic power-sharing at all administrative levels but with respective communities defined according to their sectarian majority – Bosniak, Bosnian Croat, Bosnian Serb. But apparently under pressure from the United States, the leader of the Bosnian Muslims (Bosniaks), Alija Izetbegovic, withdrew his signature and support for the agreement ten days later setting the stage for the horrific battles that ensued. The U.S. Congress also attempted to override the UN arms embargo but these efforts were vetoed by President Bill Clinton. The embargo, although often breeched through the porous mountainous borders, left the Yugoslav People's Army (JNA) with the bulk of heavy armaments including artillery and tanks. The JNA leader, General Ratko Mladic, sided with the Bosnian Serbs and the Army of Republika Srpska (VRS). These forces were responsible for the 44-month siege of Sarajevo where even the UN Protective Forces had limited results other than keeping the airport open allowing for the basic essentials to sustain the besieged population. Another failure of the UNPROFOR was the protection of Srebrenica where it is estimated that some 8,000 Bosnian Muslim men and boys were massacred from July 12-22, 1995 by the army led by Ratko Mladic. Interestingly, the forces defending Sarajevo during the siege, the Army of the Republic of Bosnia and Herzegovina (Armija RBiH; ARBiH) not only outnumbered the RS forces surrounding the city, but was comprised of all sectarian and ethnic groups residing in Sarajevo.

The Croat-Bosniak War from June 19, 1992 until February 23, 1994 engulfed 30 percent of the country into a separate war. The purpose of this war was Croatian domination of central and eastern region of BiH known historically as Herzegovina. Again this conflict involved ethnic cleansing and atrocities against both combatants and civilians. Mostar, long considered the de facto capital of Herzegovina, was held under siege for nine months by Croat forces and the destruction of the city and its religious and cultural structures including the iconic Stari Most Bridge. This time both Bosniaks and Bosnian Serbs became the targets for Croat aggression. It is widely understood that the United States favored both the Catholic Croats and Muslim Bosniaks over the Orthodox Serbs. Toward this end, the US began efforts for these two groups to settle their differences and form a coalition that would unite against the Serbian forces.

Both warring parties signed the US-initiated peace agreement (the Washington Agreement) in March 1994 leading to the creation of the joint Bosniak-Croat Federation of Bosnia-Herzegovina (FBiH) with the population divided into ten cantons (seven predominately Muslim and three predominately Bosnian Croat).6 At the same time the USA was clandestinely using private military security forces, MPRI (Military Professional Resources, Inc.) to arm and train the Croatian Army in its fight against Serbian forces as well as smuggling arms to the ARBiH. These initiatives allowed the Croats to break the stalemate with Serbian forces in the summer of 1995 in two actions, Operation Flash and Operation Storm driving the Serbs out of most of Croatia. These actions were followed by Operation Maestral, a combined Croat/Bosniak effort to push back the Bosnian Serbs in BiH. This operation, along with the ensuring NATO bombing brought the combined Croat and FBiH troops to the outskirts of Banja Luka, the de facto capital of RS. The signing of the Dayton Peace Accords on December 14, 1995 effectively ended the fighting in both Croatia and Bosnia-Herzegovina resulting in the FBiH comprising of about 51 percent of the country and RS with 49 percent with Sarajevo separated into two segments with East Sarajevo belonging to RS.

Granted, the United States played a significant role in forging the Dayton Peace Accord. Yet, the U.S. is seen by many as the party that allowed the war to rage in the first place by influencing Alkja Izetbegovic to pull out of the March 1992 EU Lisbon Agreement. Ironically, the Dayton Accord came to reflect the same basic thesis as the Lisbon Accord but with the added ingredient of nearly four years of war laced with sectarian-led atrocities on all sides leaving a festering legacy of inter-group segregation and hate even to the present. In the final analysis, Bosnia-Herzegovina became divided along sectarian lines with seven Bosniak cantons and three Bosnian-Croat cantons comprising the Federation of Bosnia-Herzegovina (FBiH) and 51 percent of the land while the Bosnian Serbs ended up with their own territory- the Republika Srpska (RS) and 49 percent of the country. A third internationally protected Brcko District was also established at the critical border areas where Croatia and Serbia and BiH meet within the greater RS region. There is also a shared, albeit weak, national assembly with representation from all three ethnic populations. Nonetheless, the prospects for a truly unified Bosnia-Herzegovina, despite the rhetoric of the Dayton Agreement, are remote, at best. It is unfortunate that the Balkans emerged as the final Cold War encounter with the former Yugoslavia being the proxy battleground for geo-political gamesmanship. Many elements of the Dayton Accord were not realized notably the return of refugees swept from their traditional homes during the ethnic cleansing forced exodus frenzy. And the war continued beyond 1995, now in the lower Slavic states of Serbia, Kosovo, Montenegro and Macedonia.[7]

The Balkan War of 1996-2002

Despite the promise of removing economic sanctions against all warring parties following the Dayton Accord, U.S. pressure resulted in continued economic reprisals against the remnants of the Federal Republic of Yugoslavia (FRY) and its leader, Slobodan Milosevic. The FRY was reduced to just two of the original six republics now consisting only of Serbia and Montenegro. Both Kosovo and Vojvodina had their provincial status upgraded by Tito with the 1974 Yugoslav Constitution which gave these autonomous units equity with the six republics. Both now had a seat on the federal presidency along with a provincial assembly, police force and national bank. However, the death of Tito on May 4, 1980 and the growing economic crisis, which was more extreme in the southern republics, led to more unrest resulting in massive protest in March of 1981. One of the demands was for Kosovo's status to be elevated to that of a republic – the seventh republic within Yugoslavia.

The demand for republic status met with strong opposition not only from Serbia but from the two republics adjacent to Kosovo – Montenegro and Macedonia. The fear here was that the ethnic Albanians would attempt to link up with Albania in the creation of a *Greater Albania*. This situation stems back to World War II and Tito's attempt to increase the size of Yugoslavia at the expense of Italy which occupied much of Yugoslavia as well as Albania during the war. The eventual quid-pro-quo arrangement was that Italy would retain its northern territory, Trieste, on the Adriatic Sea while Yugoslavia would take control over *North Albania* (Kosovo Province) separating it from Albania proper. At this time the majority of the populace in Kosovo were Albanian and sizable minorities those of Albanian descent resided in the surrounding Montenegro and Macedonia.

Discontent between the Muslim Albanians and Orthodox Serbs in Kosovo goes back to the end of World War II and continued to fester despite Tito's efforts to curtain both Albanian and Serb sectarian extremism in the region. Soon after Tito's death the Orthodox Church complained about a campaign by Kosovo Albanians extremists against Serbs and Montenegrins that resulted in harassment as well as the destruction of Orthodox Churches. The sectarian divide intensified as the economy worsened in the 1980s and 1990s when Kosovo had the poorest economy within Yugoslavia. Ibrahim Rugova, the leader of the Democratic League of Kosovo, is credited in keeping the lid on violence through his policy of peaceful resistance. His call for an independent Republic of Kosovo in 1991 did not set well with the Serbs. Milosevic's action in November 1988 obviating the autonomy of both Kosovo and Vojvodina provinces served to ignite the flames of discontent and the eventual emergence of guerrilla units and the creation of the Kosovo Army in April 1993. The following year the Albanian guerrillas became known as the *Kosovo Liberation Army* (KLA). The KLA soon overshadowed the peaceful resistance of Ibrahim Rugova.

Following the Dayton Accord, the KLA saw their opportunity to actively engage the Federal Republic of Yugoslavia without the distractions of the Bosnian and Croatian conflicts. The KLA, initiated this segment of the Third Balkan Wars when they began attacking police stations and government offices in 1996. The KLA's fortunes changed in 1998 when the US and Great Britain changed their status from that of a *terrorist group* to that of *freedom fighters*. Soon after this change the American diplomat credited with orchestrating the December 1995 Dayton Accord, Richard Holbrook, began meetings with the KLA providing them with monetary and logistics, and, many suspect, military arms. With US and British recognition, the next step was to get NATO involved in what was to become the compete dismantling of the former Yugoslavia.

Despite efforts by Russian leader, Boris Yeltsin, in May 1998 to stop the on-going sectarian fighting and bring the parties, notably Albania and the FRY, together, these efforts were undermined by Richard Holbrook's public support for the Kosovo Albanians over the Serbs, including the widely-distributed picture of him taken with the KLA. With this endorsement, the KLA stepped up their attacks on Serbs in violation of an agreed upon ceasefire. In an attempt to settle this matter, international intervention efforts began on February 6, 1999 with the NATO-sponsored Rambouillet Conference outside Paris. These talks also included Russia and Serbian president, Milan Milutinovic who represented Milosevic who did not attended fearing arrest on war crime indictments being processed by the International Court of Justice (ICJ) at The Hague. Despite his absence, a consensus on restoring Kosovo's status as an autonomous republic within the FRY was reached on February 23rd. However, the condition for an "invited international monitoring force in Kosovo" was rejected by the USA which insisted on a "forced military presence" not only in Kosovo but throughout Yugoslav territory. This obvious slant toward the Kosovo Albanians was met with considerable resistance by both the FRY and Russia, neither which signed onto these US-influenced changes. Milosevic went further by opposing all international oversight within Kosovo.

The unarmed peace monitors were withdrawn on March 22, 1999 in anticipation of the ensuing NATO offensive. The US-led NATO bombing offense, name Operation Noble Anvil by the USA and Operation Allied Force by NATO, began on March 24th and continued until June 11th involving some 1,000 aircrafts in 38,000 combat missions. This represented the first major military action for many NATO forces, including Canada, since the Korean War and it was the first for the Luftwaffe since World War II. This action was conducted without any UN Security Council approval and included both military and civilian sites. Some 20,000 bombs and missiles were deployed on targets in Kosovo, Belgrade, Vojvodina and even in Montenegro. Civilian targets included bridges, factories, power stations, homes, hospitals, schools.... Controversial targets included the Chinese Embassy in Belgrade, an Albanian refugee convey, the Dubrava prison in Kosovo, the Serbian state television broadcasting tower, and the petrochemical plants and oil refineries in Vojvodina. The latter resulted in the release of thousands-of-tons of noxious chemical into the air, onto the ground and into the water ways including the Danube River. These toxins included vinyl chloride monomer (VCM) and 1,2 dichlorethane (EDC) along with the depleted uranium (DU) used in the NATO bombs (in violation of the Geneva Convention).

The NATO action spelled the beginning of the end of Milosevic's reign but at a high cost to the civilian populations of both Serbia and Kosovo. Moreover, no major efforts have been made by the international community to clean up the contamination in Vojvodina, the bread basket of Serbia where the water and ground continue to be very toxic. The FRY army left Kosovo to be replaced by the NATO-led Kosovo Force (KFOR) under a UN Security Council Resolution (1244) while the notorious KLA was renamed the Kosovo Police Force and served alongside the KFOR troops. In 2000, Slobodan Milosevic was voted out of office resulting in the removal of economic sanctions against the FRY. Milosevic was put on trial in 2002 at The Hague for war crimes. Conflict continued in southern Serbia and northern Macedonia initiated mainly by ethnic-Albanian guerrillas during 2001 and 2002. In 2006, both leaders in the Kosovo war died – Ibrahim Rugova and Slobodan Milosevic. Also in 2006, Montenegro declared its independence from the Federation Republic of Yugoslavia – leaving only Serbia. In 2007, the International Court of Justice (ICJ) finds Serbia *not guilty* of planned genocide in Bosnia. And Kosovo declared its independence from Serbia in 2008 over the objection of Serbia. Clearly, the actions of the international community, including most members of NATO, did much to ignite the Balkan Wars which, in turn, allowed for the rise of ultra-nationalist leaders, who, by most accounts, did not represent the majority of their populace. In the end, the International Criminal Tribunal for Yugoslavia (ICTY) indicted these ultra-nationalists including Alija Izetbegovic, the ultra-Bosniak leader of BiH; Franco Tudman, ultra-Catholic Croat; Slobodan Milosevic, ultra-Orthodox Serb; Radovan Karadzic, ultra-Bosnian Serb; Ramush Haradinaj, ultra-Kosovo Albanian; and Ejup Ganic, ultra-Bosniak from BiH. And charges continue to surface including those against Hashim Thaci, leader of the KLA and Kosovo Prime Minister in 2010 for organ trafficking (human organs taken from prisoners during the 1996-1999 conflict). Another area of concern is the issue of forced prostitution for the pleasure of the international forces stationed throughout the former Yugoslavia.[8]

A conservative estimate is that over 100,000 people died, both combatants and civilians, in these conflicts with another million displaced from their traditional homes, many placed in concentration camps or prisons where tens of thousands, both men and women, were subjected to sexual assaults, starved or beaten. Thousands are still remain missing. Over 30,000 mine fields remain active today, many located around Sarajevo resulting in continued deaths and injuries inflicted mostly against children and youth. The trauma associated with these conflicts transcends ethnicity or sectarianism – affecting all those involved: Muslims/Bosniaks; Orthodox/Serbs and Bosnians; Catholic

Croats/Bosnians and Roma. The dire economic situation in these struggling, emerging states leaves many of these victims and their families untreated resulting in increased social ills including suicides. While recent efforts have been made by the leaders of Croatia and Serbia to reduce the intensity of sectarianism by publically apologizing for their country's role in the Balkan Wars, inter-group hostilities continued to be fuelled by the indictments and trials conducted or supervised by the International Criminal Tribunal for the former Yugoslavia (ICTY). While these are obviously socio-political issues, treatment needs are the same regardless of one's national, religious or ethnic identification. Toward this end, we worked with two high-risk populations – the Bosnians in the Sarajevo area and the Serbs in the Vojvodina province, notably those in Pancevo.[9]

Review of the Clinical Literature on the War's Aftermath

The Balkans Wars of 1991-2002 were the most destructive conflicts in Europe since the Second World War yet, studies on the nature and extent of war trauma associated with the Balkan Wars existed mainly in Slavic-language professional journals that covered both military and civilian victims. A review of these articles is crucial in determining assessment and treatment strategies for dealing with victims who have survived the conflict but continue to suffer from unresolved and untreated symptoms.

The Slavic-language articles deal with traumatic stress among both veterans and civilians, notably those involved in the forty-four-month-long siege of Sarajevo (April 1992-February 1996); the NATO bombing of the Federal Republic of Yugoslavia (now the States of Serbia, Montenegro and Kosovo) from March to June 1999; as well as the tens-of-thousands of refugees displaced, many still not back in their homeland, during the entire Balkan conflict (1991-2002). It is important to note that people on all sides of the Balkan conflict, veterans and civilians alike, were subjected to war-related trauma, either directly or indirectly, and that these social/clinical features pertain to anyone, regardless of their ethnic/sectarian origin. Consequently, these articles address clinical research on victims from Slovenia, Croatia, Bosnia and Herzegovina, Serbia/Montenegro, and Kosovo as well as those working in refugee camps located in Macedonia and throughout Europe (The USA accepted more than 100,000 Bosnian refugees and asylum seekers from 1991 to 2004). The literature is arranged into four categories: veterans; general war trauma; refugees; and women and children. We begin with the focus on veterans given that this is the major focus of the English-based literature pertaining to U.S. and its allies in both the Gulf wars and the NATO operations in the Balkans.

Veterans

Research specific to war veterans focuses mainly on Croatians, Bosnians and Serbs with the majority of studies done on Croatian soldiers. One reason for this may be the stronger affiliation of Croatia with Western Europe and its more abundant research resources. The major clinical and medical Slavic language journals also are located in Croatia, followed by Serbia. Bosnia-Herzegovina has no major medical or clinical journals and is dependent upon either Croatia or Serbia for local language academic and professional resources. Corruption within the medical professions is also problematic especially in Bosnia-Herzegovina. Slovenia's short ten-day war provided few injured or traumatized veterans while research on ethnic Albanians during the Kosovo war is still outstanding. However, it is reasonable to infer from the existing ethnic-specific research to combatants in general given that the war environment was consistent, differing only in degrees of intensity, across all sectarian groups involved in the Balkan conflict.

The Croatian studies focus mainly on traumatic stress and other comorbid mental and physical health factors as well as social factors. In a study conducted at the Vrapce Psychiatric Hospital and the Croatian Institute for Brain Research in Zagreb, 136 persons presenting with war-related post-traumatic Stress Disorder (PTSD) were divided in to four groups: 79 veterans, 18 former prisoners-of-war (POWs) who witnessed or were subjected to torture, 15 rape victims, and 24 refugees from Bosnian-Herzegovina. The research found significant inter-group differences relevant to the arousal and avoidance. As would be expected, rape victims had more avoidance symptoms and fewer hyper-arousal symptoms. The prisoners and veterans, on the other hand, experienced a greater degree of hyper-arousal. Additionally, the rape victims and POWs reported more symptoms overall than any of the other groups. None of the groups reported intrusive symptoms considered a hallmark of PTSD. This research challenges the use of a homogenous classification of war-related PTSD when assessing Balkan War victims. The authors suggest that a better protocol would be one that looks at specific clinical symptoms associated with war-related stress.[10]

Other studies also indicated the prevalence of depression and anxiety among Croatian war veterans. A study of 151 male veterans of the 1992-1995 war in Croatia, aged between 30 to 50, were assessed for traumatic stress at the Zagreb University Hospital Center from January 2003 to May 2005. The results indicated that those with more intense PTSD tended to present with externalized symptoms such as aggression, hostility and mistrust while those with less intense PTSD presented with depressive symptoms. The major outcome of this study was that a different intensity of PTSD resulted in different symptoms. A similar study on war stress and aggression among Croatian soldiers found that impulsive aggression was higher for those with high war stress.[11] Yet another study of 402 Croatian male veterans of the Balkan War, aged between 20 and 60, being screened for war-related compensation claims, looked at the prevalence of pre-morbid clinical conditions prior to their military service. Of the veterans screened, 346 met the criteria for PTSD. Out of this group, the most common comorbid disorder was major depression (31%), alcohol dependence (16%), and dysthymia (15%). Moreover, those with co-morbid major depression, 35% had a previous history of clinical disorders including psychiatric hospitalization. The major outcome of this study was the need to assess previous psychiatric disturbances among both veterans and their families in order to ascertain the role of combat in their current stress situation. This process also would help in weeding out those who are malingering or presenting with possible factitious disorders in order to obtain disability compensation.[12] In a similar fashion, a study conducted at the Split University Hospital and School of Medicine found that after a five-year intense treatment period for PTSD psychotherapy was successful in reducing the intensity of PTSD symptoms but did little to change pervasive personality deficits (defense mechanism) like projection, displacement, regression and intellectualization – features that are paramount for a reintegration back into society.[13]

Another study done in Croatia also addressed the issue of preexisting risk-factors linked to the severity of war trauma. Again the examinations were in regards to veterans seeking war-related disability compensation. Four-hundred and fifteen war veterans, 405 men and 10 women, were selected from 1055 that initially put in for veterans disability compensation. The mean age of the subsample was between 29 and 75 and all were receiving outpatient psychiatric services. Inadequate social support, especially from significant others; chronic unemployment; a history of mental disorders that transcends their military service, notably affective and anxiety disorders, substance abuse and/or dissociative disorders – were all significant risk factors for chronic PTSD. The study also noted that women have a higher vulnerability for PTSD than their male counterparts if they experienced sexually motivated violence or had a preexisting anxiety disorder. However, a 2007 study of male war veterans compared with a control group, conducted by the Split University Hospital and School of Medicine, found that war veterans with PTSD has less sexual activity than the control group. The PTSD sample suffered from hypoactive sexual desire and erectile difficulties and premature ejaculation.[14]

A longitudinal study of 42 severely disabled male war veterans aged 19 to 44 being treated at the VaraZdinske Toplice Rehabilitation Hospital in Croatia found that the anxiety levels of these immobile, dependent veterans increased the longer they were in the same homogenous treatment environment when that environment was deficient in social and psychological care for their clinical symptoms. A similar finding was arrived at in a study of these disabled veterans conducted by the University Hospital Center in Zagreb. They also found significantly higher anxiety levels in patients with PTSD stemming from still unprocessed traumatic experiences coupled with unsuccessful adaptation to the veteran's physical disability. And prolonged anxiety results in impaired short-term memory and visual retention according to a 2007 study conducted on Croatian war veterans at the Split University Hospital and School of Medicine.[15]

The major Bosnian veteran protests included massive protests in 2009 and 2010 regarding cuts in veterans' benefits – a situation brought about by demands of the International Monetary Fund (IMF) relevant to a 1.2 billion euro loan to help Bosnia-Herzegovina cope with the global economic crisis. Thousands of veterans, including disabled veterans, wives and children of veterans joined the protest which erupted into violence directed toward the police and the destruction of government offices – including those located adjacent to the U.S. Embassy (now replaced with a new facility located near the old Tito's Barracks). The 2010 riot forced a shut down of the U.S. Embassy which provided medical care to the injured police officers guarding the government office adjacent to the Embassy. A study of war veterans aged between 30 and 50 was conducted by the Department of Psychiatry at the University of Tuzla. In this study, 200 war veterans were divided equally into two groups – those diagnosed with PTSD and those without this diagnosis. The results showed that the PTSD sample had a significant higher rate of alcohol-related problems. It should be noted that the PTSD group was older and had a high rate of unemployment. The researchers concluded that loss of work can serve to erode the veteran's fragile social support system leading to not only untreated PTSD but substance abuse and other mental health disorders.[16]

The other major research on Balkan war veterans stems from Serbia. A study conducted by the Military Medical Academy in Belgrade found that the Serbian veterans from the Bosnian War with the greatest degree of clinical problems were those who had front line exposure, were married, had lower educational levels and had a history of family problems during their upbringing.[17] Another study of 419 wounded veterans treated at the Military Medical Centre in Karaburma indicated that those suffering from PTSD showed a higher propensity for aggression than those without PTSD symptoms. Similarly, a study of 104 male combat veterans with PTSD conducted by the Institute of Mental Health in Belgrade, found certain characteristics among those with violent tendencies. Those with violent tendencies were members of the reserve forces of the former Yugoslav Army with a mean age of 35 during the study period of 1998-2000. Most were married with children and had completed secondary school and were employed following the war. Among those assessed with aggressive tendencies secondary to their PTSD seventy (67%) committed at least one violent act subsequent to their treatment while another fifty-eight (56%) perpetrated physical violence and nine (8%) were charged with violent criminal offenses. Included in this aggressive profile was the use of dangerous firearm-related behaviors adding to the problem of effective war trauma treatment and aftercare protocols. A relationship was found between PTSD and alcoholism in a study of 62 psycho traumatized veterans treated at the Clinical Centre in Novi Sad. Twenty-one of the patients had symptoms of alcohol addiction. An interesting finding that distinguished the alcoholic veterans from those without this problem was that the former were younger veterans and a third of them had alcoholic fathers.[18]

General War Trauma

General war trauma involves the larger population engulfed in the Balkan Wars of 1991-2002, civilians as well as veterans. An area of concern here is that of increased violence including homicides and suicides. A major study conducted by the Trauma Studies Unit, Institute of Psychiatry, King's College of London from March 2000 to July 2002 and published in the *Journal of the American Medical Association* (JAMA) in August 2005, addressed the psychiatric and cognitive effects of the Balkan Wars in the former Yugoslavia by interviewing 1,358 war survivors from Belgrade, Serbia; Rijeka, Croatia; Sarajevo, Federation of Bosnian-Herzegovina, BiH; and Banja Luka, Republic of Srpska, BiH. The sample consisted of men and women including combat veterans and torture survivors, many of them refugees (Internally Displaced Persons - IDPs). A control group based on sectarianism, gender, and age was also used in the study. According to the study, the IDPs in Belgrade included Kosovo Serbs displaced due to the NATO bombardment while the IDPs in Banja Luka were the Serbs forced from Muslim and Croat sections of BiH. The IDPs in Rijeka were mostly Croats from the Vukovar region and the IDPs in Sarajevo had been displaced by Serb-controlled regions in Bosnia. Regardless of sectarian affiliation, the findings showed a common theme: that the survivors reported a sense of injustice in relations to what they perceived to be a lack of redress for their trauma. In relations to the control group, the traumatized survivors had stronger emotional responses to impunity, a greater fear and loss of control over their lives, a diminished belief in the benevolence of people, a stronger affiliation to the dictates of their sectarian beliefs and higher rates of PTSD and depression.[19]

A study conducted in Croatia by faculty at the Split University Hospital and the Canton Institute of Public Health found an increase in the number of violent deaths in South Croatia (the region most involved in the 1991-1993 conflict). Not only was there an increase in homicides (77) and suicides (254) during the war but the method of death was more violent as well, including firearms and explosives especially among the younger population and those with military background. The researchers concluded that war related trauma seems to have a direct influence on both the number and pattern of violent deaths in this population.[20]

Research on pervasive war trauma in Bosnia-Herzegovina, the region that saw the most intense and prolonged conflict during the war years of 1992-1995, include a study conducted by the University Clinical Centre in Tuzla, now part of the Federation of Bosnia-Herzegovina (FBiH). This retrospective study, published in 2008, looked at 8,329 outpatients, 617 inpatients and 301 patients in the partial hospitalization program during the period 1999-2003. More psychotraumatized women were represented in the partial hospitalization program (61%) than in either the inpatient (24%) or outpatient (18%) programs. PTSD was found to be present in the majority (65%) of the patients overall with the majority of these individuals (73%) also presenting with comorbid other mental health problems. The study also found that there is considerable stigma associated with war-related mental health issues especially among war veterans.[21]

Another retrospective study on war trauma among residents of Bosnia-Herzegovina was conducted by the Department of Psychiatry, Norwegian University of Science and Technology in 2003. Their approach was to assess the effects of the war on the three major sectarian groups caught up in the 1992-1999 conflict. Toward this end they conducted face-to-face interviews from a sample of 3,313 respondents representing Bosniac Muslims, Bosnian Croat Catholics and Bosnian Orthodox Serbs from all three divisions – Federation of Bosnian-Herzegovina, Republic of Srpska and the Brcko District. The researchers used questions related to both war-related distress and war experiences. While about half of the respondents did not relate any war-related distress symptoms at this time, those that did felt a persistent sense of a foreshortened future as well as recurrent and bothersome thoughts or memories related to the conflict. This study also found that women reported significantly more war-related distress than men while the Bosnian Croats and Bosnian Serbs scored lower that their Bosniac counterparts on the War-related Distress Scale. The conclusions drawn from this study were that war related distress continues to be problematic even eight years following the conclusion of hostilities and that direct war experiences (seeing people killed, experiencing or witnessing rape, or being held prisoner) were a more salient stressor than indirect war experiences.[22]

A 1998 study conducted in Serbia at the University Clinic in Belgrade, prior to the NATO air attacks, compared war-related trauma to non-war-trauma among patients at this facility. The total sample size consisted of 175 subjects of varying age, gender, occupation and marital status. The patients were then divided into three groups – two experimental subgroups and a control group. The first subgroup consisted of 26 veterans traumatized during service in the war in Bosnia-Herzegovina while the second subgroup comprised of 44 residents of Belgrade traumatized in occupational or traffic accidents. The control group involved 105 people of which 45 had experienced some non-war mental trauma while the other 60 had never had experienced any trauma of any kind. Those who experienced trauma of any kind were then classified as to somatic versus mental trauma and those who were suffering from mental trauma were the ones most likely to present with PTSD symptoms.23

Other Serbian studies focused on the impact of the NATO bombings that occurred on a daily (often at night) basis from March 24 to June 9, 1999 terrorizing many areas of Serbia and Montenegro notably the Belgrade and Vojvodina Province in Serbia. The capital of Yojvodina Province, Novi Sad was the first to be attacked and continued to be attacked for 77 days. During this time, the Institute of Neurology, Psychiatry and Mental Health in Novi Sad set up a crisis line. Women made the majority of calls with concerns about their mental health as well as those of their family. The most compelling symptoms were anxiety, fear, panic and insomnia. The clinic at Novi Sad also reported on suicides during this period. Interestingly, there were fewer suicides reported during the 77 days of the air attacks leading to the speculation that the external threat of the immediate crisis served to suspend suicidal behaviors instead forcing them to concentrate on their and their family's survival. The suicide rate then peaked in the months following the end of the NATO attacks. And as in the study on suicides in southern Croatia, a more violent methodology emerged with more self-inflicted deaths conducted by firearms and hangings.[24]

A 2009 article in the Journal of the American Medical Association (JAMA) looked at the association of torture and other potentially traumatic events (PTEs) with mental health outcomes among populations exposed to mass conflict and displacement. While this meta-analysis study did not pertain to the Balkans per se, it found a common theme regarding the relationship of torture and pervasive exposure to traumatic events and the prevalence of PTSD and depression among survivors. The analysis involved looking at over 5,900 research articles published in English-language journals between 1980 and May 2009. From this pool 161 articles had sufficient diagnostic data for the study. This sample involved 81, 866 subjects from 40 countries. The meta-analysis clearly indicated that torture emerged as the single, strongest factor associated with the prevalence of post-traumatic stress disorders while cumulative exposure to potentially traumatic events was the strongest factor associated with depression. The authors argued for a more rigorous analysis of clinical events surrounding conflicts so as to adequately determining the post conflict mental health needs of these victims. The authors also suggested that a more through clinical assessment could also help provide better evidence in human rights abuse cases.[25]

Refugees

Refugees and displaced persons represent a significant causality of the Balkan Wars with over a million persons fleeing their homes either forcefully or in order to avoid being caught up in these conflicts. Despite conditions in the Dayton Accord and the Kosovo treaties allowing the return of refugees and displaced persons this was not the reality for tens-of-thousands of refugees. Serbs were expelled from Slovenia and Croatia while new sectarian boundaries in Bosnia-Herzegovina and Kosovo made this an unlikely scenario for the immediate future forcing these displaced individuals to reside in camps or resettle in their sectarian section of these respective states. Ironically, Serbia emerged as the former Yugoslavian state to have a viable inter-ethnic composition. Many refugees fled to and resettled in Western Europe, Great Britain or the United States.

Studies on the mental health of these refugees have emerged over time. An especially ambitious study was the international project, "Study of Long-Term Clinical and Social Outcomes After War Experiences in Ex-Yugoslavia", also known as "The Connect Project" or "STOP" project." Funded by the European

Community this was seen as a major study on the lasting effects of war trauma on those displaced by the Balkan Wars. The project, conceptualized in 2002, was designed to have two components, the first being a study on barriers to treatment and coping strategies within the targeted samples in Croatia, Serbia, Montenegro, Germany and the United Kingdom. In the second part, outcomes of treatment were to be assessed in mental health centers in Belgrade, Rijeka, Sarajevo and Zagreb. The researcher institutions involved in this project were: The London School of Medicine, Queen Mary, University of London; Department of Psychiatry and Psychotherapy, University of Technology, Dresden, Germany; School of Medicine, University of Modena and Reggio Emilia, Italy; School of Medicine, University of Belgrade, Serbia; Faculty of Philosophy, University of Zagreb, Croatia; School of Medicine, University of Rijeka, Croatia; School of Medicine, University of Sarajevo, Bosnia-Herzegovina; Faculty of Philosophy, University of Skopje, FRY Macedonia.

The original research design called for a random sample of a minimum of 640 subjects from each of the participating countries with a minimum of 250 in each entity within these countries, where applicable. The interviewers were to be native to the former Yugoslavia. Some findings, published in 2009, looked at the subjective quality of life and care costs among those participating in the original study. In the final analysis, this aspect of the project ended up focusing on Croatia, Serbia, Germany and the United Kingdom. Germany and the United Kingdom were focused given that they apparently had the highest number of immigrants from the former Yugoslavia. The results of this scaled back study had a total of 799 participants with only 264 subjects meeting the criteria for inclusion in the study. Of these, 88 resided in Croatia (45 males; 43 females), 65 in Serbia (23 males; 42 females) while 47 lived in Germany (26 males; 21 females) and 64 in the United Kingdom (30 males; 34 females). The findings showed that 221 (84%) met the criteria for PTSD at the time of their assessment. The overall finding of this study was that delay in providing mental health services to this population not only exacerbates the likelihood and intensity of PTSD but that these delays are costly as well. Again, this study echoed the results of similar research – factors linked with the likelihood of severe mental distress among war traumatized victims include higher age, lower education and exposure to more traumatic events.[26]

Another study of Bosnian refugees residing in Australia looked at the effects of PTSD and depression on successful acculturation into new environments. The study, published in 2005, involved 63 subjects (47 females; 16 males) who were participants in the Family in Cultural Transition (FICT) program for displaced persons. Eventually nearly half (30) participants failed to complete the program. While the sample was small the failure of the program to successfully reach these individuals indicates, in this study, that resettlement agencies tend to refer its most distressed refugees abroad. A secondary finding is that those refugees with untreated PTSD, especially those comorbid with depression, are difficult clients to work with as long as these conditions are untreated. An earlier study conducted in Croatia indicated that untreated older refugees and displaced persons who had experienced war-related traumatic experiences were more likely to manifest signs of dementia than a control group sample.[27]

Part of the problem with refugees and displaced persons was the seemingly uncoordinated efforts among agencies attempting to provide for these peoples especially while war was waging throughout the region. One success story was that in Macedonia during the brief, but intense, Kosovo conflict. Part of the success of this UN response was the apparent heads up given the United Nations by the NATO forces relevant to its pre-planned war on the Federal Republic of Yugoslavia.   At any rate, Macedonia, a country of 2.2 million, was overwhelmed with some 344,500 refugees, 15 times more than was expected, during the 77 day bombing campaign. Despite coping with millions of refugees worldwide, the United Nations High Commissioner for Refugees (UNHCR) and numerous NGOs responded to the needs of this overwhelming refugee population.

Fortunately, at the conclusion of the NATO bombing in June 1999 the vast majority of the refugees (223,000) returned to Kosovo. Even then some 2,500 refugees still resided in collective centers while another 10,400 refugees stayed on with host families. Later, a new wave of over 2,000 refugees, mainly Roma, sought asylum in Macedonia including some 8,000 Serbs and ethnic Albanians due to continued fears of ethnic reprisals from either side of the conflict. Many of the health care services were provided by the World Health Organization (WHO) Humanitarian Assistance Office headquartered in Skopie. These efforts kept the mortality rate lower than similar emergencies with only 107 deaths reported. Moreover, there were no major epidemic outbreaks during the crisis except for a small-scale run of hepatitis A in two camps (Cegrane and Neprosteno).   Most potential major health outbreaks were addressed aggressively with a focus on children with bloody diarrhea, suspected cholera, acute hepatitis, and suspected meningitis and measles.   There were no substantial cases of sexually transmitted diseases. Mental health issues were also aggressively addressed in the camps with fatigue, pain, anguish and fear being the most common complaints. The success for these refugee camps are attributed to: 1) the healthy conditions of the refugees entering the camps; 2) the short duration of the crisis and the quick return of most of the refugees; 3) the strong support of the host families; and 4) the effectiveness of the international aid. Weaknesses of the refugee crisis included the fact that Macedonia had no asylum law thereby allowing for the overwhelming numbers of refugees as well as difficult communication between camps, government agencies and health care providers.[28]

Women and Children

Other studies have shown that during the Balkan Wars women appear to be more susceptible to war trauma than men. Additional studies shine more light on this phenomenon. A joint study conducted by the Department of Psychiatry, Mostar University Hospital in BiH and the Department of Psychiatry and Psychological Medicine at the Rijeka University School of Medicine in Croatia looked at 367 adult women in order to ascertain the psychological consequences of war trauma and postwar stressors. The group was divided into two samples. One group of 187 women were from West Mostar and were exposed to serious war trauma while the second group of 180 women came from other areas of western Herzegovina and were not directly exposed to war trauma. As expected, the results showed that the women from Western Mostar, those that experienced significantly more traumatic events, suffered from more posttraumatic symptoms including PTSD. Moreover, postwar stressful events continued to fuel traumatic symptoms among this population. A major outcome of this study is that long-term exposure to war and postwar stressors continues to contribute to serious psychological consequences among civilian women. This research group also looked at the issue of secondary traumatization of wives of war veterans with PTSD. Here, they looked at 56 wives of war veterans diagnoses with PTSD and treated at the Center for Psychotrauma in Rijcka, Croatia. The study results showed that more than a third of the war veterans wives suffered from secondary traumatic stress concluding that any treatment plan for veterans needs to also include family members, notably wives.[29]

Another Croatian study, conducted at the Department of Psychiatry, Zagreb University Hospital on the psychological consequences of rape on women during the 1991-1995 wars in Croatian and Bosnia-Herzegovina studied 68 rape victims. The samples consisted of both Croatian and Bosniak women with 44 of them raped more than once and 21 raped daily during their captivity. Another 18 were forced to witness rapes. Most of the rapes also involved physical torture. While none of the women had preexisting psychiatric histories before the rapes, at the time of the study 52 suffered from depression, 51 had social phobias, 21 presented with PTSD and 17 had lasting sexual dysfunctions – most of these comorbid. Suicide ideations afflicted 25 of the rape victims. Out of the 29 who got pregnant from these rapes, 17 had abortions. This study indicates that war-time rape has deep immediate and long lasting consequences on these women and with substantial clinical, social and interpersonal issues.[30]

Many articles focused on the effects of the war on children and youth. A sampling of these studies portrays the complexity of this problem within the Balkans. Clearly, while war is the most significant human stressor, children are the most vulnerable to its effects. Children and youth represent a vulnerable population in both Bosnia-Herzegovina and in Serbia, notably in the areas subjected to NATO bombings (Pancevo region within the province of Vojvodina). In addition to living with parents who suffer from untreated PTSD, children and youth around Sarajevo are subjected to the constant threat of injuries, or death, from encountering unexploded armaments in the numerous mine fields surrounding the city. The focus on unmet social/cultural and psychological needs of traumatized children and youth is important because not doing so could be costly to the society in terms of later disorganization by this group as they mature. Substance abuse, dysfunctional families, poor educational and employment records are likely to increase among this untreated population. Also, segregated sectarian education adds to the ethnic divide and inter-group prejudices further complicating not only their lives but presents challenges to clinicians attempting to treat them.

In a study on the effect of the war in Croatia on children, a study by Marina Ajdukovic indicated that 696 children were wounded and 254 killed during the 1991-1995 war. Another 4,273 children lost one parent and 54 lost both. Many more children witnessed war violence and over 100,000 children were displaced during the conflict. Ajdukovic noted that the displaced children and youth suffered the greatest loss with serious disruptions in their development due to disruptions in education, destroyed communities and family disorganization. These findings were supported by a study conducted jointly by the Albert Einstein College of Medicine and the Society for Psychological Assistance in Zagreb, Croatia. The sample consisted of 56 children, aged 10 and 11 (31 boys and 25 girls) selected to attend a summer camps on the island of Kor-ula in the Adriatic Sea away from the fighting in 1994. Among this group, refugee children showed more pathology focusing on death of a family member, forced expulsion or heavy bombardment while the non-refugee children focused mainly on the bombardment.[31]

A lingering aftermath of the Balkan Wars is the number of active mine field (estimated at over 30,000) and uncleared, unexploded munitions. Studies done both in Banja Luka, BiH and at the Split University School of Medicine in Croatia addressed this problem that afflicts mostly children and youth. In the Bosnia-Herzegovina study, conducted by the Faculty of Philosophy at the University of Banja Luka, they looked at the psychosocial consequences suffered by adolescent victims of landmines in the post-war period. For those youth who survive these unsuspected explosions, their life-long injuries are traumatic events not only for the victim but for his/her family and the community – often rekindling memories of the intense sectarian conflict. The research conducted in Split, Croatia analyzed the effects of war-related injuries inflicted on children during the 1991-1995 conflict in Croatia and the 1992-1995 war in Bosnia-Herzegovina treated at the hospital in Split. The sample consisted of 94 youth aged between 10 and 16 including both boys and girls. Most of these children were wounded during bombardments or by leftover explosive devices. Boys in upper elementary grades and high school were at greatest risk of being wounded by leftover explosive devices than younger boys or girls. Extremities were the most commonly found wounds with injuries to the head/neck and abdomen being the most serious. In this study three children died and 39% were on permanent disability.[32]

Studies on children in Bosnia-Herzegovina, the region which sustained the longest involvement in the Balkan Wars include studies from both the Bosnian Serbs (Republic of Srpska/RS) and the mixed populations of what is now the

Federation of Bonsia-Herzegovina (Bosniaks and Bosnian Croats/FBiH). The RS study conducted at the Faculty of Philosophy at the University of Banja Luka studied the effect of "war psychic trauma syndrome" (WPTS) on 1,085 elementary (5th to 8th grade) school children, aged between 10 and 16, in November and December of 1995 at a time that the war was most intense. The research team found that the effects of WPTS, notably psychophysiological, emotional and cognitive impairments were more frequent among females that males and that these effects were more intense and frequent among those youth who lost somebody close to them in the conflict. This finding is in concert with other research findings: that the prolong nature of the conflict, in conjunction with the unpredictability of their situation, contributed to the intensity of post-traumatic crisis within vulnerable populations such as children and youth.[33]

A similar study was conducted among pubic school children in the Sarajevo Canton by Pecs University of Arts and Humanities in Pecs, Hungry. This study looked at 310 children from 6 public schools as well as parents (280) and teachers (156) four years following the Dayton Accord (October-November, 1999). The study found that many school-age children continued to live in unhealthy and dangerous environments including overcrowded living conditions, unsafe playgrounds and general poverty. The researchers noted that parents and teachers also lived and worked in stressful environments which impacted the children under their care. Nonetheless, the researchers found that most of the children tended to employ healthy strategies in coping with stressful events in their everyday lives. In this sense, the children seemed the least impaired group among this population.[34]

Exceptions to the resilience of children and youth in Bosnia-Herzegovina include two select populations, that of children of war veterans with PTSD and those living in foster homes. In a study conducted jointly by the Department of Psychiatry, University Hospital in Mostar, BiH and the Psychiatric Clinic at the Rijeka University Medical School in Rijeka, Croatia, the researchers looked at 154 veterans with PTSD treated at the Mostar University Hospital with a control group of 77 war veterans without signs of PTSD selected from veterans associations. The veterans presenting with PTSD showed a greater likelihood of having children with developmental disorders and behavioral and emotional problems than did the control group leading to the impression that the father's mental health problems afflicted their children as well. And most likely their wives as well as other studies have indicated. The study on the psychological disturbances of war-traumatized children from foster settings in BiH was conducted by the Department of Psychiatry, Tuzla University Medical Center. This study, conducted in March 2002, included 186 (93 boys and 93 girls) elementary school children aged 12 and 13 who were screened for the prevalence of PTSD and depression. The results showed that 90 (48%) of the children were forced into refugee status due to the war, mainly due to the loss of family members. Regarding PTSD, these symptoms were found to be highest among children who lost a parent but continued to reside with the surviving parent. This was higher than those children living in orphanages or residing with both parents. Besides, the loss of a parent was also associated with the prevalence of both PTSD and depression with no differences in rates between boys and girls within these strata. Interesting, the loss of both parents was associated with higher frequency of PTSD but not with depression. The researchers conclude that while all the children in the study experienced war trauma, those who lost one or both parents had the highest prevalence of PTSD, often comorbid with depression. The sample recording the lowest rate of psychological disturbances were those living with both parents.[35]

The situation of traumatized children and youth in the Federation of Yugoslavia (Serbia and Montenegro) focused mainly on the NATO bombing attacks of 1999. Petrovic, a faculty of the School of Philosophy at the University of Novi Sad, in a study of 1,934 primary school children, aged 11 to 14, in Vojvodina, Serbia, compared war-related traumatization (NATO bombings) with that of single-event non-war childhood trauma finding that repeated (chronic) stress leads to a higher level of traumatization coupled with serious personality changes. The study showed that children with war related trauma run a serious risk for problems of self-respect and personality disorders. Petrovic concluded that it is imperative that trauma intervention and monitoring be provided for these children. Another study out of the School of Philosophy at the University of Novi Sad, by Maija Zotovic, looked at the relationship of PTSD and depression among a sample of 629 children and youth in Vojvodina, 14 months following the end of the NATO bombing attacks. The research results found that nearly 60 percent of the children and youth showed signs of trauma which impacted on their everyday coping skills. An outcome of this study was that the best indicators of clinical symptoms among this population are changes in personality especially those patterns that reflect negative affectivity. Along similar lines, a joint study conducted by the University of Novi Sad and Charles de Gaulle University in France, found that children (aged 7 at the time of the NATO bombings) from towns that were directly hit by the air campaign showed more marked signs of personal distress five years later, in comparison to those children not directly impacted by these attacks. This phenomenon was more common in male subjects than in females.[36]

A study of traumatized children in Prishtina, conducted by the Faculty at Pecs University of Arts and Sciences, Pecs, Hungry, in 2000 found similarities among this population to that of a sample taken from Sarajevo. The Kosovo sample differed from the besieged Sarajevo study in that the Prishtina children involved refugees relocated to camps in Macedonia hence having the additional feature of socio-cultural anomie – a common factor among all groups of refugee children regardless of ethnic/sectarian/national origin. The study reported three major groups of stressor: 1) a lack of cultural and social security resources they once enjoyed in their native homeland; 2) poor mental and physical health conditions; and 3) school-related stressors. The study, conducted by the Canadian International Children's Institute (ICI), warned that environmental, educational and social/cultural circumstances need to be taken into account when addressing traumatized children, especially those who were refugees.[37]

Reconciliation

Few would argue that hate is the antithesis to healing and reconciliation. Yet reconciliation is a big challenge in the former Yugoslavia where societies remain segmented generally along sectarian lines. Perhaps this difficulty is best illustrated by the situation in Bosnian-Herzegovina. The UN, NATO and the EU have attempted to implement change in Bosnia and Herzegovina in preparing it for potential membership in both the North Atlantic Treaty Organization the European Union. The major obstacle toward realizing these goals is the rigid ethnocentrism and sectarian entrenchment of the three major ethnic groups comprising Bosnia and Herzegovina. Indeed, the main institutions for sustaining sectarian ethnocentrism outside of the family and community are security agencies (public and private) and education.

On the surface, the Republic of Srpska (RS) appears to have unified its police and educational institutions. But this impression is misleading since these institutions are dominated by Bosnian Serbs and maintain a strong affiliation with Serbia. In the Federation of Bosnia and Herzegovina (FBiH) the Muslim Bosniak majority share a fragile coexistence with the minority Bosnian Croat Catholics with each attempting to reinforce their own ethnic separatism through the school system and the complex political structure. Despite a call for an end to sectarian education, dual educational socialization systems exist, often under the same roof, within the primary and secondary schools. These divided schools promote their own sectarian history and language curricula widening the cultural divide within the Federation portion of Bosnia and Herzegovina. This sectarian separatism extends to institutions of higher education as well posing a serious challenge to the Bologna Accord stipulating a common European educational format in colleges and universities.

A complicated and convoluted political structure obviates any realistic attempts at a meaningful centralized government. In FBiH there is the Entity level with a House of Representatives and a House of People, a president and two vice-presidents. Then there is the Cantonal level with each of the ten cantons having its own assembly and security forces. Lastly, there is the Municipal level each with its own municipal council and police. The Republic of Srpska (RS) has a National Assembly, the Council of Peoples, a president, two vice-presidents and a prime minister. There are no cantons in RS, only municipalities. At the state level there is the Parliamentary Assembly (Skupstina) comprised of the National House of Representatives (Predstavnike Dom) with 28 seats from the Federation of BiH and 14 from the Republic of Srpska. A similarly complex and ethnically divided national court system has emerged but is basically ineffective. The only national (multi-ethnic) police forces are the Federal Bosnian State Investigation and Protection Agency (SIPA) and the Border Patrol both recently created and supervised by the EU Police

Mission. Most policing, however, falls within the 15 different police forces under 13 different Ministers of Interior. Corruption and ethnic preference predominates within these forces. Promises for reconciliation within BiH are contingent upon certain fundamental changes that are needed to radically transform the existing situation including adopting the Bologna Standards for higher education which should then filter through both law enforcement agencies and education facilities. Other studies support this analysis.

Collectively, psychological crisis among children and youth serve to impede any reconciliation efforts within the various ethnic/sectarian groups caught up in the Balkan conflicts. Studies on ethnic stereotypes in Bosnia-Herzegovina measured the nature of continued out-group negative images harbored by Bosniak and Serbian youth. One study, conducted by the faculty at the University of Banja Luka, RS compared attitudes of youths in Sarajevo (Bosniaks) and Banja Luka (Serbs). These results showed significant inter-group negative stereotypes between the two groups – a clear reflection of their respective socialization within a polarized society Another study, conducted by Srdan Puhalo also from Banja Luka, focused on the ethnical distance of citizens of Republic of Srpska (RS) and the Federation of Bosnia and Herzegovina (FBiH) indicating a broader spectrum of ethnic dislikes among adults within these two entities. The FBiH sample disliked Romas the most followed in descending order: Albanians, Macedonians, Serbs and Montenegrians. Slovenians and Croats were the least rejected by the citizens of FBiH. The Croats were most adamant about their ethnic rejections than their more populous Bosniaks within the greater FBiH sample. The RS sample rejected the Bosniaks the most followed, in descending order: Romas, Croats, Slovenians, and Macedonians. They rejected Montenegrians the least. The RS sample was more adamantly against inter-ethnic/sectarian marriages as well.[38]

A study conducted by the faculty of psychology at the University of Novi Sad examined the relationship of war trauma and the process of reconciliation. The authors noted the difficulty associated with this process given that the Balkan Wars of 1991-1995 between Serbs, Croats and Bosniaks were known for their cruelty, ethnic cleansing and war crimes. Given these parameters they wondered if reconciliation was possible. And if so, what are the chances and obstacles for this process. In order to ascertain an answer they sampled 800 individuals in 2000-2002, 400 from Vukovar in Croatia (Serbs and Croats) and 400 in Mostar in BiH (Croats and Bosniaks). A promising outcome of the study was that the level of traumatic experience in itself was not correlated with someone's readiness for reconciliation. One of the strongest positive variables was having friends from and positive relations with members of other sectarian groups. On a collective basis, the authors felt that schools teaching tolerance and the media offering positive examples of all groups could do much to foster reconciliation.   It was also noted that war crime trials are a positive factor leading toward reconciliation.[39] Hjort and Frisen added to this discussion noting that intergroup intolerance may be reduced by intergroup contact providing: (1)

that the groups were seen as being equal; (2) that intergroup cooperation was fostered in these interactions; (3) that they shared common goals; and (4) shared supportive values and norms. They attempted to test this thesis among females aged 13 to 24 participating in Koraci Nade social clubs in Herzegovina and RS. While the participants felt that their Koraci Nade involvement was a positive one, it did little to influence either ethnic identity or cross-ethnic friendships. Hence, the results remain mixed on particular methods for reconciliation while, at the same time, offering means for progressing on this needed social factor.[40]

Chapter Six

Assessment and Treatment of Trauma

Introduction: Reliability & Validity

The process involved in evaluating a mental health problem to its effective treatment involves a number of steps from the initial intake interview to providing an individualized treatment protocol. A distinction is made between an initial, brief screening and that of more reliable assessment protocols. The initial screening can be done by just about any mental health professional or paraprofessional while the administration of an assessment protocol requires specialized training usually by a certified/licensed professional such as a psychiatrist or psychologist. The assessment tools used in determining a definitive diagnosis varies with their effectiveness based on their test construction reliability and validity.

Reliability refers to the accuracy of the instrument in measuring what it purports to assess. Accuracy refers to the consistency of score obtained by people taking the same test. Score consistency is usually measured by a correlation coefficient which is the expression of the degree of correspondence, or relationship, between two sets of scores. Here a +1 reflects a perfect correlation. The most common way of computing the correlation coefficient is using the Pearson Product-Movement Correlation Coefficient. Types of reliability are "Test-Retest Reliability" (repeating the same test to the same subjects on a second occasion), "Alternate-Form Reliability" (two different versions of the same test are administered to the same subjects – e.g., Forms L and M),"Split-Half Reliability" (a single test, consisting of equivalent halves, is administered once and the scores determined by comparing the corresponding responses) and "Kuder-Richardson Reliability and Coefficient Alpha" (a single administration of a test is administered to the subjects with the correlation coefficient determined by inter-item consistency). The coefficient of stability is the measure linked with test-retest reliability while the coefficient of equivalence is the measure associated with alternate forms reliability and the coefficient of internal consistency is used with split-half reliability. The reliability of a test is usually expressed in terms of the "Standard Error of Measurement" (SEM). It is calculated by dividing the standard deviation for the test into the reliability coefficient. Using IQ test results, if a person has a SEM of 5 and an IQ result of 100 then we would state that the person's IQ is most likely 100 + or – 5; that is between 95 and 105.[1]

Validity, on the other hand, addresses the instruments utility – how useful is it in the assessment process. That is, does the test measure what it purports to measure (its content) and if so, how well does it measure it? Content validity is not the same as "Face Validity." Face validity is the extent to which test items appear to measure what it purports to measure but is not substantiated by a more rigorous procedure. Actually the more direct the questions in an assessment, the less valid its outcome. There are three basic ways to ascertain content validity: (1) Criterion-Related Validity; (2) Content Validity; and (3) Construct Validity.

Criterion-Related Validity is determined by correlating predictor and criterion scores. This form of validity depends on a mathematical correlational analysis (Pearson's r) termed the "coefficient of determination." There are two types of criterion-related validity – predictive and concurrent. Predictive validity is established by administering the predictor (like the MMPI) to all applicants/candidates and then later assessing the scores/profiles with those who are successful or who failed the program. Concurrent validity is when you administer the predictor to current applicants/candidates based on the data derived from the predictive validity process. Criterion-related concurrent validity often uses cutting scores to determine if someone is accepted into a program.

Content Validity refers to the extent to which an instrument adequately measures the content domain that it was designed to measure (IQ, personality, aptitude, attitude...). This is generally determined by a blind review of experts in the field, a process known as *judgment of experts.*

Construct Validity refers to the extent to which an instrument measures the theoretical construct it was designed to measure. Here the test scores are compared to similar instruments whose reliability and validity has been determines to be accurate. Often the *multitrait-multimethod matrix* is used in this process measuring the convergent and discriminant validity of the instrument in relation to other similar instruments.[2]

Obviously the strength of an assessment tool is contingent upon its reliability and validity. Sometimes a number of instruments are used in a battery of tests. The collective result comes to constitute the client's "baseline" data. Certain assessments can then be used during the treatment process in order to measure the effectiveness of the intervention protocol (s). Hence, these assessments provide "outcome" measures. Within this process the screening/assessment procedure should help determine a definitive diagnosis or diagnoses which, in turn, drives the treatment protocol. Treatment can include individual or group therapies, psychotherapies, cognitive-behavioral therapies, medical procedures (acupuncture...) and psychopharmacological interventions, or a combination of these clinical approaches.

Screening & Assessments

Assessment of mental illness, including traumatic stress, includes initial screening instruments as well as more detailed clinical protocols. The (MSE) most common screening instrument used by the medical profession is the Mental Status Exam. If mental pathology is suspected, then the next major reference resource is the DSM (Diagnostic and Statistical Manual of Mental Disorders) and the SCID (Structured Clinical Interview for the DSM). The DSM series follows a multi-axel format with the first three axes being the most relevant to the diagnosis of mental disorders. As stated earlier, Axis I includes Major Mental Disorders as well as conditions that may result in a mental disorder if left unattended or untreated while Axis II addresses Personality Disorder and Mental Retardation. Axis III provides the etiology and associated medical conditions along with the appropriate ICD codes.

Numerous assessment instruments have been developed over the years for PTSD, Depression, Anxiety and Personality Disorders. Most have been influenced by either the MSE or DSM, or both. A stand alone clinical protocol, however, is the MMPI (Minnesota Multiphasic Personality Inventory). Indeed, the MSE and MMPI are perhaps the most widely used mental health assessment tools used throughout the world. The administration and interpretation of these assessment require professionally trained individuals, mainly those with doctoral degrees (MD, Ph.D, PsyD...), and are not to be used by lay personnel, including those within the military. Other brief assessment protocols lend themselves to lesser qualified technicians and clinical assistants.

Mental Status Exam

The MSE covers six categories of mental status that are generally observed during the initial clinical consultation. There are various methods of conducting the MSE with most trained clinicians using the casual conversational approach so as to not startle the interviewee and further elevating their stress level.

Appearance, Attitude, and Activity: Appearance is the assessment of the physical characteristics of the client including physical disabilities or abnormalities as well as the client's dress, hygiene, grooming. This observation needs to be in concert with the client's cultural norms and social class and not necessarily that of the clinician. Attitude is how the client reacts to the questions during the intake process – the factors here are cooperativeness, hostility, or over dependency.... Activity looks at the client's physical demeanor during the interview. What is their activity level especially that which seems abnormal for the situation – sitting rigidly, involuntary tics or tremors, fidgeting, unique mannerisms....

Mood and Affect: Mood and affect are sometimes difficult to distinguish from each other. Mood is how the person describes his/her feelings while affect is the external manifestation of these feelings. The continuum for mood and affect runs from depression to mania. Generally speaking mood and affect fall into six categories: euthymic (calm, friendly, pleasant...); angry (belligerent, confrontational, hostile, irritable, oppositional, outraged...); euphoric (cheerful, elated, ecstatic...); apathetic (flat affect, dull, bland...); dysphoric (despondent, grieving, hopeless, distraught, sad, overwhelmed...); and apprehensive (anxious, fearful, nervous, tense, panicked, terrified...).

Speech and Language: Speech looks at fluency of the language spoken. Also note if this is the client's original language or a second language. This category of the MSE looks at the following language functions: fluency of speech, repetition, comprehension, naming, writing, reading, prosody (variations in rate, rhythm and stress in speech), and quality of speech. Portions of standardized intelligence tests such as the Weschler batteries and the Standford-Binet test can be used to determine many of these features. Disorders to look out for during this phase of the MSE include cluttering, dysgraphia, dyslexia, echolalia, mutism, palialilia, pressured speech, stuttering, and word salad, among others.

Thought Process, Thought Content, and Perception: Thought process involves evaluating the organization, flow and production of thought looking for abnormalities such as flight of ideas, loose associations, tangentiality, clang associations, echolalia, perseveration, thought blocking and word salad. Thought content and perception looks for delusions, homicidal or suicidal ideations, magical thinking, overvalued ideas, obsessions, paranoia, phobias, preoccupation, rumination, suspiciousness, depersonalization, derealization, hallucinations and illusions.

Cognition: Cognition is the ability to think using one's intellect, logic, reasoning and memory. The cognitive testing sequence involves: (1) orientation X 4 – person, place, time and situation; (2) attention and concentration; (3) registration and short-term memory; (4) long-term memory (verbal and non-verbal); (5) constructional and visuospatial ability; and (6) abstraction and conceptualization. Standardized tests used for attention and concentration include the Trail-making Tests, Symbol Digit Test, and the Stroop Color-Word Test while the Digit Span (forward and backwards) sub-test of the Weschler IQ batteries are used for attention. Short-term memory is usually tested by giving the client 3 common words (cat, blue, bike...) at the beginning of the session and then having them repeat these words back to you at least 15 minutes into the session. Visual memory and construction and visuospatial ability can be tested with the Bender-Gestalt, Draw-A-Clock, Rey-Osterrieth Complex Figure Test or Trail-making Tests.

Insight and Judgment: Insightfulness includes the capacity for abstraction and the ability to communicate effectively with appropriate cognitive functioning while having a stable mood and affect and not manifesting any thought disorder. Insight and judgment are seen as being interrelated in that the ability to make sound judgments or decisions is dependent upon an adequate level of insight. Insight is the ability to be self-aware - being conscious of one's feelings, ideas, and motives. Intrusive defense mechanisms such as repression, displacement, dissociation, reaction formation and intellectualization often arise during this portion of the MSE as well as acting out, externalization, idealization, projection and denial and distortions. These are features that impair one's insight and judgment.[3]

The *Mini-Mental Exam* is an abbreviated form that is often used in hospital intakes. It consists of five categories: Orientation; Registration; Attention and Calculation; Recall; and Language. Under orientation the client is asked what is the year, month, season, day and month as well as where he/she is at that time. Under registration the client is asked to name 3 objects that you present them and ask them to repeat them back to you.. In attention and calculation have the client count back from 100 by 7s. Stop after 5 answers. Under recall, ask for the 3 objects repeated earlier. With language, have the client name a pencil, and watch; have them repeat "No ifs, ands, or buts; and then have them follow a 3-stage command (take a paper in your right hand and fold it in half and put it on the floor). Then have them read a sentence and then write it followed with having the client copy a geometric design. These are usually scored and are used primarily with people suspected of brain damage including those with TBIs.[4]

The DSM-V proposed PTSD draft revisions

The following conditions regarding the duration of the PTSD disorder along with the fact that these disturbances cause clinically significant distress or impairment in social, occupational, or other important areas of functioning, remains the same as stated in the original 1980 DSM-III PTSD diagnosis.

A. Exposure to one or more of the following event(s): death or threatened death, actual or threatened serious injury, or actual or threatened sexual violation, in one or more of the following ways:
   1. Experiencing the event(s) him/herself.
   2. Witnessing, in person, the event(s) as they occurred to others.
   3. Learning that the event(s) occurred to a close relative or close friend; in such cases, the actual or threatened death must have been violent or accidental.
   4. Experiencing repeated or extreme exposure to aversive details of the event(s) (e.g., first responders collecting body parts; police officers repeatedly exposed to details of child abuse); this does not apply to exposure through electronic media, television, movies, or pictures, unless this exposure is work related.

B. Intrusion symptoms that are associated with the traumatic event(s) (that began after the traumatic event(s)), as evidenced by one or more of the following:
   1. Spontaneous or cued recurrent, involuntary, and intrusive distressing memories of the traumatic event(s) – in children, repetitive play may occur in which themes or aspects of the traumatic event(s) are expressed.

2. Recurrent distressing dreams in which the content and/or affect of the dream is related to the event(s) – in children these may be frightening dreams without recognizable content.
3. Dissociative reactions (e.g., flashbacks) in which the individual feels or acts as if the traumatic event(s) were recurring – in children, trauma-specific reenactment may occur in play.
4. Intense or prolonged psychological distress at exposure to internal cues that symbolize or resemble an aspect of the traumatic event(s).
5. Marked physiological reactions to reminders of the traumatic event(s).

C. Persistent avoidance of stimuli associated with the traumatic event(s) (that began after the traumatic event(s)), as evidenced by efforts to avoid one or more of the following:
1. Avoids internal reminders (thoughts, feelings, or physical sensations) that arouse recollections of the traumatic event(s).
2. Avoids external reminders (people, places, conversations, activities, objects, situations) that arouse recollections of the traumatic event(s).

D. Negative alterations in cognition and mood that are associated with the traumatic event(s) (that began or worsened after the traumatic event(s)), as evidenced by three or more of the following – in children, as evidenced by two or more:
1. Inability to remember an important aspect of the traumatic event(s) (typically dissociative amnesia, not due to head injury, alcohol or drugs).
2. Persistent and exaggerated negative expectations about one's self, others, or the world.
3. Persistent distorted blame of self or others about the cause or consequences of the traumatic event(s).
4. Pervasive negative emotional state – fear, horror, anger, guilt, or shame.
5. Markedly diminished interest or participation in significant activities.
6. Feeling of detachment or estrangement from others.
7. Persistent inability to experience positive emotions (e.g., unable to have loving feelings, psychic numbing).

E. Alterations in arousal and reactivity that are associated with the traumatic event(s) (that began or worsened after the traumatic event(s)), as evidenced by three or more of the following – in children, as evidenced by two or more:
1. Irritable or aggressive behavior.
2. Reckless or self-destructive behavior.
3. Hypervigilance.

4. Exaggerated startle response.
5. Problems with concentration.
6. Sleep disturbance...difficulty falling or staying asleep, or restless sleep.5

Accompanying the DSM, beginning with the 1987 DSM-III-R version, is the SCID, or Structured Clinical Interview for the DSM, a semi-structured interview schedule, like the MSE. The SCID-I is a diagnostic tool used to determine Axis I disorders – major mental disorders including mood disorders, psychotic disorders, anxiety disorders and the substance-use disorders. The SCID-II, on the other hand, is a diagnostic tool for assessing personality disorders. The current edition is the DSM-RV edition of SCID-I and SCID-II which was modified in 2010. In 2007, revisions in SCID-I were made to better discern between Acute Stress Disorder and PTSD.[6]

The MMPI's

The Minnesota Multiphasic Personality Inventory (MMPI)is one of the most widely used tools, along with the MSE, for screening for mental illness and is the leading assessment for predicting occupational success, including mental health professionals, and law enforcement and legal professionals. The MMPI was first standardized in 1943 and readied for use. Its reliability and validity is not so much due to its original construction validation sample, which was poor by current standards, but to the numerous sets of predictive data generated by the MMPI during its nearly 70 years of retrospective research relevant to both concurrent and predictive studies. Its predictive strength comes from the instrument being administered to all individuals entering academic and/or professional studies at the time of their entry into these programs. This represented the concurrent study data whereby aggregate profiles were later developed reflecting those who were successful or unsuccessful in these professions – hence leading to the MMPI's predictive strength. These retrospective studies have led to a wealth of data in the areas of professional aptitude and mental health status. Clearly, this is one of the most studied assessment tools with thousands of published reports including samples worldwide. All versions of the MMPI (MMPI-2; MMPI-A; MMPI-2 RF) provide a graphic profile on the basis clinical and validity scales using a bell-distribution based T-score analysis where 50 is the mean and the standard deviation is 10 and where two standard deviations above the mean generally indicates statistical significance relevant to pathology.

The Validity Scales

The original MMPI consists of three validity scales (Lie, Validity, and Corrections). The Lie score (L) is based on a group of items that place the respondent in a favorable light but are unlikely to be truthfully answered as being true. The Validity Scale (F) consisted of unfavorable items unlikely for any respondent to answer all as relevant to his/her life. Accordingly, high F scores reflect a number of responding errors: carelessness in responding, gross eccentricity or deliberate malingering (faking bad). The Correction Scale (K) again uses specifically chosen items that measure test-taking attitudes. A high K score most likely indicates defensiveness or an attempt to fake good. A low K score, on the other hand, may reflect frankness and self-analysis or yet another attempt to fake bad. Besides, the K score provides a computed correction factor that is added to certain of the clinical scales in order to provide a weighted adjusted scale: scale 1 (Hs) = +.5 K; scale 4 (Pd) = +.4K; scale 7 (Pt) = +1K; scale 8 (Sc) = +1K; and scale 9 (Ma) = +.2K. These weighted factors are provided on the MMPI *Profile and Case Summary* sheet which presents a graphic representation of the MMPI scores based on a T-score distribution.

The Clinical Scales
The body of the original MMPI consists of 10 clinical scales that correspond to the major clinical syndromes posited by the DSMs.

1. Hypochondriasis Scale (Hs). This scale measures the level of preoccupation with illnesses and health as well as long-term fears and worries about one's health.

2. Depressive Scale (D). This scale measures self-worth ranging from hopelessness (high T-score), to effortless optimism (low T-score). High scores, with suicidal ideations, represent a red flag for suicide potential.

3. Hysteria Scale (Hy). This scale measures one's preoccupation with body pain including conversion disorders (psychosomatic illnesses with no biological basis). At the other end of the continuum, low T-scores indicate levels of trustfulness and a lack of hostility.

4. Psychopathic Deviant Scale (Pd). This scale is designed to measure amoral, asocial behavior and levels of empathy. Also measured are family conflicts, feelings of alienation, and problems with authority. This is a critical item when assessing law enforcement or military personnel. It is important to discern if a high score is indicative of a transitory event in the past or if the score reflects a pervasive characterological feature of one's personality.

5. Masculine-Feminine Interests Scales (Mf). This scale measures sexual identification and sexual occupational/professional identification. It focuses on contrasts of action versus feeling and expressions of aggression (verbal versus physical). This scale does not identify homosexuality or lesbianism. Instead it tends to identify certain personality traits including competitiveness and aggressiveness, as well as being outgoing, uninhibited, and self-confident.

6.　　　　Paranoia Scale (Pa).　This scale measures ideas of mistreatment and persecution (higher T-scores) versus heightened interpersonal sensitivity and moral righteousness (lower T-scores).　It combines with other scales to indicate critical personality disorders, including Paranoid PD, and certain dangerous clinical disorders such as Paranoid Schizophrenia and Paranoid Delusional Disorder.

7.　　　　Psychasthenia Scale (Pt).　In contemporary terms, this scale measures obsessive and compulsive tendencies including Obsessive Compulsive Personality Disorder and Obsessive Compulsive Anxiety Disorder.　It also indicates excessive fears and other forms of rumination secondary to anxiety. It a good index of psychological turmoil, discomfort and agitation.

8.　　　　Schizophrenia Scale (Sc).　This scale measures the degree of personal confusion, including serious thought disorders such as alienation from one's own feelings and from others, impaired concentration and attention, uncontrolled impulses, excitability, peculiar body experiences, delusions, depersonalization and hallucinations.　A number of personality disorders are indicted by elevated T-scores on this item (schizoid, Schizotypal, Borderline, Antisocial…) as well as Schizophrenia.　Extremely high T-scores, however, are more likely to reflect transitory psychosis secondary to Substance-Use Disorders.

9.　　　　Hypomania Scale (Ma).　This scale measures a person's activity from intense autonomic over-activity (high T-scores) to a markedly slow personal temperament (low T-scores).　Autonomic endocrine/limbic dysregulation can result in an override of the executive functioning of the frontal lobe, thereby falsely presenting hypermania as a thought disorder or psychosis.　The manias are associated with a number of disorders including bipolar affective disorders, paraphilias, and impulse control disorders.　They can also emerge as secondary features of Substance-Use Disorders, and organic brain damage including dementia and TBIs.

10.　　　Social Introversion-Extroversion Scale (Si).　This scale indicates one's level of introversion versus extroversion. In western societies where 75 percent of the people are extroverted and only about 25 percent introverted, extremes of the latter reflect pathology.　However, extremely low T-scores can be problematic in that these

11.   individuals can be overly dependent on others for their
                       social motivation and interaction. Indeed, being
                       slightly socially introverted may prove to be a virtue for
                       clinicians assessing and/or treating victims of traumatic
                       stress.

Supplemental Scales
A number of additional scales, many outside the clinical
criteria outlined in the DSM, are apart of the more recent
MMPI-2. Even with about 20 years of data available, most of
these additional scales are not yet considered to have the
reliability and validity of the original 13 scales. However, four
supplementary scales are common to both the MMPI and the
MMPI-2. These scales appeared as a modification to the
original MMPI and many practitioners used to the expanded
MMPI continue to draw on these items when using the MMPI-
2.
A Scale. High T-score on this item reflects miserable and
unhappy individuals.
R Scale. On the other hand, high scores on this scale reflect
individuals who are careful and cautious.
Combined A/R Scales. U.S. Veterans Administration data
profiled the A/R combinations among its patients. Depressive
diagnoses were associated with the high A-high R profile
while personality disorders were mostly associated with the
low A-low R profile.
Es Scale. High scores on this item are indicative of stability
and good mental health.
MAC-R scale. This scale does not measure if a person is a
problem drinker as much as it indicates his/her potential to
exhibit problems if he/she drinks. High T-scores on this item
indicate individuals who present themselves as being socially
extroverted, self-confident, and assertive but are also likely to
be exhibitionistic and risk takers.[7]

Political Correctiveness and MMPI Revisions

The genesis of the current review of the predictive effectiveness of
psychological testing was rooted in the U.S. Civil Rights Act of 1964, Section H
of Title VII which specifically makes reference to the use of nondiscriminatory
tests for employment decisions. This, and other civil rights cases, led to the
restructuring of the original MMPI. A major decision was the *Soroka v.
Dayton-Hudson* case, better known as the Target case, which was filed as a class
action on September 7th, 1989. The case involved the use of a pre-employment
psychological screening device for security officers working for Target stores.

The significant of the Soroka case was that it coincided with passage of the *Americans with Disabilities Act of 1990* which underscored the importance of keeping the invasiveness of psychological inquiries in pre-employment testing to a minimum. At that time the Target Stores used the Rodgers Condensed CPI-MMPI which was developed in 1966. The California Psychological Inventory (CPI) augmented the MMPI by looking at attributes on one's personality using a 20 scale format compared to the MMPI's traditional 10 clinical scales. However, the CPI also used 194 MMPI items in its 462-item measure. Security officer applicants screened out by Rodgers CPI-MMPI claimed that the inventory was not job related and was offensive and intrusive. Part of the problem with the Rodgers assessment tool was that no empirical data was available related to its administration, norming, standardization, and interpretation even though such standards existed independently for the CPI and the MMPI. Hence, in August 1989, the MMPI-2 was introduced. This version came 46 years following the original MMPI. The reason for a change in the MMPI was not that it needed renorming (subsequent normings of the original has greatly increased its reliability and validity) but was to replace outdated items. Toward this end, the MMPI-2 omitted the 16 repeat items, religious and sexual preference items and what was felt to be outdated items. In all 107 items were eliminated due to these reasons, but 108 items were added. Some of these new items pertain to revisions in the validity scales while others pertain to new scales and measures such as family dynamics, Type A behavior, eating disorders, substance abuse, and suicide.

The MMPI-2 is even longer (567 items) than the original MMPI (566 items). The norming sample for the MMPI-2 consisted of respondents who had higher educational levels than that of the general public, thereby contributing to a T-score distribution flaw where now T=65 (a standard deviation and a half) indicates statistical significance instead of the traditional two-standard deviations (T=70 or more). In order to use the decades of reliability and validity associated with the original MMPI, the first 370 items of the revised MMPI-2 are said to correspond to the three-validity and ten-clinical scales of the MMPI, without of course the items measuring religiosity and sexuality. Given the significant changes reflected in the MMPI-2, many clinicians question the transferability of the original MMPI's predictive validity, especially when measuring mental pathology and critical occupational suitability to the new versions. For one, hyper-religiosity and hyper-sexuality are common features of manic episodes. A protocol used by forensic psychologists who prefer the greater reliability, validity and predictability of the original MMPI is to alert those being tested as to archaic terms and the flexibility of tense (past or present). The authors found that 10 of the 566 items raised the most questions among those taking the MMPI:

Item 48:   When I am with people I am bothered by hearing very *queer* things.

Item 57:   I am a good *mixer.*

Item 70:   I used to like *drop-the-handkerchief.*

Item 105:	Sometimes when I an not feeling well I am *cross.*
Item 118:	In school I was sometimes sent to the principal for *cutting up.*
Item 129:	Often I can't understand why I have been so *cross* and *grouchy.*
Item 236:	I *brood* a great deal.
Item 381:	I am often said to be *hotheaded.*
Item 471:	In school my marks in *deportment* were quite regularly bad.
Item 506:	I am a *high-strung* person.

Being able to define these terms in contemporary terms is the only adjustment that is needed for the continued of the original MMPI and its 50 years of post facto predictive validity. The original MMPI assessment, at the time of job entry, should be conducted along with a Mental Status Exam, with the MMPI score constituting a baseline profile. Subsequent, the abbreviated MMPI assessment, consisting of the first 360 items covering the three validity scales and ten clinical scales, can then be administered as needed with these profiles compared with the initial MMPI baseline profile.

In 1992, the MMPI-A (adolescent version) was introduced based mainly on the items from the original MMPI. The MMPI-A comes in both a long form (478 items) and a short form consisting of 350 items. Most recently, the MMPI-2-RF (restructured form) is an attempt to give the MMPI-2 clinical scales the same validity of those in the original MMPI. Yet, many clinicians see these efforts as further complicating the assessment role of the MMPI, especially regarding major clinical syndromes and personality disorders. The added content scales of the MMPI-2, such as the Dominance Scale, Addiction Potential Scale, Addiction Acknowledgement Scale, Social Discomfort Scale, Type A scale, Over-Controlled Hostility Scale, Marital Distress Scale and Psy-5 scales all seem to add to the original problem as to why the MMPI was changed in the first place – claiming intrusive attributes of human behavior that may not stand up in a court-of-law when their reliability and validity is challenged, let alone what they purport to measure. Indeed, this controversy over the MMPI-2-RF prompted a special issue of the *Journal of Personality Assessment* (Vol. 87, Issue No. 2, October, 2006).[8]

Other Tests for Depression and Anxiety

The Projectives

Many European clinicians are trained in psychoanalysis and rely more heavily on projective assessment techniques than do their American counterparts. The major projective techniques were developed in the early part of the 20th century and relied heavily on clinical training and clinical judgment while the instruments developed in the United States were more quantified relying on standard scores and statistical significance. Both types of assessments are quite useful as long as they are administered and interpreted by qualified clinicians. Included in the category of projective assessment protocols is The Rorschach developed by the Swiss psychiatrist, Hermann Rorschach in 1921. He was the first to apply the inkblots projective technique and relating to dimensions of personality, including pathology. The Rorschach Inkblot Test consists of 10 cards or plates each consisting of one ink block. Five are black or gray and five are colored. Clients are asked to project what they see in each card. The American psychologist, Henry Murray developed a similar projective technique, one involving hazy pictures and a blank sheet, known as the Thematic Apperception Test (TAT) in 1938 by Murray and Christina Morgan. The TAT uses an interview approach using certain of the pool of 30 black-and-white picture cards and a blank white card. In 1938, Loretta Bender developed the Bender Visual Motor Gestalt Test, also know as the Bender-Gestalt Test. Initially the gestalt (geometric figures) drawings were aggregated and used to determine a student's appropriate grade level. The Bender-Gestalt Test consists of nine cards showing geometric designs presented as dots, curves or lines. There is a copy and a recall component to the assessment with the recall done by memory. The Bender Gestalt Test is now a viable component of neurological test batteries. Florence Goodenough developed a Draw-A-Man test in 1926 which was revised in the 1960s by Dale Harris resulting in the popular "Draw-a-Person" techniques. Others soon followed suit with the House-Tree-Person and other variations of the Draw-a-Person tests. Another popular and widely used projective technique is the Sentence-Completion technique. Of these techniques, the Rotter Incomplete Sentence Bland (ISB) is perhaps the most widely used. It consists of 40 sentence stems that need to be completed.[9]

Brief Assessment Tools for Anxiety and Depression

Aaron Beck has developed a number of short self-or clinician -administered screening instruments that are widely used. These instruments include his Depression Inventory; Hopelessness Scale; Anxiety Inventory and the Scale for Suicide Ideation – all currently published by the Psychological Corporation. Other self-administered screening questionnaires used with traumatic stress include: the Impact of Events Scale (IES-R); General Health Questionnaire (GHQ 60); Symptom Checklist 90; Traumatic Symptom Inventory (TSI); and the Davidson Trauma Scale (DTS), to mention a few. Other screening instruments are designed to be administered by trained clinicians and are not designed for self-reporting. Included in this category are: the Mississippi Scale for PTSD (Military Version); the Historical, Clinical, Risk Management – 20 (HRC-20); the Detailed Assessment of Posttraumatic Stress (DAPS); the Clinician-Administered PTSD Scale (CAPS); and the PTSD Checklist – Military Version (PLC).[10]

Other screening and assessment protocols attempt to measure either particular items associated with traumatic stress or are broader in their approach to the topic. The McCormick TBI (traumatic brain injury) Interview (Military Version) is a specialty screening instrument again administered only by trained clinicians. This instrument was designed to determine the presence of TBIs among military personnel including discerning the nature of the injury: blast (IED, landmine, grenade, RPG...); land-based vehicle accident; air-based vehicular crash (helicopter, airplane); fall; fragment; physical confrontation (fight, assault...); or other accident(s).   The TBI Interview also looks at experiences following the injury: memory problems or lapses; balance problems or dizziness; sensitivity to bright light; sleep problems; change in work function; ringing in the ears; irritability; headaches or personality changes.   More detailed assessments can be determined from this initial screening instrument in order to focus on the particular nature and extent of the TBI as well as secondary problems associated with the injury.[11]

Another instrument, this one a self-reporting questionnaire, the Global Assessment Tool (GAT) is designed to measure the psychological status of military personnel of all ranks and experience in four domains: emotional fitness; social fitness; family life; and spiritual fitness.   It is part of the Unites States Army's "Comprehensive Soldier Fitness" (CSF) program.   This inventory, the GAT, is administered to all U.S. Army personnel thereby attempting to minimize the negative status associated with any mental health inventory within the military.   Here, emotional fitness attempts to ascertain the degree of life satisfaction, freedom from depression, optimism, character strengths, coping styles and resilience.   Social fitness is conceptualized as how one feels about the Army, the soldier's unit and his/her fellow soldiers. Family fitness looks at family and personal relationships while spiritual fitness attempts to see if the individual has a sense of meaning, purpose and goals that extend beyond the self. How this data is used is another matter.[12]

A major criticism of the U.S. military and veteran's administration has been the post-facto labeling of psychologically impaired veterans as having personality disorders and therefore exempting them from a military-connected disability along with any treatment consideration.   Indeed, many such labeled veterans are given a "general discharge" which may further deflate their self-image as well as set up barriers to educational and occupational pursuits. The problem of untreated psychologically damaged veterans is a problem with both Gulf War and Balkan War veterans.   This problem is more significant during economically challenging times like that which exists in much of the former Yugoslavia and, to a lesser extent, among the coalition (NATO) nations, including the United States. Since 2009, the authors have been working with clinicians within war-torn Balkan War nations in order to provide standardized assessment tools that address the clinical picture of youth aged 12-19; adult family members including traumatize victims, both civilians and veterans.

Training Protocols in Bosnia-Herzegovina and Serbia

At an international conference (International Police Executive Symposium) in Macedonia in June 2009, sponsored by the Minister of the Interior, it became clear that there was a shortage of Slavic-language clinical assessment tools, and that those that did exist, were insufficient for the task of addressing the clinical needs of the multitude of untreated victims of the Balkan Wars. Toward this end we set about translating and norming assessment tools that could be used in addressing these unmet needs in those states with the greatest needs – Bosnia-Herzegovina, Croatia, Macedonia and Serbia. Consultations with psychologists in both Serbia and Bosnia-Herzegovina (most of the psychologist in these states were trained in Belgrade) led to the conclusion that testing protocols would be most beneficial in the areas of: (1) assessing mental health issues associated with traumatic stress; (2) determining the needs of troubled youth; and (3) measuring the quality of adult family relations.

The Slavic-Language Personality Inventory-360

For the purpose of diagnosing mental health issues such as Post-traumatic Stress Disorder (PTSD) and its associated co-morbid clinical features (depression, panic-disorders, disassociation...), we developed the Slavic-Language Personality Inventory-360 (SLPI-360) based on the first 360 items in the original MMPI (Minnesota Multi-Phasic Personality Inventory) along with an "Interpretation Manual". The first 360 items of the MMPI are known as the *short form* and adequately measure the three validity scales and the ten clinical scales. The only advantage of administering the entire 566 items is for the three add-on supplementary scales which are not clinical in nature. The short form best lends itself to people suffering from traumatic stress and its related syndromes because of concentration issues associated with the longer.[13]

Although Slavic language models of the MMPI exists – the MMPI-201 & 202 – the psychologists we collaborated with on this project felt that these instruments were weak in that they did not correspond with the original MMPI therefore lacking the rich predictive material that makes the MMPI a viable and strong assessment tool. The MMPI-201 and 202 profiles do not correspond to the original MMPI sequence of questions therefore do not lend themselves to the rich resource of "factorial analysis" associated with the original MMPI or the "critical items" or forensic analysis. The MMPI-201 also lacks two critical scales; (#5), Masculine-Feminine Interest Scale and (#10) Introversion/Extroversion Scale (the MMPI 202 does include this latter scale but still does not address scale #5). Moreover, the Slavic-language MMPI 201 and 202 interpretation and diagnostic manuals lack the reliability, validity and predictability of the original MMPI.

The Slavic-Language Personality Inventory-360 upgraded archaic terminology while, at the same time, making it culturally-sensitive to major ethnic populations within the former Yugoslavia – Catholics, Muslims and Orthodox Christians. Test-retest and alternate test validity was conducted with students who understood English at the Faculties of Criminology and Political Sciences at the University of Sarajevo during the 2010 spring semester 2010 where the same cohort of students took both the first 360 items of the original (English version) MMPI followed later with the SLPI-360. The aggregate profiles were similar for both sets of tests.

By following the format of the original MMPI over 60 years of profiling and predictability are available associated with both the validity and clinical scales. The inclusion of religious and sex items makes it a stronger measure than its replacement the MMPI-2 which cleansed the MMPI of these items in a response to the *political correct movement*. Clearly, hyper-religiosity and hyper-sexuality are strong indicators of the mental classifications associated with impulse-control dysregulation. Thus, the SLPI-360 allows the clinical practitioner to assess *General Profile Characteristics* based on a combination of validity and clinical scales as well as using the *two-point code types* and the *critical items*. There is also considerable interest in the SLPI-360 by law enforcement agencies in the former Yugoslavia due to the serious problem of police corruption and abuses of authority. The original MMPI is the strongest instrument for sorting out mental illnesses and personality disorders among police personnel.[14]

The Problem-Oriented Screening Instrument
for Teenagers (POSIT)

Children and youth represent a vulnerable population in both Bosnia-Herzegovina and in Serbia, notably in the areas subjected to NATO bombings (Pancevo region within the province of Vojvodina). In addition to living with parents who have suffer from untreated PTSD, children and youth around Sarajevo are subjected to the constant threat of injuries, or death, from encountering unexploded armaments in the numerous mine fields surrounding the city. Also, segregated sectarian education adds to the ethnic divide and inter-group prejudices further complicating not only their lives but presenting challenges to clinicians attempting to treat them.

The problem in the province of Vojvodina, in addition to the trauma of constant NATO bombings in 1999, is the ground, atmospheric and water contamination due to the destruction of the areas petrochemical plants and oil refineries resulting in the initial release of 2,000 tons of noxious chemicals and contamination of the Danube River above Belgrade. Among the long-lasting toxins released due to the bombings are vinyl chloride monomer (VCM) and 1,2-dichloroethane (EDC) along with the depleted uranium (DU) used in the NATO bombs. This occurred in the *bread basket* of Serbia contaminating both the soil and groundwater of this agricultural region. Clearly, parental fears associated with these environmental issues affects their children's psychological well-being in addition to their worries associated with the potential for health problems.[15]

It is under these circumstances that the Slavic-language Problem Oriented Screening Instrument for Teenagers (POSIT) was developed. The POSIT was developed in 1991 by the National Institute on Drug Abuse (NIDA), a component of the United States National Institute of Health. It is a 139-item, forced choice ("yes/no") screening questionnaire assessment that measures ten domains: Substance use/abuse; Physical health; Mental health; Family relations;

Peer relations; Educational status (learning disabilities/disorders); Vocational status; Leisure/recreation; and Aggressive behavior/delinquency. It is designed

for use among teens aged 12 to 19. It is important to note that the POSIT is not copyrighted and is free-of-charge readily lending itself to its translation and norming for the Slavic-language population of the former Yugoslavia.

In the mid-1990s, French adapted the POSIT for aggregate use among school-aged populations providing a class profile that could assist schools in getting a better feel for their students' needs. Here, French devised the *minimum mean score* (MMS) based on the cutting scores associated with the original POSIT. Now students could be assessed along these 10 domains according to age, gender, ethnicity etcetera. The POSIT could also be used to measure the effectiveness of a class-wide clinical intervention by administering it as an aggregate pre-test prior to the intervention and later as a post-test once the program ended. It could also be used as an indicator of mass trauma following a school-wide crisis like a school shooting or suicide. Psychologists in both Bosnia-Herzegovina and in Serbia (Pancevo/Belgrade region) are being trained on the administration and interpretation of the Slavic-language POSIT and are working with the schools in both states.[16]

Partner/Relationship Inventory (PRI)

The third related area that requires assessment was at the parental level. The *Marital Satisfaction Inventory* (MSI) was our choice for this task in that it was revised in 1997 (MSI-R) allowing for the original instrument to be translated and normed to the cultures comprising the former Yugoslavia (Snyder, 1979; 1997; Snyder, et al., 1981). The strength of this instrument is that its eleven (11) scales are plotted on a single profile sheet where both participant's profile can be superimposed and compared based on a T-score format like that of the SLPI-360 profiles where the Mean is 50 and the Standard Deviation is 10. And like the SLPI-360 this is a forced-choice inventory where the participant marks each of the 280 items either "T" (true) or "F" (false). In general, the eleven scales measure truthfulness in partner disclosures and effective communication, the strength of the relationship, common interests, perceptions regarding finances, sex and domestic, role satisfaction, perceptions about having children and agreement or conflict over childrearing. We decided to name this the *Partner/Relationship Inventory* due to the more informal partnership arrangement within the former Yugoslavia, notably in Bosnia-Herzegovina and Serbia, where couples often declare their *marriage* without actually having the relationship formally sanctioned by either civil or religious authorities.[17]

Summary

Together the POSIT and Partner/Relationship Inventory (PRI) provide the clinician with a better idea of the overall dynamics of their client's family. Moreover, the training for these two instruments is easier than that for the SLPI-360. Essentially, administration of the POSIT and the PRI provide first-stage assessments from which referrals can be made to doctoral-level psychologists trained in the SLPI-360 for developing a more refined diagnostic and treatment

protocol. It should be noted that these training sessions were sponsored by the U.S. Embassy in Sarajevo through the Office of Public Affairs (OPA/U.S. State Department. OPA provided the certificates for each of the clinical training sessions. This work is still in progress.

Treatment Protocols

Treatment for veterans of the Gulf and Balkan wars has not been effective leading to complaints and protests in Bosnia-Herzegovina, Canada and the United States as well as from other countries caught up in these conflicts. The current world-wide economic recession does not help matters while most of the former Yugoslavian states never recovered from the 1991-2002 wars. Indeed, the recession only compounds the issue in Croatia, Bosnia-Herzegovina, Macedonia, Montenegro, Serbia and Kosovo where mental health services for both veterans and civilians are low priorities. Part of the problem is discerning between adequate and timely care versus the demands by veterans for monetary compensation in the form of disability payments. Hence, a common practice among veteran agencies and administrations has been to delay the assessment process so as not to officially classify current or former service personnel as "disabled veterans" until the vast majority of these individuals have died thereby drastically reducing the availability pool. Even then the numbers remain high as does the cost to the society.

In an April 2011 issue of the Third Marine Division Association newsletter, *Caltrap,* it noted that more than 150,000 U.S. veterans are expected to submit Agent Orange claims to the Veterans Administration within the next year and a half with many being eligible for retroactive disability payment on their claim. These are Vietnam-era veterans and this does not include the tens-of-thousands of Gulf War veterans also filing claims that extend to 1991 and the First Gulf War who suffer from the Gulf War Syndrome.[18] Canadian Force members who served with NATO and the United Nations in both the Balkan Wars and in the current Gulf War have also protested the lack of adequate health care and disability benefits. In November 2010, thousands of Canadian veterans marched against the Harper's Conservative government over benefits and care when the government attempted to end benefits by providing a lump-sum settlement to the disabled soldiers. The government's own investigations and recommendations regarding the incidence of PTSD states that Canadian Forces members return home from deployments without sufficient de-briefings, support or time to adjust – all factors that exacerbate the level of traumatic stress among these veterans.[19]

Moreover, the authors (French & Nikolic-Novakovic) witnessed the riot of April 21st, 2010 in Sarajevo when disgruntled veterans of the 1992-95 war attacked the government offices adjacent to the then U.S. Embassy with stones and firebombs resulting in a "close down" of the U.S. Embassy and over 30 police officers injured and cared for in the Embassy. Their cause was a lack of health care and delays and obstacles regarding disability status and payments.

Untreated veterans are a volatile subculture throughout the Balkans especially in those regions that experienced the bulk of the conflict. While veterans usually have a stronger voice than their civilian counterparts who also experienced traumatic stress, both populations suffer from an inadequate mental health system especially in comparison to Britain, Canada and the United States. The Sarajevo incident is emblematic of things to come along with a continued high suicide rate unless there is consorted effort to improve the mental health services for war trauma veterans in this region as well as for NATO and coalition force veterans.

The RAND Corporation, *Invisible Wounds* project noted that: "the most powerful message of the accumulated research on the lives of individuals afflicted with PTSD, depression, or TBI is that, on average, these disorders are associated with great suffering and impaired functioning across multiple domains."[20] The report goes on to say that effective treatment for war trauma is contingent upon eliminating the negative stigma associated with mental health treatment within the military milieu. One way for the military to accomplish this is to provide positive and concrete incentives for seeking treatment. Moreover, the military and/or veterans administration needs to make viable treatment options available to all service members suffering from mental disorders, including the National Guard and Reserve members. The core message from the RAND study is that the consequence of untreated mental disorders gives rise to long-term and costly consequences. One approach toward reducing the incidences of war-related mental disorders is the development of policies and programs that promote resilience toward the symptoms associated with depression and anxiety. Their research showed that policies aimed at alleviating the suffering of afflicted veterans expand the focus beyond treating the disorders per se. Important here is involving the family as a source of social support for afflicted service members including incorporating them into the treatment plan itself. The main point here is that the veteran should not be treated in a vacuum. Effective treatment protocols need to take into account the multiple aspects of the veterans' lives. The issue of effectively detecting and treating TBIs is more complex given the limited research on the prevalence of traumatic brain injuries.[21] It was not until May 2007 that Congressional Brain Injury Task Force required that the U.S. Department of Defense screen all U.S. troops for TBI, before and after they deploy. Prior to this mandate, the military only recorded obvious head injuries omitting most closed head injuries and mild TBIs. A major problem with getting accurate numbers of mental health problems within the U.S. military is a lack of any consistent across-the-board assessment protocols. Few studies look at both Army and Marine personnel and even then it is usually unit-specific eliminating support personnel or those who were separated due to injuries or for other reasons during deployments to Iraq or Afghanistan. Even then, the instrument used was components of the 17-item

PTSD Checklist (PCL). Obviously, better screening and assessment is needed in order to develop viable treatment protocols for war trauma victims, not only within the U.S. forces but in all coalition forces. The determination of viable

treatment for Balkan War victims is even more challenging. A review of the literature shows that therapies for traumatic stress fall into two broad categories – psychotherapies and psychopharmacology or a combination of both approaches.

Psychotherapies

Cognitive-behavioral therapies pretty much dominate the psychotherapies. Much of the literature links assessment to therapeutic recommendations. A 2009 study in *Addictive Behaviors* looked at gender differences relevant to PTSD and substance-use disorder (SUD) comorbidity where substance abuse most likely reflects attempts at self-medication for the symptoms associated with PTSD. The research noted that women with comorbid PTSD-SUD were more likely to experience difficulties controlling impulsive behaviors when distressed hence being more vulnerable to arousal. The authors in this study recommend treatments such as Dialetical Behavioral Therapy (DBT) since it promotes skills training specific to distress tolerance and emotion regulation that address impulsive behaviors relevant to situations of hyperarousal. The study, on the other hand, found that men with the PTSD-SUD comorbid condition suffer more from a lack of emotional awareness and clarity. For men, the authors of the study recommend Acceptance and Commitment Therapy that focuses on emotional awareness and education. Both of these approaches should be seen as adjuncts to other viable treatment protocols that most likely involves some psychoactive medications.[22]

The noted Canadian psychologist Donald Meichenbaum promotes Cognitive Behavioral Therapies (CBT)-based interventions for anxiety management, anger management and stress inoculation. He is especially skeptical of many other approaches for the treatment of PTSD including Eye Movement Desensitization and Reprocessing (EMDR), Thought Field Therapy and Critical Incident Stress Debriefing (CISD) with the latter being seen as exacerbating traumatic symptoms. It is important to note that Meichenbaum focused primarily on PTSD associated with rape, sexual molestation and childhood physical abuse – conditions that may or may not affect war trauma victims. In his therapeutic approach, Meichenbaum looks at how the survivor reacts to the traumatic event, the pre-existing characteristics of the survivor and the recovery environment. His form of CBT addresses these factors and then attempts to restructure the person's definition of the situation.[23]

Other studies follow suit advocating Cognitive Processing Therapy (CPT) for sexual assault survivors suffering from PTSD. CPT attempts to change the fear networks, what CPT terms schemata, which are associated with the aftermath of a traumatic sexual assault. Through information processing CPT attempts to resolve schema conflicts doing so by revealing, and correcting, distorted or dysfunctional thinking patterns and ways of coping with emotions associated by the assault. The recommended CPT treatment for sexual assault consists of 12 weekly groups of an hour-and-a-half duration. Other studies indicate that the effectiveness of CTP is contingent upon age, intelligence and education with those of a younger age, lower IQ and less education associated with a higher dropout rate while clients suffering from higher depression and guilt at pretreatment were associated with better results regarding the alleviation of PTSD symptoms. Moreover, clients with high anger at pretreatment were more likely to drop out of prolonged exposure treatment modalities. Most sexual assault studies focus on female victims with little done for male victims – a phenomenon just now being seriously studied. This is a needed area of treatment research given the incidences of male rapes during both the Gulf and Balkan wars.24 Furthermore, a 2008 Serbian study on the treatment of refugees who suffered from multiple stressors, including violence, ethnic conflict, bombing, and being expelled from their homes, found that Group Cognitive Behavioral Therapy worked well with these traumatized victims. The cognitive group work helped these victims (70 refugees) process their grieving as well as increasing their coping skills. The client's treatment effectiveness was measured by the Impact Event Scales-Revised, Ways of Coping-Revised, Scale of Cognitive Self-regulation and Scale of Coping Strategies with testing done following six-months of group cognitive-behavioral therapy.[25]

Additional studies looked at the effectiveness of Brief Cognitive Behavioral Therapy with patients suffering from acute PTSD. In a 2007 article in *The American Journal of Psychiatry,* the authors found that brief early behavioral therapy accelerated recovery from symptoms of acute PTSD while not influencing long-term results. It was most effective with clients with baseline comorbid depression. Thus, while brief early cognitive behavioral therapy helped during the initial recovery of symptoms of PTSD, anxiety and depression, after four months these improvements melted away, placing this cohort in the same category as those without this treatment intervention.[26] These findings are similar to a 1996 study in the same journal that looked at the outcome of Intensive Inpatient Treatment for combat-related PTSD. In this study comprehensive measures of PTSD and associated symptoms as well as social functioning were assessed at admission (baseline), discharge and at 6, 12 and 18 months later. The overall study showed an increase in symptoms from admission to follow-up but a decrease in violence and legal problems. The study found that family and interpersonal relationships improved by the time of discharge but returned to pretreatment (baseline) levels at 18 months leaving the authors to conclude that the chronic nature of combat-related PTSD is complicated and that intensive inpatient treatment may not be a viable solution.[27]

Little of the treatment literature addresses the needs of children and youth relevant to traumatic events, including sexual abuse and war trauma as was evident among the civilian populations caught in both the Gulf and Balkan wars. French put forth an adaptive projective assessment/treatment protocol that was published in 1993 in *Psychological Reports.* Here, he adapted elements of both the Goodenough-Harris Draw-A-Person protocol with Murray's Thematic Apperception Test (TAT) in a way that was basically cultural-free, while, at the

same time, allowing for the therapeutic effects of projection while involved in the assessment process.   This culturally modified procedure involves the following stages. During the first stage the child is asked to draw a picture of him/her so as to have a baseline assessment of his/her drawing skills. At the next session have the child tell you something about the person he/she drew (self-portrait). This is much like the Bender-Gestalt "recall" stage. The purpose of this step is to verify the child's interpretation of drawing characteristics and trait indicators. At the third session, ask the child to "draw a picture of you and your family" asking him/her to identify the participants. This drawing lends itself to D-A-P analysis regarding spacing, boldness of lines, additions and omissions and the like. The family drawing also serves as the TAT plate whereby you ask the client to: Tell me a story about this family. What is happening in the story? Who is the hero? What are the people thinking, feeling? What is the outcome of the story?[28]

The literature showed that a similar approach was used for war-traumatized children in Croatia. In the article published in the *Croatian Medical Journal,* the Department of Health Psychology at the Zagreb University School of Medicine employed a series of art therapy programs for the war-traumatized children from 1991to 1995. The program was administered to over 100,000 children in Croatia, including refugees living abroad. Interestingly most of the children benefitted from the opportunity to express their feelings about the war through their drawings – a form of therapeutic projection, hence the externalization of traumatic stress.[29] In Serbia, the Machover Human Figure Test was used by clinics in Belgrade to diagnosis traumatic symptoms of 201 subjects of whom 109 were refugees from the war. Their findings showed that the Machover Test was most effective with tailoring treatment plans for the somatically traumatized clients. On the other hand, aggressiveness was discerned by the drawings among the refugees, again allowing for a differential treatment plan for these war-trauma victims.[30]

Psychopharmacology

Traumatic stress disorders are complex in nature obviating any single "magic bullet" treatment approach. Indeed, the most common approach to traumatic stress is to address the most compelling symptoms. In many cases this requires medicines designed to alleviate these symptoms with often the best treatment protocol being a combination of psychotherapies and psycho-active agents.

An article entitled, "Myths and Realities of Pharmacotherapy in the Military" in the 2009 book, *Living and Surviving in Harm's way: A Psychological Treatment Handbook for Pre- and Post-deployment of the Military* notes that treatment with a Beta-adrenergic blocker within six hours of an acute traumatic event with continued treatment for 10 days has been shown to reduce the development of PTSD symptoms. This intervention most likely prevents the activation of the sympathetic mode of the Autonomic Nervous System, hence keeping the traumatic event within the realm of an Acute Stress situation – one that the Central Nervous System is better suited to address adequately. The authors of this article go on to say that there are three avenues for medications to control the negative-feedback cortisol activation route so critical to PTSD. One approach is to block the glutamate receptors so that threatening information associated with the trauma is not transmitted to the central nucleus of the amygdale – the emotional center of the brain. Another intervention is to increase the GABA activity which also acts to inhibit the action at the glutamate receptor, while the third intervention is to increase serotonin which serves to activate GABA producing additional inhibition of the glutamate receptor. Medications indicated for these inhibitory processes include the class of mood stabilizers such as carbamazepine (Tegretol), divalproex (Depakote), gabopentin (Neurontin), lamotrigine (Lamictal), and topiramate (Topamax). Of the anxiety medicines, clonidine (Catapress) and guanfacine (Tenex), alpha-2 agonists, work by reducing the presynaptic release of norepinephrine. Also helpful are the atypical antipsychotics like risperidone (Risperdal), olanzapine (Zyprexa) and quetiapine (Seroquel).[31] A study on the use of pharmacotherapy with Croatian war veterans suffering from PTSD with psychotic features, published in 2006 in the *Croatian Medical Journal*, found that the psychotic symptoms were greatly reduced with the introduction of atypical antipsychotic medications such as fluphenazine (Prolixin), risperidone (Risperdal), and olanzapine (Zyprexa).[32]

Select Serotonin Reuptake Inhibitors (SSRIs) are widely used with trauma victims to address a number of associated symptoms including anxiety, depression and obsessive-compulsiveness. SSRIs are often dosed for depression but work as an anti-anxiety medication at lower doses and as anti-compulsive agent at higher doses. Sertraline (Zoloft) is the most widely prescribed SSRI used with the U.S. Veterans Administration for PTSD and related symptoms. It has a relatively short half-life. Paroxetine (Paxil), however, has the shortest half-life and can be out of the system within eight hours. Because of this, Paxil is often used for situations where its effectiveness will not compromise other longer-acting medications hence reducing the drug-drug interaction process. For sustained relief of depressive or anxious symptoms, long-acting SSRI's are often used including fluoxetine (Prozac) and citalopram (Celexa). Fluvoxamine (Luvox) was approved in the United States specifically as an anti-obsessional agent. SSRIs are generally as effective as quick-acting benzodiazepines for the treatment of panic attacks. Here, alprazolam (Xanax) and lorazepam (Ativan) are used PRN (as needed). Buspirone (BuSpar) has been shown to be effective for low-level, but pervasive, anxiety and can be taken on a regular basis since it does not have the addictive qualities of the benzodiazepines. Buptopion (Wellbutrin) is also gaining in use for both depression and anxiety disorders. It is also used to suppress smoking addiction. Veteran Administration hospitals in the northwest region have been reporting success with prazosin (Minipress), an antihypertensive, like beta-blockers and ace-inhibitors, in reducing some of the unpleasant symptoms of PTSD including nightmares and sleep disturbances.[33]

   Combination Therapies
   Combination therapies involving both pharmacotherapies and psychotherapies have long been recommended for a better treatment outcome. It is common practice to combine elements of classical conditioning with rapid-acting anti-anxiety medications for the treatment of panic disorders. Psychotherapy, notably cognitive-behavior approaches, helps the client understand the purpose and expected outcomes of their psycho pharmacotherapy. A 2005 article in *The Journal of Clinical Psychiatry* addressed the effectiveness of sequential treatment of mood and anxiety disorders using both antidepressants and cognitive-behavioral therapy (CBT). The authors found that when CBT is used, following the administration of antidepressants (SSRIs), the relapse rate over time is greatly reduced. For the best results the authors recommended two sequential psychotherapeutic approaches – cognitive-behavioral therapy (CBT) and well-being therapy (WBT). This approach was used with clients diagnosed with panic attacks, obsessive-compulsive disorder, or generalized anxiety disorder. The overall purpose of the sequential approach is to add therapeutic ingredients as long as they are needed. With depressed clients not responding to a single agent, the sequential use of an augmentative agent such as a low-dose of lithium is often tried. It is imperative that the initial antidepressant be given an adequate trial prior to changing it or adding an augmentative agent. Adverse drug-drug interactions need to be closely watched as well. At any rate, client-reports, using instruments like the Yale-Brown Obsessive Compulsive Scale and the Hamilton Depression Inventory, help determine the effectiveness of both medications and corresponding psychotherapies.[34]

Preventive and Aftercare Protocols

   The United States Army Master Resilience Training (MRT) is a part of the Comprehensive Soldier Fitness program. It is a 10-day course for non-commissioned officers (NCOs) whereby they will learn skills that they are, in turn, to teach to the men under them. The program was developed at the University of Pennsylvania through its Penn Resilience Program (PRP) and is based on the concepts stemming from those developed in the Positive Psychology Center. The program focuses on a number of factors that are believed to better prepare the solider for encounters that may be stressful. These factors include optimism, problem solving, self-efficacy, self-regulation, emotional awareness, flexibility, empathy, and strong relationships. These skills are designed to enhance the soldiers' ability to handle adversity, prevent depression and anxiety, prevent PTSD and enhance overall well-being and performance. The four modules include:
   (1) Resilience: The core competencies of this training module are self-awareness (identifying one's thoughts, emotions, and behaviors); self-regulation (ability to regulate impulses, thinking, emotions, and
   (2)

behaviors in order to achieve goals); optimism (noticing the goodness
    in self and others, identifying what is controllable and challenging

(3) counterproductive beliefs); mental agility (thinking flexibly and accurately, perspective taking, willingness to try new strategies); character strengths (identifying top strengths and using them to overcome challenges and to meet goals); and connection (building strong relationships through positive and effective communication, empathy, and wiliness to ask for help and to offer help).

(4) Building Mental Toughness: These skills derive from the work of Aaron Beck, Albert Ellis, and Martin Seligman and are based on the field of cognitive-behavioral therapy. It relies on the ABCs of behavioral therapy where A is the activating event and (B) is our beliefs about the activating event and (C) are our emotional and behavioral consequences surrounding the activating event. The goal of this module is to have the soldier distinguish activating events, thoughts, and consequences.

(5) Identifying Character Strengths: In this module, soldiers identify their top character strengths, practice indentifying strengths in others, and also practice using individual strengths and team strengths to overcome a challenge and reach a goal. The module is linked to the Army's "Be, Know, Do" model of leadership stated in the Army Field Manual where it states that leadership begins with what the leader must be – the values and attributes that shape character.

(6) Strengthening Relationships: This final module focuses on strengthening relationships among soldiers and between soldiers and their family members. This training involves three skills: active constructive responding (ACR); praise; and communication styles (passive, aggressive, and assertive communication). The module is designed to provide soldiers with practical tools that help in building relationships and that challenge beliefs that interfere with positive communication.

This is a new program outlined in the January 2011 special issue (Comprehensive Soldier Fitness) of the *American Psychologist.* Its success in combat situations has yet to be tested. And one has to ask how NCOs can adequately perform after only a 10-day training course. A common theme regarding crisis situations is that rationality is its first casualty.[35]

The U.S. Army is also testing its Army Post-Deployment Reintegration Scale (APDRS). In a study appearing in the July 2009 issue of *Military Psychology,* the authors found that reintegration is not solely about returning to a garrison environment but it is also about returning to one's family. Toward this end, researchers need to consider both positive and negative aspects of reintegration. The researchers found strong links among negative post-deployment work reintegration attitudes, affective commitment, negative and positive job-related affect and intentions to leave the military within the next year. The authors recommend expanding the groups of military personnel who complete the APDRS to include not only Regular Army personnel deployed to combat zones but also those soldiers serving in high-stress occupations (such as medical) and to include National Guard and Reservists which it currently omits. Moreover, as it now stands, the APDRS is an anonymous self-report measure posing a question regarding its overall validity as well as its usefulness in screening individuals who may require additional assessment and treatment.[36]

Donald Meichenbaum's Case Conceptualization Model, designed for Canadian and U.S. soldiers, has nine basic components for a treatment plan.
1.   Background Information and Reason for Referral;
2.   Presenting Problems and Symptomatic Functioning;
3.   Presence of Comorbid Disorder;
4.   Stressors (Present/Past);
5.   Treatments (Current./Past);
6.   Strengths and Signs of Resilience;
7.   Summary of Risk and Protective Factors;
8.   Possible Outcomes; and
9.   Barriers or Possible Roadblocks to Maintaining Improvement.
This format would fit into the investigations and recommendations made regarding the Systemic Treatment of Canadian Force Members with PTSD. These recommendations include the following:
-The Canadian Forces develop a database on suicides among members and former members.
-The Canadian Forces initiate a program whereby all units receive outreach training about post-traumatic stress disorder.
-Specific and detailed education and training objectives dealing with post-traumatic stress disorder be included in the curricula of all Canadian Forces educational and training establishments, and that the performance measurement criteria for these organizations reflect these objectives.
-Canadian Force units be mandated to provide ongoing continuation training about post-traumatic stress disorder to all members at regular intervals, in addition to any deployment-related training.
-The Canadian Forces make post-traumatic stress disorder a mandatory part of education and training at all ranks and that educating Canadian Forces members about post-traumatic disorder be made a priority.
-The Office of the Post-Traumatic Stress Disorder Coordinator play a central role in the education and training process by acting as a resource and advisor for bases, formations and commands.
-The Canadian Forces include members or former members who have experience of post-traumatic stress disorder in all education and training initiatives relating to post-traumatic stress disorder.
-Multidisciplinary teams that include all of the professional specialties with an interest in post-traumatic stress disorder diagnosis and treatment, including using experienced soldiers, be used to deliver outreach training. To enhance

training effectiveness and ensure standardization, such training should fall under the control of the Office of the Post-Traumatic Stress Disorder Coordinator.

-The Canadian Forces develop a standardized screening process that involves all of the pertinent specialists and that is under the control of a single point of contact.

-The Canadian Force provide sufficient incremental resources to permit all mental health caregivers, including padres and social workers, access to training required to deal with mental health issues.

-The Canadian Forces prioritize and accelerate the efforts toward standardizing treatment of members diagnosed with post-traumatic stress disorder.

-The Canadian Forces take steps to deal with the issues of stress and burn-out created by lack of resources and high caseloads among Canadian Forces caregivers.

-The Canadian Forces create the position of Post-Traumatic Stress Disorder Coordinator, reporting directly to the Chief of the Defence Staff and responsible for coordinating issues related to post-traumatic stress disorder across the Canadian Forces.[37]

The Croatia response to traumatized war victims, many of them refugees, consisting of displaced women and children, illustrates a coordinated effort from the Balkan Wars. It is estimated that the 1991-1995 component of the Balkan Wars resulted in more than 250,000 refugees in Croatia alone. In response to this overwhelming need the National Program of Psychosocial Help to War Victims was created in 1994. The program was developed in collaboration with the World Health Organization and the United Nations International Children's Fund (UNICEF)leading to the development of a pyramidal model with a National Center for Psychotrauma and four Regional Centers located in Rijeka, Osijek, Zagreb, and Split. The role of the National Center for Psychotrauma was redefined in 1999 accordingly: (1) to provide diagnostic assessment for hospitalized victims including assessing their work ability; (2) provide treatment for psychotraumatized persons; (3) develop differential diagnostic methods for PTSD and related disorders; (4) develop high quality treatment programs that correspond with these diagnoses; (5) establish a 24/7 counseling service for couples, children and demobilized veterans; (6) establish a referral center for PTSD and related disorders along with a database; and (7) provide relevant seminars and lectures for medical students, psychologists, social workers, educators, the Police Academy, and those working in rehabilitation services as well as for members of the Regional Psychosocial Teams and other psychiatric institutions working in the area of psycotrauma. This response was needed given that the demands for these services greatly increased after the war and continues to the present. Obviously the challenge for all societies with military and civilian war trauma victims is to establish a viable screening/assessment/diagnostic and treatment program and, most significantly, to adequately fund these programs.[38]

Chapter Seven

International Trauma Bibliography

Aardal-Eriksson, E., Eriksson, T.E., & Thorell, L.H. (2001). Salivary cortisol, posttraumatic stress symptoms, and general heath in the acute phase and during 9-months follow-up. *Biological Psychiatry,* Vol. 50(12): pp. 986-993.

Abu Hein, F., Qouta, S., Thabet, A., & El Sarraj, E. (1993). Trauma and mental health of children in Gaza. *British Medical Journal,* Vol. 306: pp. 1129-1131.

Adams, R.L., et al. (1996). *Neuropsychology for Clinical Practice.* Washington, DC: American Psychological Association Press.

Adler, A.B., Vaitkus, M.A., & Martin, J.A. (1996). Combat exposure and posttraumatic stress symptomatology among U.S. soldiers deployed to the Gulf War. *Military Psychology,* Vol. 8(1): pp. 1-14.

Agger, I. (1989). Sexual torture of political prisoners: an overview. *Journal of Traumatic Stress,* Vol. 2(3): pp. 305-318.

Agger, I., & Jensen, S. (1990). Testimony as ritual and evidence in psychotherapy for political refugees. *Journal of Traumatic Stress,* Vol. 3: pp. 115-130.

Ahearn, E.P., Krohn, A., Connor, K.M., & Davidson, J.R. (2003). Pharmacologic Treatment of Posttraumatic Stress Disorder: A focus on antipsychotic use. *Annals of Clinical Psychiatry,* Vol. 15: pp. 193-201.

Aikins, D.E., Johnson, D.C., Borelli, J.L., et al. (2009). Thought suppression failures in combat PTSD: A cognitive load hypothesis. *Behaviour Research and Therapy,* Vol. 47: pp. 744-751.

Ajdukovic, D., Arambasic, L., & Ljubotina, D. (1992). *Posttraumatic Stress Reaction Scale.* Zagreb, Croatia: The Society for Psychological Assistance.

Ajdukovic, M. (1995). Children in War in Croatia. *Croatian Journal of Social Policy,* Vol. 2 (4): pp. 295-304.

Albucher, R.C., & Liberzon, I. (2002). Psychopharmacological treatment in PTSD: Critical review. *Journal of Psychiatric Research,* Vol. 36: 355-367.

Allodi, F.A. (1991). Assessment and treatment of torture victims: a critical review. *Journal of Nervous and Mental Disease*, Vol. 179: pp. 4-11.

Ambady, N., & Bharucha, J. Culture and the brain, *Current Directions in Psychological Science*, Vol. 18: pp. 342-345.

Anticevic, V., & Britvic, D. (2008). Sexual functioning in war veterans with posttraumatic stress disorder. *Croatian Medical Journal*, Vol. 49: pp. 449-505.

APA (1980). *Diagnostic and Statistical Manual of Mental Disorder – Third Edition (DSM-III)*. Washington, DC: American Psychiatric Association.

APA (1987). *Diagnostic and Statistical Manual of Mental Disorders – Third Edition-Revised (DSM-III-R)*. Washington, DC: American Psychiatric Association.

APA (1994). *Diagnostic and Statistical Manual – Fourth Edition (DSM-IV)*. Washington, DC: American Psychiatric Association.

APA (2000). Practice guideline for the treatment of patients with major depressive disorders (revision). *American Journal of Psychiatry*, Vol. 157 (Suppl. 4): pp. 1-45.

APA (2002). *Diagnostic and Statistical Manual of Mental Disorders- Fourth Edition-Text Revision (DSM-IV-TR)*. Washington, DC: American Psychiatric Association.

Avdibegovic, E,, & Sinanovic, O. (2006). Consequences of domestic violence on women's mental health in Bosnia and Herzegovina. *Croatian Medical Journal*, Vol. 47: pp. 730-741.

Avdibegovic, E., et al. (2008). Mental health care of psychotraumatized persons in post-war Bosnia-Herzegovina – experiences from Tuzla Canton. *Psychiatria Danubina*, Vol. 20: pp. 474-484.

Babic, D., et al. (2007). Metabolic syndrome and combat posttraumatic stress disorder intensity: preliminary findings. *Psychiatria Danubina*, Vol. 19: pp. 68-75.

Bailey, R.H., et al. (1990). *Brother against Brother*. New York, NY: Prentice-Hall.

Baker, C.K., Norris, F.H., Jones, E.C., & Murphy, A.D. (2009). Childhood trauma and adulthood physical health in Mexico. *Journal of Behavioral Medicine*, Vol. 32(3): pp 255 - 270.

Baker, D.G., Mendenhall, C.L., Simbartl, L.A., et al. (1997). Relationship between posttraumatic stress disorder and self-reported physical symptoms in Persian Gulf War veterans, *Archives of Internal Medicine*, Vol. 157: pp. 2076-2078.

Ballenger, J.C., et al. (2004). Consensus statement update on posttraumatic Stress disorder from the international consensus group on depression and anxiety, *Journal of Clinical Psychiatry*, Vol. 65 (Suppl. 1): pp. 55-62.

Barath, A. (1996). Creative therapies for war-traumatized children: 1991-95 Croatian Experience. *Croatian Medical Journal*, Vol. 37: pp. 355-368.

Barath, A. (2002). Children's well-being after the war in Kosovo: Survey 2000. *Croatian Medical Journal,* Vol. 43: pp. 199-208.

Barath, A. (2002). Psychological status of Sarajevo children after war: 1999-2000 survey. *Croatian Medical Journal,* Vol. 43: pp. 213-220.

Barefoot, J.C., Dodge, K.A., Peterson, B.L., et al. (1989). The Cook-Medley hostility scale: item content and ability to predict survival. *Psychosomatic Medicine,* Vol. 51: pp. 46-57.

Barrett, D.H., Doebbeling, C.C., Schwartz, D.A., et al. (2002). Posttraumatic stress disorder and self-reported physical health status among US military personnel serving during the Gulf War Period: A population-based study. *Psychosomatics,* Vol. 43: pp. 195-205.

Bartzokis, G., Freeman, T., & Roca, V. (2001). Risperidone treatment for PTSD, *European Journal of Neuropsychopharmacolgy,* Vol. 11 (Suppl. 3): p. 262.

Basoglu, M., et al. (2005). Psychiatric and cognitive effects of war in former Yugoslavia: association of lack of redress for trauma and posttraumatic stress reaction. *Journal of the American Medical Association (JAMA),* Vol. 294: pp. 580-590.

Beals, J., Novins, D.K., Spicer, P., et al. (2004). American Indian services utilization, psychiatric epidemiology, risk and protective factors project team: Challenges in operationalizing the DSM-IV clinical significance criterion. *Archives of General Psychiatry,* Vol. 61: pp. 1197-1207.

Bear, M.F., Connors, B.W., & Paradiso, M.A. (1996). *Neuroscience: Exploring the Brain.* Baltimore, MD: Williams & Wilkins.

Beck, A.T., Rush, A.J., Shaw, B.F., & Emery, G. (1979). *Cognitive Therapy of Depression.* New York, NY: Guilford Press.

Beck, A.T., Steer, R.A., & Brown, G. (1996). *Beck Depression Inventory-2.* San Antonio, TX: Psychological Corporation.

Beck, A.T. (1999). *Prisoners of Hate: The Cognitive basis of Anger, Hostility and Violence.* New York, NY: Harper/Collins.

Becker, D., et al. (1999). Case series: PTSD symptoms in adolescent survivors of "ethnic cleansing". Results from a 1-year follow-up study. *Journal of the American Academy of Child & Adolescent Psychiatry,* Vol. 38: pp. 775-781.

Beckham, J.C., Moore, S.M., Feldman, M.E., et al. (1998). Health status, somatization and severity of posttraumatic stress disorder in Vietnam combat veterans with posttraumatic stress disorder. *American Journal of Psychiatry,* Vol. 155: pp. 1565-1569.

Begic, D., & Jokic-Begic, N. (2007). Heterogeneity of posttraumatic stress disorder symptoms in Croatian war veterans: Retrospective study. *Croatian Medical Journal,* Vol. 48: pp. 133-139.

Begovac, I., et al. (2004). Self-image, war, psychotrauma and refugee status in adolescents. *European Child & Adolescent Psychiatry,* Vol. 13: pp. 381-388

Bell, K.M., & Orcutt, H.K. (2009). Posttraumatic Stress disorder and male-perpetrated intimate partner violence. *Journal of the American Medical Association (JAMA),* Vol. 302: pp. 562-.

Berger, J. (1989). *Projective psychology – the Rorschach personality test.* Belgrade, Serbia: Nolit.

Bernstein, E.M., & Putnam, F.W. (1986). Development, reliability, and validity of a dissociation scale. *Journal of Nervous and Mental Disease,* Vol. 174: pp.727-735.

Beslija, A. (1997). Psychotherapy with refugees from Bosnia-Herzegovina. *Transactional Analysis Journal,* Vol. 27: pp. 49-54.

Bidzinska, E.J. (1984). Stress factors in affective diseases. *British Journal of Psychiatry,* Vol. 144: pp. 161-166.

Birmes, P., Raynaud, J-P., Daubisse, L., et al. (2009). Children's enduring PTSD symptoms are related to their family's adaptability and cohesion. *Community Mental Health Journal,* Vol. 45: pp 290-299.

Biro, M. (1992). War stress syndrome. *Psychology,* Vol. 25: pp. 78-84.

Biro, M., & Novovic, Z. (1994). Psychotherapy of war stress syndrome. *Social Thought,* Vol. 1: pp. 64-72.

Biro, M., & Milin, P. (2005). Traumatic Experience and the process of reconciliation. *Psychology,* Vol. 38: pp. 133-148.

Bisson, J.I., Roberts, N., & Macho, G.S. (2003). The Cardiff Traumatic Stress initiative: an evidence -based approach to early psychological intervention following traumatic events. *Psychiatric Bulletin,* Vol. 27: pp. 145-147.

Bisson, J.I., Shepherd, J.P., Joy, D., et al. (2004). Early Cognitive-behavioural therapy for post-traumatic stress disorder symptoms after physical injury: Randomised controlled trial. *British Journal of Psychiatry,* Vol. 184: pp. 63-69.

Bisson, J.I., & Cohen, J. (2006). Disseminating early interventions following trauma. *Journal of Traumatic Stress,* Vol. 19: pp. 583-595.

Bisson, J.I. (2007). Pharmacological treatment of post-traumatic stress disorder. *Advances in Psychiatric Treatment,* Vol. 13: pp. 119-126.

Bisson, J.I. (2007). Post-traumatic stress disorder. *British Medical Journal,* Vol. 334: pp. 789-793.

Bisson, J.I., Brayne, M., Ochberg, F.M., & Everly, G.S., Jr. (2007). Early psychosocial intervention following traumatic events. *American Journal of Psychiatry,* Vol. 164: pp. 1016-1019.

Bisson, J.I., Ehlers, A, Matthews, R., et al. (2007). Psychological treatments for chronic post-traumatic stress disorder: Systematic review and meta-analysis. *British Journal of Psychiatry,* Vol. 190: pp. 97-104.

Black, D.W., Carney, C.P., Peloso, P.M., et al. (2004). Gulf War veterans with anxiety: Prevalence, comorbidity, and risk factors. *Epidemiology,* Vol. 15: pp. 135-142.

Blair, R. (2000). Rick factors associated with PTSD and major depression among Cambodian refugees in Utah. *Health and Social Work,* Vol. 25: pp. 23-30.

Blais, A-R, Thompson, M.M., & McCreary, D.R. (2009). The Development and validation of the Army Post-Deployment Reintegration Scale. *Military Psychology,* Vol. 21: pp. 365-381.

Blake, D.D., Weathers, F.W., Nagy, L.M., et al. (1990). A clinician rating scale for assessing current and lifetime PTSD: The CAPS-1. *Behavioral Therapy,* Vol. 13: pp. 187-188.

Blake, D.D., Weathers, F.W., Nagy, L.M., et al. (1995). The development of a Clinician-Administered PTSD Scale. *Journal of Traumatic Stress,* Vol. 8: pp. 75-90.

Blanchard, E.B., Jones-Alexander, J., Buckley, T.C., & Forneris, C.A. (1996). Psychometric properties of the PTSD Checklist (PCL). *Behavioral Research Therapist,* Vol. 34: pp. 669-673.

Bleich, A., & Moskowits, L. (2000). Post traumatic stress disorder with psychotic features. *Croatian Medical Journal,* Vol. 41: pp. 442-445.

Boman, B. (1986). Combat Stress, Post-traumatic stress disorder, and associated psychiatric disturbances. *Psychosomatics,* Vol. 27: pp. 567-573.

Bolibok, B. (2001). The plural "self": Group therapy with Bosnian women survivors of war. *Smith College Studies in Social Work,* Vol. 71: pp. 459-472.

Bonanno, G.A. (2004). Loss, trauma, and human resilience: have we underestimated the human capacity to thrive after extremely aversive events? *American Psychologists,* Vol. 59: pp.20-28.

Borisev, L,D., Stajic-Soldatovic, B.S., Drezgic-Vukic, S.M., & Dasovic, A. (1995). Socio-demographic and other characteristics of refugees hospitalized at psychiatric clinic at Novi Sad. *Current Topics in Neurology, Psychiatry and Related Disciplines,* Vol. 3: pp. 37-42.

Bornovalova, M.A., Quimette, P., Crawford, A.V., & Levy, R. (2009). Testing gender effects on the mechanisms explaining the association between post-traumatic stress symptoms and substance use frequency. *Addictive Behaviors,* Vol. 34: pp. 685-692.

Boston University School of Public Health. (2007). Military recruiters offer more waivers for drug offenses. *Join Together* (February 15th): www.jointogether.org.

Bourne, P.G. (1970). *Men, Stress, and Vietnam.* Boston, MA: Little Brown.

Bourne, P.G. (1970). Military psychiatry and the Vietnam experiences. *American Journal of Psychiatry,* Vol. 127: pp. 481-488.

Brackbill, R.M., Hadler, J.L., DiGrande, L., et al. (2009). Asthma and posttraumatic stress symptoms 5 to 6 years following exposure to the World Trade Center terrorist attack. *Journal of the American Medical Association (JAMA),* Vol. 302(5): pp. 502-516.

Brady, K.T. (1997). Posttraumatic stress disorder and comorbidity: Recognizing the many faces of PTSD. *Journal of Clinical Psychiatry,* Vol. 58 (Suppl. 9): pp. 12-15.

Bremner, J.D., Southwick, SM, Johnson, D.R., et al. (1993). Childhood physical abuse and combat-related posttraumatic stress disorder in Vietnam veterans. *American Journal of Psychiatry,* Vol.150: pp. 235-239.

Bremner, J.D., Randall, P., Scott, T.M., et al. (1995). Combat-related posttraumatic-stress-disorder. *American Journal of Psychiatry,* Vol. 152: pp. 973-981.

Bremner, J.D., Randall, P., Vermetten, E., et al. (1997). Magnetic Resonance Imaging-based measurement of hippocampal volume in posttraumatic stress disorder related to childhood physical and sexual abuse – a preliminary report. *Biological Psychiatry,* Vol. 41: pp. 23-32.

Brende, J.O., & Parson, E.R. (1985). *Vietnam Veterans: the Road to Recovery.* New York, NY: Plenum Press.

Brewin, C.R., Andrew, B., & Valentine, J.D. (2000). Meta-analysis of risk factors for posttraumatic stress disorder in trauma-exposed adults. *Journal of Consulting Clinical Psychology,* Vol. 68: pp. 748-766.

Briere, J. (2005) *Trauma Symptom Inventory* (TSI). www.parinc.com.

Briere, J. (2009). *Trauma Symptom Checklist for Children* (TSCC). www.parinc.com.

Britvic, D., Radelic, N., & Urlic, I. (2006). Long-term Dynamic-oriented Group Psychotherapy of posttraumatic stress disorder in war veterans: Prospective study of five-year treatment. *Croatian Medical Journal,* Vol. 47: pp. 76-84.

Brown, L.S. (2008). *Cultural Competence in Trauma Therapy: Beyond the Flashback.* Washington, DC: American Psychological Association Press.

Brown, T.A. & NcNiff, J. (2009). Specificity of autonomic arousal to DSM-IV panic disorder and posttraumatic stress disorder. *Behaviour Research and Therapy,* Vol. 47: p. 487.

Brownmiller, S. (1975). *Against Our Will: Men, Woman and Rape.* New York, NY: Simon and Schuster.

Bryant, R.A., Sackville, T, Dang, S.T., et al. (1999). Treating acute stress disorder: an evaluation of cognitive behavior therapy and supportive counseling techniques. *American Journal of Psychiatry,* Vol. 156: pp. 1780-1786.

Bryant, R.A., Moulds, M., Guthrie, R., & Nixon, R.D. (2003).Treating acute stress disorder following mild traumatic brain injury. *American Journal of Psychiatry,* Vol. 160: pp. 585-587.

Bryant, R.A., Moulds, M.L., Guthrie, R.M., & Nixon, R.D. (2005). The additive benefit of hypnosis and cognitive-behavioral therapy in treating acute stress disorder. *Journal Consulting and Clinical Psychology,* Vol. 73: pp. 334-340.

Bryant-Davis, T. (2005). *Thriving in the Wake of Trauma: a Multicultural Guide.* Westport, CT: Praeger Publishers.

Budden, A. (2009). The role of shame in posttraumatic stress disorder: a proposal for a socio-emotional mode for DSM-V. *Social Science & Medicine,* Vol. 69: pp. 1032-1039.

Burke, A., Heuer, F., & Reisberg, D. (1992). Remembering emotional events. *Memory & Cognition,* Vol. 20: pp. 277-290.

Buttollo, W.H. (2000). Asocial interaction model for war traumatization: Self-processes and postwar recovery in Bosnia in subjects with PTSD and other psychological disorders. *Dialogues in Clinical Neuroscience,* Vol. 2: pp. 71-81.

Buydens-Branchey, N., Noumair, D.,& Branchey, M. (1990). Duration and intensity of combat exposure and posttraumatic stress disorder in Vietnam Veterans. *Journal of Nervous and Mental Disorders,* Vol. 178: pp. 582-587.

Byrne, C.A., Hyman, I.E.,Jr., & Scott, K.L. (2001). Comparisons of Memories for traumatic events and other experiences. *Applied Cognitive Psychology,* Vol. 15: pp.119-133.

Cabarkapa, M.M., & Markovic, N. (1998). Indicators of the stress syndrome on the Rorscharch test applied to the war participants. *Psychology,* Vol. 4: pp. 437-448.

Cabarkapa, M.M. (2004). The most frequent stress syndromes in soldiers in war. *Military-Medical and Pharmaceutical Review,* Vol. 6: pp. 675-682.

Calhoun, P.S., Boggs, C.D., Crawford, E.F., & Beckham, J.C. (2009). Diagnostic efficiency of the personality assessment inventory LOGIT function for posttraumatic stress disorder in women. *Journal of Personality Assessment,* Vol. 91: pp. 409-415.

Carballo, M., et al. (2004). Mental health and coping in a war situation: the case of Bosnia-Herzegovina. *Journal of Biosocial Science,* Vol. 36: pp.463-477.

Card, J.J. (1987). Epidemiology of PTSD in a national cohort of Vietnam veterans. *Journal of Clinical Psychology,* Vol. 43: pp. 6-17.

Carlier, I.V., Laamberts, R.D., Van Uchelen, A.J., & Gersons, B.P. (1998). Disaster-related post-traumatic stress in police officers: a field study of the impact of debriefing. *Stress and Health,* Vol. 14: pp. 143-148.

Carlson, E.B. (2001). Psychometric study of a brief screen for PTSD: Assessing the impact of multiple traumatic events. *Assessment,* Vol. 8: pp. 431-441.

Carver, C.S., Scheier, M.F., & Weintraub, J.K. (1989). Assessing coping strategies: A theoretical based approach. *Journal of Personality and Social Psychology,* Vol. 56: pp. 267-283.

Castro, C.A., & McGuik, D. (2007). The intensity of combat and behavioral health status. *Traumatology,* Vol. 13: pp. 6-13.

Cavic, T. (2001). Refugees at the Avala Psychiatric Clinic: Role of cognitive restructuring in the treatment of psychological trauma. *Engrami - Journal of Clinical Psychiatry, Psychology and Related Disciplines,* Vol. 23: pp. 71-75.

Cavic, T., Lecic-Tosevski, D., & Pejovic, M. (2008). Post-traumatic stress disorder and coping strategies in psychotraumatized refugees. *Medical Review,* Vol. 61: pp. 11-15.

Center for Stress Recovery (1986). *Brecksville Semi-Structured Diagnostic Interview.* Brecksville, OH: Veterans Administration Medical Center.

Ceranic, S. (2003). Psycho-social consequences in adolescents: Victims of landmines. *Engrami - Journal of Clinical Psychiatry, Psychology and Related Disciplines,* Vol. 25: pp. 49-54.

Ceric, I., et al., (1999). Reconstruction of mental health services in the Federation of Bosnia and Herzegovina. *Medical Archives,* Vol. 53: pp. 127-130.

Charney, D.S. (2004). Psychobiological mechanisms of resilience and vulnerability: Implications for successful adaptation to extreme stress. *American Journal of Psychiatry,* Vol. 161: pp. 195 -216.

Charney, ME., & Keane, T.M. (2007). Psychometric analysis of the Clinician-Administered PTSD Scale (CAPS) - Bosnian translation. *Cultural Diversity & Ethnic Minority Psychology,* Vol. 13: pp. 161-167.

Chartier-Otis, M., Guay, S., & Marchand, A. (2009). Psychological and relationship distress among partners of civilian PTSD patients. *Journal of Nervous and Mental Disease,* Vol. 197: pp. 543-546.

Chemtob, C.M., Thomas, S., Law, W., & Cremniter, D. (1997). Postdisaster psychosocial intervention: a field study of the impact of debriefing on psychological distress. *American Journal of Psychiatry,* Vol. 154: pp. 415-417.

Chiao, J.Y., & Ambady, N. (2007). (Cpt. 9) Cultural neuroscience: Parsing universality and diversity across levels of analysis. *Handbook of Cultural Psychology* (Kitayama, S, & Cohen, D., eds.). New York, NY: The Guilford Press: pp. 237-254.

Chodoff, P. (1963). Late effects of the concentration camp syndrome. *Archives of General Psychiatry,* Vol. 8: pp. 323-333.

Christianson, S-A., Loftus, E.F., (1987). Some characteristics of people's traumatic memories. *Bulletin of the Psychosomatic Society,* Vol. 28: pp. 195-198.

Cizmic, S.M., & Petrovic, I.B. (1994). On the psychic condition of workers who have returned from the battlefield. *Psychology,* Vol. 27: pp. 83-96.

Clancy, C.P., Graybeal, A, Tompson, W., et al. (2006). Lifetime trauma exposure in veterans with military-related posttraumatic stress disorder: Association with current symptomatology. *American Journal of Psychiatry,* Vol. 67: pp. 1346-1353.

Cloitre, M., Koenen, K.C., Gratz, K.L., & Jakupeak, M. (2002). Differential diagnosis of PTSD in women. *Gender and PTSD* (Kimerling, R., Ouimette, P., & Wolf, J., ed.s). New York, NY: The Guilford Press: pp. 117-150.

Cloitre, M., Stovall-McClough, K.C., Miranda, R., et al. (2004). Therapeutic alliance, negative mood regulation, and treatment outcome in child abuse-related posttraumatic stress disorder. *Journal of Consulting and Clinical Psychology,* Vol. 72: pp. 411-416.

Coffey, S.F.B., Gudnumdsdottir, J.G., Beck, S.A., et al. (2006). Screening for PTSD in motor vehicle accident survivors using the PSS-SR and IEP. *Journal of Trauma and Stress,* Vol. 19: pp. 119-128.

Coleman, P. (2006). *Flashback: Posttraumatic Stress Disorder Suicide and the Lessons of War.* Boston, MA: Beacon Press.

Conway, M.A., Anderson, S.J., Larsen, S., et al. (1994). The formation of flashbulb memories. *Memory & Cognition,* Vol. 22: pp. 326-343.

Cooper, J.R., Bloom, F.E., & Roth, R.H. (1991). *The Biochemical Basis of Neuropharmacology.* New York, NY: Oxford University Press.

Cook, R. (2005). One in four foster children suffers from post-traumatic stress, study finds. *The Associated Press* (April 7th).

Coser, L. (1955). *The Functions of Social Conflict.* Glencoe, IL: The Free Press.

Coser, L. (1956). *Continuities in the Study of Social Conflict.* Glencoe, IL: The Free Press.

Costa, D.L. (1993). Height, weight, wartime stress, and older age mortality: evidence from the Union Army records. *Explorations in Economic History,* Vol. 30: pp. 424-449.

Cramer, P. (1991). *The Development of Defense Mechanisms: Theory, Research, and Assessment.* New York, NY: Springer-Verlag.

Creamer, M., Morris, P., Biddle, D., & Elliott, P. (1999). Treatment outcome in Australian veterans with combat-related posttraumatic stress disorders: a cause for cautious optimism? *Journal of Traumatic Stress,* Vol.12: pp. 545-558.

Creasey, H., et al. (1999). Is experience as a prisoner of war a risk factor for accelerated age-related illness and disability? *Journal of American Geriatrics Society,* Vol. 47: pp. 60-64.

Dahl, S., Mutapscic, A., & Schei, B. (1998). Traumatic events and predictive factors for posttraumatic symptoms in displaced Bosnian women in a war zone. *Journal of Traumatic Stress,* Vol. 11: pp. 137-145.

Danes, V., & Horvat, V. (2005). Psychological consequences of war stress in the developing population in Bosnia and Herzegovina. *Psychiatria Danubina,* Vol. 17: pp. 225-229.

Das, R.R., Moorthi, R.N., Warden, D.L., & French, L. (2005). Traumatic brain injury in the war zone. *New England Journal of Medicine,* Vol. 353: 633-634.

Davidson, J.R, & Swartz, M. (1985). A diagnostic and family study of posttraumatic stress disorder. *American Journal of Psychiatry,* Vol. 142: pp. 9-93.

Davidson, J.R., Book, S.W., Colket, J.T., et al. (1997). Assessment of a new self-rating scale for posttraumatic stress disorder: the Davidson Trauma Scale. *Psychological Medicine,* Vol. 27: pp. 153-160.

Davidson, J.R. (2000). Pharmacotherapy of posttraumatic stress disorder: Treatment options, long-term follow-up, and predictors of outcomes. *Journal of Clinical Psychiatry,* Vol. 61 (Suppl. 5): pp. 52-56.

Davidson, J.R., Baldin, D., Stein, D.J., et al. (2006). Treatment of posttraumatic stress disorder with Venlafaxine extended release: A 6-month randomized controlled trial. *Archives of General Psychiatry,* Vol. 63: pp. 1158-1165.

Davidson, I.R.T., & Foa, E.B. (ed.s). (1993). *Posttraumatic Stress Disorder: DSM-IV and Beyond.* Washington, DC: American Psychiatric Press.

Dean, E.T., Jr. (1991). "We will all be lost and destroyed": Post-traumatic stress disorder and the Civil War. *Civil War History,* Vol. 38: pp. 138-153.

Dean, E.T., Jr. (1997). *Shook Over Hell - Post-Traumatic Stress, Vietnam, and the Civil War.* Cambridge, MA: Harvard University Press.

Defense Health Board Task Force on Mental Health. (2007). *An Achievable Vision: Report of the Department of Defense Task Force on Mental Health.* Falls Church, VA: Defense Health Board.

Definis-Gojanovic, M., Capkun, V., & Smoljanovic, A. (1997). Influence of war on frequency and patterns of homicides and suicides in south Croatia (1991-1993). *Croatian Medical Journal,* Vol. 38: pp. 59-63.

de Jong, J.T., et al. (2001). Lifetime events and posttraumatic stress disorder in 4 postconflict settings. *Journal of the American Medical Association (JAMA),* Vol. 286: pp. 555-562.

de Kloer, E., Joels, E., & Holsboer, F. (2005). Stress and the brain: from adaptation to disease. *Nature Reviews Neuroscience,* Vol. 6: pp. 463-475.

Desai, R.A., Dausey, D., & Rosenheck, R.A. (2008). Suicide among discharged psychiatric inpatients in the Department of Veterans Affairs. *Military Medicine,* Vol. 173: pp. 721-728.

DeSilva, P. (1993). Post-traumatic stress disorder: cross-cultural aspects. *International Review of Psychiatry,* Vol. 5: pp. 217-229.

Dijanaic-Plasc, I., Peraica, T., Grubisic-Ilic, M., et al. (2007). Psychiatric heredity and posttraumatic stress disorder: Survey study of war veterans. *Croatian Medical Journal,* Vol. 48: pp. 146-156.

Dobie, D.J., Kivlahan, D.R., Maynard, C., et al. (2004). Posttraumatic stress disorder in female veterans: association with self-reported health problems and functional impairment. *Archives of Internal Medicine,* Vol. 164: pp. 394-400.

Dollard, J., et al. (1939). *Frustration and Aggression.* New Haven, CT: Yale University Press.

Domash, M. D., & Sparr, L. F. (1982). Post-traumatic stress disorder in female veterans: association and self-reported health problems and functional impairment. *Archives of Internal Medicine,* Vol. 147: pp. 772-774.

Donev, D., Onceva, S., & Gligorov, I. (2002). Refugee crisis in Macedonia during the Kosovo Conflict in 1999. *Croatian Medical Journal,* Vol. 43: pp. 184-189.

Donovan, B., Padin-Rivera, E., Dowd, T., et al. (1996). Childhood factors and war zone stress in chronic PTSD. *Journal of Traumatic Stress,* Vol. 9: pp. 361-368.

Dor-Shav, N.K. (1978). On the long-range effects of concentration camp internment on Nazi victims: Twenty-five years later. *Journal of Consulting and Clinical Psychology,* Vol. 46: pp. 1-11.

Drescher, K.D., & Foy, W.D. (1995). Spirituality and trauma treatment: Suggestions for including spirituality as a coping resource. *National Center for PTSD Clinical Quarterly,* Vol. 5: pp. 4-5.

Drezgic-Vukic, S.M., Knezevic, A., Siladi Den, B., et. al. (1996). War stress and alcoholism in veterans. *Current Topics in Neurology, Psychiatry and Related Disciplines,* Vol. 4: pp. 35-39.

Drozdek, B. (1997). Follow-up study of concentration camp survivors from Bosnia Herzegovina: Three years later. *Journal of Nervous and Mental Disease,* Vol. 185: pp. 690-694.

Dubester, K.A. & Braun, B.G. (1995). Psychometric properties of the Dissociative Experience Scale. *Journal of Nervous and Mental Disease,* Vol. 183: pp. 231-235.

Dupue, R.A., & Spoont, M.r. (1989). Conceptualizing a serotonin trait: A behavioral model of constraint. *Annals of the New York Academy of Sciences,* Vol. 12: pp. 47-62.

Durakovic-Belko, E., Kulenovic, A., & Dapic, R. (2003). Determinants of posttraumatic adjustment in adolescents from Sarajevo who experienced war. *Journal of Clinical Psychology,* Vol.59: pp. 27-40.

Durkheim, E. (1951). *Suicide: A Study in Sociology.* (Spaulding, J.A., & Simpson, G., trans.). New York NY: Free Press.

Dybdahl, R. (2001). Children and mothers in war: an outcome study of a psychosocial intervention program. *Child Development,* Vol. 72: pp. 1214-1230.

Dyer, K.F.W., Dorahy, M.J., Hamilton, G., et al. (2009). Anger, aggression, and self-harm in PTSD and complex PTSD. *Journal of Clinical Psychology,* Vol. 65: pp. 1099-1114.

Edgerton, J.E. (1999). *American Psychiatric Glossary,* American Psychiatric Press.

Edmonds, I.J. (2005). Mainstreaming community based rehabilitation in primary health care in Bosnia-Herzegovina. *Disability and Society,* Vol. 20: pp. 293-309.

Eisson, J.I., Roberts, N., & Macho, G.S. (2003). The Cardiff Traumatic Stress Initiative: an evidence-based approach to early psychological intervention following traumatic events. *Psychiatric Bulletin,* Vol. 27: pp. 145-147.

Eitinger, I. (1961). Pathology of the concentration camp syndrome, *Archives of General Psychiatry,* Vol. 5: pp. 371-380.

Elder, G.H., Clipp, E.C. (1989). Combat experience and emotional health: impairment and resilience in later life. *Journal of Personality,* Vol.57: pp. 311-341.

Elder, G.H., Shanahan, M.J., & Clipp, E.C. (2000). Linking combat and physical health: the legacy of World War II in men's lives. *American Journal of Psychiatry,* Vol. 154: pp. 330-336.

Elliot, D.M., Mok, D.S., & Briere, J. (2004). Adult sexual assault: prevalence, symptomatology, and sex differences in the general population. *Journal of Traumatic Stress,* Vol. 17: pp. 203-211.

Emery, P.E., & Emery, V.O.B. (1989). Psychoanalytic considerations on post-traumatic stress disorder. *Journal of Contemporary Psychotherapy,* Vol. 19: pp. 39-53.

Emery, V.O., Emery, P.E., Shama, D.K., et al. (1991). Predisposing variables in PTSD patients. *Journal of Traumatic Stress,* Vol. 4: pp. 325-343.

Engelhard, I.M., Van Den Horn, M.A., Weerts, J., et al. (2007). Deployment-related stress and trauma in Dutch soldiers returning from Iraq. *British Journal of Psychiatry,* Vol. 191: pp. 140-145.

Erbes, C., Westermeyer, C.J., Engdahl, B., & Johnson, E. (2007). Post-traumatic stress disorder and service utilization in a sample of service members from Iraq and Afghanistan. *Military Medicine,* Vol. 172: pp. 359-363.

Erikson, E.H. (1950). *Children and Society.* New York, NY: Norton.

Erikson, E.H. (1964). *Insight and Responsibility.* New York, NY: Norton.

Evans, L., & Cowlishaw, M.H. (2009). Family functioning predicts outcomes for veterans in treatment for chronic posttraumatic stress disorder. *Journal of Family Psychology,* Vol. 23: pp. 531-539.

Evans, S., Patt, I., Giosan, C., et al. (2009). Disability and posttraumatic stress disorder in disaster relief workers responding to September 11, 2001 World Tade Center Disaster. *Journal of Clinical Psychology,* Vol. 65: pp. 684-694.

Fall, B. (1973). *Street Without Joy.* New York, NY: Schocken.

Fanon, F. (1963). *The Wretched of the Earth.* New York, NY: Grave Weidenfeld.

Fauerbach, J.A., Lawrence, J.W., Fogel, J., et al. (2009). Approach-avoidance coping conflict in a sample of burn patients at risk for posttraumatic stress disorder. *Depression and Anxiety,* Vol. 26: pp. 838-850.

Fear, N.T., Rubin, G.J., Hatch, S., et al. (2009). Job strain, rank, and mental health in the UK armed forces. *International Journal of Occupational and Environmental Health,* Vol. 15: pp. 291-298.

Feeny, N.C., Zoeliner, L.A., & Foa, E.B. (2000). Anger, dissociation, and posttraumatic stress disorder among female assault victims. *Journal of Traumatic Stress*, Vol. 13: pp. 89-100.

Figley, C.R. (1988). A five-phase treatment of post-traumatic stress disorder in families. *Journal of Traumatic Stress*, Vol. 1: pp. 127-141.

Fejzic, J.B., & Tett, S. (2004). Medication management reviews for people from the former Yugoslavia now resident in Australia. *Pharmacy World & Science*, Vol. 26: pp. 271-276.

Ferren, P. (1999). Comparing perceived self-efficacy among adolescent Bosnian and Croatian refugees with and without posttraumatic stress disorder. *Journal of Traumatic Stress*, Vol. 12: pp. 405-420.

Filice, I., et al. (1994). Women refugees from Bosnia-Herzegovina: Developing a culturally sensitive counseling framework. *International Journal of Refugee Law*, Vol. 6: pp. 207-226.

First, M.B., Spitzer, R.L., Gibbon, M., & Williams, J.B.W. (1996). *Structured Clinical Interview for Axis I DSM-IV, patient version, with psychotic screen (SCID-I/P w/ psychotic screen), Version 2.* New York, NY: Biometrics Research Department, New York State Psychiatric Institute.

Fischbach, G.D., et al. (1993). *Mind and Brain.* New York, NY: W.H. Freeman and Company.

Fischer, H. (2006). *United States Military Casualty Statistics: Operation Iraqi Freedom and Operation Enduring Freedom.* Washington, DC: Library of Congress, Congressional Research Service.

Foa, E.B., & Meadows, E.A. (1997). Psychosocial treatments for posttraumatic stress disorder: A critical review. *Annual Review of Psychology*, Vol. 48: pp. 449-480.

Foa, E.B., Davidson, J.R.T., & Frances, A. (1999). The Expert Consensus Guidelines: Treatment of posttraumatic stress disorder. *Journal of Clinical Psychiatry*, Vol. 60 (suppl. 16): pp. 4-76.

Foa, E.B., Keane, T.M., Friedman, M.J., & Cohen, J.A. (ed.s) (2009). *Effective Treatment for PTSD: Practice Guidelines* (2nd. Ed.). New York, NY: Guilford Press.

Folnegovic-Smalc, V., Folnegovic, Z.,Uzun, S., et al. (1997). Psychotrauma related to war and exile as a risk factor for the development of dementia of Alzheimer's Type in refugees. *Croatian Medical Journal*, Vol. 38: pp. 273-276.

Fontana, A., & Rosenheck, R. (1994). Posttraumatic stress disorder among Vietnam theater veterans: a causal model of etiology in a community sample. *Journal of Mental Disorders*, Vol. 182: pp. 677-684.

Fontana, A., & Rosenheck, R. (1999). A model of war zone stressors and posttraumatic stress disorder. *Journal of Traumatic Stress*, Vol. 12: pp. 111-126.

Ford, J.D., Campbell, K.A., Storzbach, D., et al. (2001). Posttraumatic stress symptomatology is associated with unexplained illness attributed to

Persian Gulf War military service. *Psychosomatic Medicine,* Vol. 63: pp. 842-849.

Foy, D.W., Sipprelle, RC., Rueger, D.B., & Carroll, E.M. (1984). Etiology of posttraumatic stress disorder in Vietnam veterans: Analysis of premilitary, military, and combat exposure influences. *Journal of Consulting and Clinical Psychology,* vol. 52: pp. 1323-1328.

Franciskovic, T., Stevanovic, A., Jelusic, I., et al. (2007). Secondary traumatization of wives of war veterans with posttraumatic stress disorder. *Croatian Medical Journal,* Vol. 48: pp. 177-184.

Freeman, S.M., Moore, B.A., & Freeman, A. (2009). *Living and Surviving in Harm's Way: A Psychological Treatment Handbook for Pre- and Post-Deployment of Military Personnel.* New York, NY: Routledge - Taylor & Francis Group.

French, L.A., & Bryce, F. (1978). Suicide and female aggression. *Journal of Clinical Psychiatry,* Vol. 39: pp. 346-352.

French, L.A., Lessard, C., & Williams, R. (1982). Marginality, suicides and suicide attempts. *Psychological Reports,* Vol. 51: p. 264.

French, L.A. (1982). Rage, marginality and suicide among forensic patients. *Corrective and Social Psychiatry,* Vol. 28 (3): pp. 116-119.

French, L.A. (1983). The post-Vietnam traumatic stress disorder. *International Journal of Offender Therapy and Comparative Criminology,* Vol. 27 (3): 218-225.

French, L.A. (1985-86). Forensic suicides and attempted suicides. *Omega,* Vol. 16 (4): pp. 335-345.

French, L.A. (1991). Neuropsychology of violence. *Corrective and Social Psychiatry,* Vol. 37: pp.12-17.

French, L.A. (1994). Early trauma, substance abuse and crime. *Police and Criminal Psychology,* Vol. 10: pp. 64-67.

French, L.A. (1997). Suicide: A biopsychosocial Review. *The Forensic Examiner,* Vol. 6: pp. 11-15.

French, L.A. (1998). Psychopharmacological interventions vs. correctional treatment for violent offenders. *Journal of the Mental Health in Corrections Consortium,* Vol. 44: pp. 5-10.

French, L.A. (2000). *Addictions and Native Americans.* Westport. CT: Praeger Publishers.

French, L.A., & deOca, B. (2001). The neuropsychology of impulse control: New insights into violent behaviors. *Journal of Police and Criminal Psychology,* Vol. 16: pp. 25-32.

French, L.A. (2003). Neurophysiology and neuropsychology of child and adolescent impulsivity. *Encyclopedia of Juvenile Justice* (Mcshane, M., & Williams, III, F., ed.s) New York, NY: Sage Publications: pp. 253-254.

French, L.A. (2005). Understanding hate, violence & vigilantism: Mitigation clinical/social factors. *American Association of Behavioral and Social Sciences Journal,* (Fall): pp. 21-30.

French, L.A. (2008). Combat stress among North American veterans serving in Iraq/Afghanistan. *IX Congreso Internacional de Estres Traumatico 2008.* (Mosca, D., Cazabat, E., & Lescano, R., ed.s). Buenos Aires, Argentina: Librenia Akadia Editiorial: pp. 205-214.

Freud, S. (1915/1957). Repression. *The Standard Edition of the Complete Psychological Works of Sigmund Freud.* (Vol. 14). (Strachey, J., ed.). London, England: Hogarth Press: pp. 142-158.

Freud, S. (1918). *Reflections on War and Death* (Brill, A.A., & Kuttner, A.B., Trans.). New York, NY: Moffat, Yard & Company.

Freud, S. (1937/1968). *The Ego and the Mechanisms of Defense.* London, England: Hogarth Press and Institute of Psychoanalysis.

Friedrich, M. (1999). Addressing mental health needs of Balkan refugees. *Journal of the American Medical Association (JAMA).* Vol. 282. pp.422-423.

Friedman, M.J. (2004). Acknowledging the psychiatric cost of war. *New England Journal of Medicine,* Vol. 351: pp. 75-77.

Friedman, M. J. (2006). Posttraumatic stress disorder among military returnees from Afghanistan and Iraq. *American Journal of Psychiatry,* Vol. 163: pp. 586-593.

Fruch, B.C., Gold, P.B., Dammeyer, M., et al. (2000). Differentiation of depression and PTSD symptoms in combat veterans. *Depression and Anxiety,* Vol. 11: pp. 175-179.

Fruch, B.C., & Kinder, B.N. (1994). The susceptibility of the Rorschach inkblot test to malingering of combat-related PTSD. *Journal of Personality Assessment,* Vol. 62: pp. 280-298.

Fruch, B.C. , Leverett, J.P., & Kinder, B.N. (1995). Interrelationship between MMPI-2 and Rorschach variables in a sample of Vietnam veterans with PTSD. *Journal of Personality Assessment,* Vol. 64: pp. 312-318.

Fry, S., & Stockton, A. (1982). Discriminate Analysis of Posttraumatic Stress Disorder among a group of Vietnam Veterans. *American Journal of Psychiatry,* Vol. 139: pp. 52-56.

Fullerton, C.S., (ed.). (1997). *Posttraumatic Stress Disorder: Acute and Long-Term Responses to Trauma and Disaster.* Washington, DC: American Psychiatric Press.

Galea, S., Ahern, J.,Resbucj, K.H., et al. (2002). Psychological sequelae of the September 11 terrorist attacks in New York City. *New England Journal of Medicine,* Vol. 346: pp. 982-987.

Galea, A., Viahov, D., Resnick, H., et al. (2003). Trends of probable post-traumatic stress disorder in New York City after the September 11 terrorist attacks. *American Journal of Epidemiology,* Vol. 158: pp. 514-524.

GAO (2006). *Posttraumatic Stress Disorder: DoD Needs to Identify the Factors Its Providers Use to Make Mental Health Evaluation Referrals for Service Members.* Washington, DC: Government Accountability Office.

Gavrilovic, J.J., Lecic-Tosevski, D., & Jovic, V. (1998). Actual symptomatology, defense mechanisms and childhood traumatic experience in war traumatized patients. *Psychiatry Today,* Vol. 30: pp. 509-521.

Gavrilovic,J.J., Lecic-Tosevski, D., Colovic, O., et al. (2005). Association of posttraumatic stress and quality of life in civilians after air attacks. *Journal of the Association of Posttraumatic Stress and Quality of Life,* Vol. 37: pp. 297-305

Gegax, T.T., & Thomas, E. (2005). Walking among the dead. *Newsweek* (August 29-September 5 issues): pp: 34-36.

Gelkopf, M., & Berger, R. (2009). A school-based, teacher-mediated prevention program (ERASE-Stress) for reducing terror-related traumatic reactions in

Israeli youth: a quasi-randomized controlled trial. *Journal of Child Psychology and Psychiatry,* Vol. 50: pp. 962-971

Gellers, J., Foy, D.W., Donahoe, C.P., & Goldfarb, J. (1988). Post-traumatic stress disorder in Vietnam combat veterans: Effects of traumatic violence exposure and military adjustment. *Journal of Traumatic Stress,* Vol. 1: pp. 181-192.

Geltman, P., et al. (2000). War trauma experience and behavioral screening of Bosnian refugee children resettled in Massachusetts. *Journal of Developmental & Behavioral Pediatrics,* Vol. 21: pp. 255-261.

Gersons, B.P., Carlier, I.V., Lamberts, R.D., & van der Kolk, B.A. (2000). Randomized clinical trial of brief eclectic psychotherapy for police officers with Posttraumatic Stress Disorder. *Journal of Traumatic Stress,* Vol. 13: pp. 333-347.

Ghaziuddin, M., Ghaziuddin, N., & Stein, G.S. (1990). Life events and the recurrence of depression. *Canadian Journal of Psychiatry,* Vol. 35: pp. 239-242.

Gibson, K. (1989). Children in political violence. *Social Science and Medicine,* Vol. 28: pp. 659-668.

Giller, E.L. (Ed.). (1990). *Biological Assessment and Treatment of PTSD.* Washington, DC: American Psychiatric Press.

Ginzburg, K., Butler, L.D., Giese-Davis, J., et al. (2009). Shame, guilt, and posttraumatic stress disorder in adult survivors of childhood sexual abuse at risk for human immunodeficiency virus: Outcomes of a randomized clinical trial of group psychotherapy treatment. *Journal of Nervous and Mental Disease,* Vol. 197: pp. 536-542.

Goldberg, D.P., & Hillier, V. (1979). A scaled version of the General Health Questionnaire. *Psychological Medicine,* Vol. 9: pp 139-145.

Goldberg, D.P., Gater, R., Sartorius, N., et al. (1997). The validity of two versions of the GHQ in the WHO study of mental illness in general healthcare. *Psychological Medicine,* Vol. 27: pp. 191-197.

Goldstein, R., Wampler, N., & Wise, P. (1997). War experiences and distress symptoms of Bosnian children. *Pediatrics,* Vol. 100: pp. 873-878.

Goleman, D. (1997). *Emotional Intelligence.* Belgrade, Serbia: Geopoetika.

Goodman, W.K., Prince, L.H., Rasmussen, S.A., et al. (1989). The Yale-Brown Obsessive Compulsive Scale, I: development, use, and reliability. *Archives of General Psychiatry,* Vol. 46: pp. 1006-1011.

Gone, J.P. (2009). A Community-based treatment for Native American historical trauma: Prospects for evidence-based practice. *Journal of Consulting and Clinical Psychology,* Vol. 77: pp. 751-762.

Goulston, K.J., et al. (1985). Gastrointestinal morbidity among World-War 2 prisoners of war – 40 years on. *Medical Journal of Australia,* Vol. 143: pp. 6-10.

Grabe, H.J., Spitzer, C., Schwahn, A.M., et al. (2009). Serotonin transporter gene (SLC6A4) promoter polymorphisms and the susceptibility to posttraumatic stress disorder in the general population *American Journal of Psychiatry,* Vol. 166: pp. 926-933.

Graham, J.R. (2000). *MMPI-2: Assessing Personality and Psychopathology.* New York, NY: Oxford University Press.

Grayman, J.H., Good, M.D., & Good, B.J. (2009). Conflict nightmares and trauma in Aceh. *Culture, Medicine and Psychiatry,* Vol. 33: pp. 290-312.

Green, B.L., Goodman, L.A., Krupnick, J.L., et al. (2000). Outcomes of single versus multiple trauma exposure in a screening sample. *Journal of Traumatic Stress,* Vol. 13: pp. 271-286.

Green, R.L. (2000). *The MMPI-2: An Interpretive Manual.* Boston, MA: Allyn & Bacon.

Gregurek, R.Vukusic, H., Baretic, V., et al. (1996). Anxiety and post-traumatic stress disorder in disabled war veterans. *Croatian Medical Journal,* Vol. 37: pp. 38-41.

Gregurek, R. (1999). Countertransference problems in the treatment of a mixed group of war veterans and female partners of war veterans. *Croatian Medical Journal,* Vol. 40: pp. 493-497.

Gregurek, R., Pavic, L., Vuger-Kovacic, D., et al. (2001). Increase of frequency of post-traumatic stress disorder in disabled war veterans during prolonged stay in a rehabilitation hospital. *Croatian Medical Journal,* Vol. 42: pp. 161-164.

Grieger, T.A., Cozza, S.J., Ursano, R.J., Hoge, C., et al. (2006). Posttraumatic stress disorder and depression in battle-injured soldiers. *American Journal of Psychiatry,* Vol. 163: pp. 1777-1783.

Grinker, R.R., & Sppeigel, J.J. (1945). *Men under stress.* New York, NY: McGraw-Hill.

Guilmette, T.J. (1997). *Pocket Guide to Brain Injury, Cognitive, and Neurobehavioral Rehabilitation.* San Diego, CA: Singular Publishing Group, Inc.

Gurvits, T.V., et al. (1996). Magnetic Resonance Imaging study of Hippocampal volume in chronic, combat-related Posttraumatic Stress Disorder. *Biological Psychiatry,* Vol. 40: pp. 1091-1099.

Gutierrez, P.M., Brenner, L.A., & Huggins, J.A. (2008). A preliminary investigation of suicidality in psychiatrically hospitalized veterans with Traumatic Brain Injury. *Archives of Suicide Research,* Vol. 12: pp. 336-343.

Hamilton, R.J., Anderson, A., Frater-Mathieson, K., et al (2003). Interventions for refugee children in New Zealand schools: Models, methods, and best practice. *Research Centre for Interventions in Teaching and Learning (RCITL).* Auckland, New Zealand: University of Auckland Press.

Hamilton, S., Goff, B.S.N., Crow, J.R., & Reisbig, A.M. (2009). Primary trauma of female partners in a military sample: Individual symptoms and relationship satisfaction. *The American Journal of Family Therapy,* Vol. 37: pp. 336-346.

Hamner, M.B. (2007). Long-term treatment of posttraumatic stress disorder. *Psychiatric Times,* Vol. 24: pp. 1-4.

Hanson, R.K. (2003). Who is dangerous and when are they safe? Risk assessment with sexual offenders. *Protecting Society from sexually dangerous offenders: Law, justice, and therapy* (Winick, B., & Lafond, J., eds.). Washington, DC: American Psychological Association: pp. 101-117.

Hariri, A.R., Mattay, V.S., Tessitore, A., et al. (2002). Serotonin transporter genetic variation and the response of the human amygdala. *Science,* Vol. 297: pp. 400-404.

Hasanovic, M., Sinanovic, O., & Pavlovic, S. (2005). Acculturation and psychological problems of adolescents from Bosnia and Herzegovina during exile and reparation. *Croatian Medical Journal,* Vol. 46: pp. 105-115.

Hasanovic, M., et al. (2006). Psychological disturbances of war-traumatized children from different foster and family settings in Bosnia and Herzegovina. *Croatian Medical Journal,* Vol. 47: pp. 85-94.

Hasanaovic, M., et al. (2006). Post-war mental health promotion in Bosnia and Herzegovina. *Psychiatria Danubina,* Vol. 18: 74-78.

Hasanovic, M., & Herenda, S. (2008). Post-traumatic stress disorder, depression and anxiety among family medicine residents after 1992-95 war in Bosnia and Herzegovina. *Psychiatria Danubina,* Vol. 20: pp. 277-285.

Helmer, D.A., Rossignol, M., Blatt, M., et al. (2007). Health and exposure concerns of veterans deployed to Iraq and Afghanistan. *Journal of Occupational and Environmental Medicine,* Vol. 49: pp. 475-480.

Helmus, T.C., & Glenn, R.W. (2005). *Steeling the Mind: Combat stress reactions and their implications for urban warfare.* Santa Monica, CA: RAND Corporation.

Helzer, J.E., Robins, L.N., & McEnvoy, L. (1987). Posttraumatic stress disorder in the general population. *New England Journal of Medicine,* Vol. 317: pp. 1630-1634.

Hendin, H., & Haas, A. (1984). Posttraumatic stress disorder in veterans of early American wars. *Psychological Review,* Vol. 12: pp. 25-30.

Henisberg, N., Folnegovic-Smalc, V., & Moro, L.J. (2001). Stressor characteristics and post-traumatic stress disorder symptom dimensions in war victims. *Croatian Medical Journal,* Vol. 42: pp. 543-550.

Henderson, D.C., et al. (2008). Building primary care practitioners' attitudes and confidence in mental health skills in post-conflict Bosnia and Herzegovina. *International Journal of Culture and Mental Health,* Vol. 1: pp. 117-133.

Henry, J.P., & Wang, S. (1998). Effects of early stress on adult affiliative behavior. *Psychoneuroendocrinology,* Vol. 23: pp. 863-875.

Herceg, M., Melamed, B.G., & Pregrad, J. (1996). Effects of war on refugee and non-refugee children from Croatia and Bosnia Herzegovina. *Croatian Medical Journal,* Vol. 37: pp. 105-111.

Herman, J.L. (1992). *Trauma and Recovery.* New York, NY: Basic Books.

Hendin, H., & Haas, A.D. (1984). *The Psychological Aftermath of Combat in Vietnam.* New York, NY: Basic Books.

Herlihy, J., Scragg, P., & Turner, S. (2002). Discrepancies in autobiographical memories – implications for the assessment of asylum seekers: Repcated interviews study. *British Medical Journal,* Vol. 324: pp. 324-327.

Hersh, S.M. (1970). *My Lai: A Report on the Massacre and Its Aftermath.* New York, NY: Random House.

Heuer, F., & Reisberg, D. (1990). Vivid memories of emotional events: the accuracy of remembered minutiae. *Memory & Cognition,* Vol. 18: pp. 496-506.

Harpaz-Rotem, I., & Rosenheck, R.A. (2009). Tracing the flow of knowledge: Geographic variability in the diffusion of Prazosin use for the treatment of posttraumatic stress disorder nationally in the Department of Veterans Affairs. Arch Gen Psychiatry, Vol. 66: pp. 417-421.

Hjort, H., & Frisen, A. (2006). Ethnic identity and reconciliation: two main tasks for the young in Bosnia-Herzegovina. *Adolescence,* Vol. 41: pp. 141-163.

Hodgetts, G., et al. (2003). Posttraumatic stress disorders among family physicians in Bosnia and Herzegovina. *Family Practice,* Vol. 20: pp. 489-491.

Hogben, G.L., & Cornfield, R.B. (1981). Treatment of war neuroses with Phenelzine. *Archives of General Psychiatry,* Vol. 38: 440-445.

Hoge, C.W., Lesikar, S.E., Guevara, R., et al. (2002). Mental disorders among U.S. military personnel in the 1990s: Association with high levels of health care utilization and early military attrition. *American Journal of Psychiatry,* Vol. 159: pp. 1576-1583.

Hoge, C.W., Castro, C.A., Messer, S.C., et al. (2004). Combat duty in Iraq and Afghanistan, mental health problems, and barriers to care. *New England Journal of Medicine,* Vol. 351: pp. 13-22.

Hoge, C.W., Auchterlonie, J.L., & Milliken, C.S. (2006). Mental health problems, use of mental services, and attrition from military service after returning from deployment in Iraq or Afghanistan. *Journal of the American Medical Association (JAMA),* Vol. 295: pp. 1023-1032.

Hoge, C.W., et al. (2007). Association of posttraumatic stress disorder with somatic symptoms, health care visits, and absenteeism among Iraq war veterans. *American Journal of Psychiatry,* Vol. 164: pp. 150-153.

Hoge, C.W., Clark, J.C., & Castro, C.A. (2007). Commentary: Women in combat and the risk of post-traumatic stress disorder and depression. *International Journal of Epidemiology,* Vol. 36: pp. 327-329.

Hoge, C.W., et al. (2008). Mild traumatic brain injury in U.S. soldiers returning from Iraq. *New England Journal of Medicine,* Vol. 358: pp. 453-463.

Hoge, C.W., et al. (2008). Association of posttraumatic stress disorder with somatic symptoms, health care visits, and absenteeism among Iraq war veterans. *American Journal of Psychiatry,* Vol. 164: pp. 150-153.

Horowitz, M.J. (1986). *Stress Response Syndromes* (2nd Ed.). New York, NY: Jason Aronson.

Hosek, J., Kavanagh, J., & Miller, L. (2008). *How Deployments Affect Service Members.* Santa Monica, CA: RAND Corporation (MG-432-RC).

Hotopf, M., et al. (2006). The health of UK military personnel who deployed to the 2003 Iraq War: A cohort study. *Lancet,* Vol. 367 (9524): pp. 1731-1741.

Hollingshead, A.B.,& Redlich, F.C. (1958). *Social Class and Mental Illness: A Community Study.* New York, NY: John Wiley & Sons.

Holmes, T.H., & Rahe, R.H. (1967). The Social Readjustment Rating Scale. *Journal of Psychosomatic Research,* Vol. 11: pp. 213-218.

Homeless, A. (1990). Developmental impact of combat exposure: comparison of adolescent and adult Vietnam veterans. *Smith College Studies in Social Work,* Vol. 60: pp. 185-195.

Hovanesian, S., Isakov, I., & Cervellione, K.L. (2009). Defense mechanisms and suicide risk in major depression. *Archives of Suicide Research,* Vol. 13: pp. 74-86.

Huethner, G. (1996). The Central Adaptation Syndrome: Psychosocial stress as a trigger for adaptive modifications of brain structure and brain function. *Progress in Neuropsychology,* Vol. 48: pp. 569-612.

Humphrey, J.A., French, L.A., & Niswander, D. (1974). Process of suicide. *Diseases of the Nervous System,* Vol. 35: pp. 215-219.

Hunt, N., & Gakenyi, M. (2005). Comparing refugees and nonrefugees: The Bosnian experience. *Journal of Anxiety Disorders,* Vol. 19: pp. 717-723.

Hyams, K.C., Wignall, F.S., & Roswell, R. (1996). War syndromes and their evaluation: from the US Civil War to the Persian Gulf War. *Annuals of Internal Medicine,* Vol. 125: pp. 398-405.

Ilic, Z.P., Jovic, V., & Lecic-Tosevski, D.M. (1998). Post-traumatic stress in war prisoners. *Psychiatry Today,* Vol. 30: pp. 73-85.

Ilic, Z.P., et al. (1999). EMDR: Cognitive behavior methods for posttraumatic stress disorder in torture victims. *Psychiatry Today,* Vol. 31: pp. 245-269.

ICD-9. (1977). *International Classification of Diseases – 9th Edition.* World Health Organization.

ICD-9-CM. (1979 -). *International Classification of Diseases-9th Edition-Clinical Modification.* U.S. National Center for Health Statistics.

ICD-10. (1992). *International Classification of Diseases – 10th Edition.* World Health Organization.

Inkelas, M., et al. (2000). Dimensionality and reliability of the Civilian Mississippi Scale for PTSD in a post-earthquake Community. *Journal of Traumatic Stress,* Vol. 13: pp. 149-167.

Institute of Medicine, Committee on Treatment of Posttraumatic Stress Disorder, Board on Population Health and Public Health Practice. (2007). *Treatment of Posttraumatic Stress Disorders: An Assessment of the Evidence.* Washington, DC: National Academic Press.

IMT-FE (1948). 20,000 rape cases. *Judgment of the International Military Tribunal for the Far East.* p. 1012.

Iowa Persian Gulf Study Group. (1997). Self-reported illness and health status among Gulf War veterans: a population-based study. *Journal of the American Medical Association (JAMA),* Vol. 277: pp. 238-245.

Ispanovic-Radojkovic, V. (2003). Youth clubs: psychosocial intervention with young refugees. *Intervention,* Vol. 1: pp. 38-44.

Jacobson, L., Lagerquist, B., & Eriksson, B. (2000). Swedish health care support to Bosnia-Herzegovina: Changing outpatient psychiatry and social work. *Lakartidningen,* Vol. 97: pp. 4153-4157.

Janet, P. (1889). *The Psychological Automatism.* Paris, France: Allcan.

Jatzko, A., et al. (2006). Hippocampal volume in chronic posttraumatic stress disorder (PTSD): MRI study using two different evaluation methods. *Journal of Affective Disorders,* Vol. 94: pp. 121-126.

Jaycox, L.H., Marshall, G.N., & Schell, T. (2004). Use of mental health services by men injured through community violence. *Psychiatric Services,* Vol. 55: pp. 415-420.

JBBC (1946). Pattern of first-phase violence. *The Black Book: The Nazi Crime Against the Jewish People.* New York, NY: The Jewish Black Book Committee. pp. 301, 329,340, 342, 366, 436.

Jenkins, S.C., & Hansen, M.R. (1995). *Pocket Reference for Psychiatrists* (Second Edition). Washington, DC: American Psychiatric Press.

Jensen, B.S., & Ceric, I. (1994). Community-oriented mental health care in Bosnian and Herzegovina: Strategy and model project – Sarajevo. *WHO Office for Bosnia and Herzegovina.*

Johnson, D.R., et al. (1996). Outcome of intensive inpatient treatment for combat-related posttraumatic stress disorder. *American Journal of Psychiatry,* Vol. 153: pp. 771-777.

Jones, E.E., & Harris, V.A. (1967). The attribution of attitudes. *Journal of Experimental Psychology,* Vol. 3: pp. 2-24.

Jones, E.E., & Palmer, I.P. (2000). Army psychiatry in the Korean War: The experience of 1 Commonwealth Division. *Military Medicine,* Vol. 165: pp. 256-260.

Jones, E.E., et al. (2002). Post-combat syndromes from the Boar War to the Gulf War: a cluster analysis of their nature and attribution. *British Medical Journal,* Vol. 324: pp. 1321-1324.

Jones, E.E., Fear, N.T., & Wessely, S. (2007). Shell shock and mild traumatic brain injury: A historical review. *American Journal of Psychiatry,* Vol. 164: pp. 1641-1645.

Jones, L. (1998). Adolescent groups for encamped Bosnian refugees: Some problems and solutions. *Clinical Child Psychology and Psychiatry,* Vol. 3: pp.541-551.

Jones, L. (2002). Adolescent understandings of political violence and psychological well-being: a qualitative study from Bosnia-Herzegovina. *Social Science & Medicine,* Vol. 55: pp. 1351-1371.

Jones, L., & Kafetsios, K. (2005). Exposure to political violence and psychological well-being in Bosnian adolescents: A mixed method approach. *Clinical Child Psychology and Psychiatry,* Vol. 10: pp. 157-176.

Jordan, B.K., et al. (1991). Lifetime and current prevalence of specific psychiatric disorders among Vietnam veterans and controls. *Archives of General Psychiatry,* Vol. 48: pp. 207-215.

Jordan, B.K., et al. (1992). Problems in families of male Vietnam veterans with posttraumatic stress disorder. *Journal of Consulting and Clinical Psychology,* Vol. 60: pp. 916-926.

Jovanovic, A.A., et al. (2009). Predicting violence in veterans with posttraumatic stress disorder. *Military-Medical and Pharmaceutical Review,* Vol. 66: pp. 13-21.

Jovicevic, M. (1981). *Psychological Stress in War.* Belgrade, Serbia: Vojnoizdavacki zavod.

Kaplan, H.I., & Sadock, B.J. (1996). *Pocket Handbook of Clinical Psychiatry* (second edition). Baltimore, MD: Williams & Wilkins.

Kapor, G. (1982). *War Psychiatry.* Belgrade, Serbia: Vojnoizdavacki zavod.

Kalayjian, A,, & Eugene, D. (2009). *Mass Trauma and Emotional Healing around the World.* Santa Barbara, CA: Praeger-ABC-CLIO press.

Kandido-Jaksic, M. (2008). Social distance and attitudes towards ethnically mixed marriages. *Psychology,* Vol. 41: pp.149-162.

Kang, H.K., et al. (2003) Posttraumatic stress disorder and chronic fatigue syndrome-like illness among Gulf War veterans: a population-based survey of 30,000 veterans. *American Journal of Epidemiology,* Vol. 157: pp. 142-148.

Kardiner, A. (1941). *The Traumatic Neurosis of War.* New York, NY: Paul Hoeber.

Kardiner, A., & Speigel, H. (1945). *War Stress and neurotic Illness.* New York, NY: Paul Hoeber.

Karstedt, S. (2002). Emotions and criminal justice. *Theoretical Criminology,* Vol. 6: pp. 299-317.

Karstedt, S. (2006). Emotions, crime and justice: Exploring Durkheimian themes. *Sociological Theory and Criminological Research: Views from Europe and the United States* (Deflem, M., ed.). Amsterdam, Netherlands: Elsevier: pp. 223-248.

Katz, R., et al., (1995). Pharmacotherapy of posttraumatic stress disorder with a novel psychotropic brofaromine in PTSD. *Anxiety,* Vol. 1: pp. 169-174.

Kaufer, D., Friedman, A., Seldman, S., & Soreq, H. (1998). Acute stress facilitates long-lasting changes in cholinergic gene expression. *Nature,* Vol. 393: pp. 373-377.

Keane, T.M., Malloy, P.F., & Fairbanks, J.A. (1984). Empirical development of an MMPI subscale for the assessment of combat-related PTSD. *Journal of Consulting and Clinical Psychology,* Vol. 52: pp. 888-891.

Keane, T.M., Caddell, J.M., & Taylor, K.L. (1988). Mississippi Scale for Combat-Related Posttraumatic Stress Disorder: three studies in reliability. *Journal of Consulting and Clinical Psychology,* Vol. 56: pp. 85-90.

Keane, T.M., Fairbanks, J.A., Caddell, J.M., et al. (1989). Clinical evaluation of a measure to assess combat exposure. *Psychological Assessment,* Vol. 1: pp. 53-55.

Keane, T.M., Kaloupek, D.G., & Weathers, F.W. (1996). Ethnocultural considerations in the assessment of PTSD. In *Ethnocultural aspects of posttraumatic stress disorder* (Marsella, A.J., Friedman, M.J., Gerrit, E.T., & Scurfield, R.M., editors). Washington, DC: American Psychological Association: pp. 183-208.

Keller, M.B., et al. (2006). Untangling depression and anxiety: Clinical challenges. *Journal of Clinical Psychiatry,* Vol. 66: pp. 1477-1487.

Kelley, H.H. (1973). The process of causal attribution. *American Psychologist,* Vol. 28: pp. 107-128.

Kenny, L.M., Bryant, R.A., Silove, D., & Creamer, M. (2009). Distant memories: A prospective study of vantage point of trauma memories. *Psychological Science,* Vol. 20: pp. 1049-1052.

Kessler, R.C., Sonnega, A., Bromet, E., et al. (1995). Posttraumatic stress disorder in the national comorbidity survey. *Archives of General Psychiatry,* Vol. 52: pp. 1048-1060.

Kessler, R.C. (2000). Posttraumatic stress disorder: The burden to the individual and to society. *Journal of Clinical Psychiatry,* Vol. 61 (Suppl. 5): pp. 4-14.

Keyes, E., & Kane, C. (2004). Belonging and adapting: Mental health of Bosnian refugees living in the United States. *Issues in Mental Health Nursing,* Vol. 25: pp. 809-831.

Khouzan, H.R., & Kissmeyer, P. (1997). Antidepressant treatment, post-traumatic Stress disorder, survivor guilt, and spiritual awakening. *Journal of Traumatic Stress,* Vol. 10: pp. 691-696.

Kilpatrick, D.G., Veronen, L.J., & Best, C.L. (1985). Factors predicting psychological distress in rape victims. *Trauma and its wake* (Figley, C., Ed.). New York, NY: Brunner/Mazel: pp. 113-141.

Kilpatrick, D.G., et al. (2007). The serotonin transporter genotype and social support and moderation of posttraumatic stress disorder and depression in hurricane-exposed adults. *American Journal of Psychiatry,* Vol. 164: pp. 1693-1699.

Kimerling, R., Ouimette, P., Wolfe, J. (eds.). (2002). *Gender and PTSD.* New York, NY: The Guilford Press.

King, D.W., King, L.A., Gudanowski, D.M., & Vreven, D.L. (1995). Alternative representations of war zone stressors: Relationships to posttraumatic stress disorder in male and female Vietnam veterans. *Journal of Abnormal Psychology,* Vol. 104: pp. 184-196.

King, D.W., King, L.A.,& Foy, D., & Gudanowski, D.M. (1996). Prewar factors in combat-related posttraumatic stress disorder: structural equation modeling with a national sample of female and male Vietnam veterans. *Journal of Consulting and Clinical Psychology,* Vol. 64: pp. 520-531.

King, D.W., Leskin, G.A., King, L.A. & Weathers, F.W. (1998). Confiratory factor analysis of the Clinician-Administered PTSD Scale: Evidence for the dimensionality of posttraumatic stress disorder. *Psychological Assessment,* Vol. 10: pp. 90-96.

King, D.W., et al. (1998). Resilience-recovery factors in posttraumatic stress disorder among female and male Vietnam veterans: Hardiness, postwar social support, and additional stressful life events. *Journal of Personality and Social Psychology,* Vol. 74: pp. 420-434.

King, D.W., et al. (1999). Posttraumatic stress disorder in a national sample of female and male Vietnam veterans: risk factors, war-zone stressors, and resilience-recovery variables. *Journal of Abnormal Psychology,* Vol. 108: pp. 164-170.

Kinzie, D., Boehnlein, J.,Leung, P., et al. (1990). The Prevalence of posttraumatic stress disorder and its clinical significance among Southeast Asian refugees. *American Journal of Psychiatry,* 147: pp. 913-917.

Kitayama, S., & Cohen, D. (2007). *Handbook of Cultural Psychology.* New York, NY: The Guilford Press.

Kitchiner, N.J. Bisson, J.I., Phillips, B., & Roberts, N. (2007). Increasing access to trauma focused Cognitive-Behavioral Therapy for post traumatic stress disorder through group clinical supervision. *Behavioural and Cognitive Psychotherapy,* Vol. 35: pp. 251-254.

Klaric, M., Klaric, B., Stevanovic, A., et al. (2007). Psychological consequences of war trauma and postwar social stressors in women in

Bosnia and Herzegovina. *Croatian Medical Journal,* Vol. 48: pp. 167-176.

Klaric M., Franciskovic, T., Klaric, B., et at. (2008). Psychological problems in children of war veterans with posttraumatic stress disorder in Bosnia and Herzegovina: Cross-sectional study. *Croatian Medical Journal,* Vol. 49: pp. 491-498.

Klayman, J., & Ha, Y.W. (1987). Confirmation, disconfirmation, and information in hypothesis testing. *Psychological Review,* Vol. 94: pp. 211-228.

Kluznick, J.C., et al. (1986). Forty-year follow-up of United States prisoners of war. *American Journal of Psychiatry,* Vol. 143: pp. 1443-1446.

Knezovic, Z., & Bunjevac, T. (2006). War stress and aggression. *Contemporary Psychology,* Vol. 6: pp. 45-53.

Knipuohcer, J., & Kleber, R. (2006). The relative contribution of posttraumatic and acculturative stress to subjective mental health among Bosnian refugees. *Journal of Clinical Psychology,* Vol. 62: pp. 339-353.

Koenen, K.C. (2007). Genetics of posttraumatic stress disorder: review and recommendations for future studies. *Journal of Traumatic Stress,* Vol. 20: pp. 737-750.

Kolb, L., & Mutalipassi, L. (1982). The conditional emotional response: A sub-class of the chronic and delayed post-traumatic stress disorder. *Psychiatric Annals,* Vol. 12: pp. 979-999.

Kolkow, T.T., Spira, J.L., Morse, J.S., & Grieger, T.A. (2007). Post-traumatic stress disorder and depression in health care providers returning from deployment to Iraq and Afghanistan. *Military Medicine,* Vol. 172: pp. 451-455.

Kopinak, J. (1999). The health of Bosnian refugees in Canada. *Ethnicity & Health,* Vol. 4: pp. 65-82.

Koren, D., et al. (2005). Increased PTSD risk with combat-related injury: a matched comparison study of injured and uninjured soldiers experiencing the same combat event. *American Journal of Psychiatry,* Vol. 162: pp. 276-282.

Kostic, P. (1994). War experience and behavior of war veterans. *Psychology,* Vol. 27: pp. 97-110.

Kostic, P. (1996). An addendum to the war crimes psychology. *Psychology,* Vol. 29: pp. 447-464.

Kozaric-Kovacic, D., Kocijan-Hercigonja, D., & Jambrosic, A. (2002). Psychiatric help to psychotraumatized persons during and after war in Croatia. *Croatian Medical Journal,* Vol. 43: pp. 221-228.

Kozaric-Kovacic, D., Kocijan-Hercigonja, D., & Grubisic-Ilic, M. (2001). Posttraumatic stress disorder and depression in soldiers with combat experiences. *Croatian Medical Journal,* Vol. 42: pp. 165-170.

Krashin, d., & Oates, E.W. (1999). Risperidone as an adjunct therapy for post-traumatic stress disorder. *Military Medicine,* Vol. 164: pp. 605-606.

Kroenke, K., & Spitzer, R.L. (2002). The PHQ-9: A new depression diagnostic and severity measure. *Psychiatric Annals,* Vol. 32: pp. 1-7.

Kroenke, K., Spitzer, R.L., & Williams, J.B. (2003). The Patient Health Questionaire-2: Validity of a two-item depression screener. *Medical Care,* Vol. 41: pp. 1284-1292.

Krystal, J.H., et al. (1989). Neurobiological aspects of PTSD: Review of clinical and preclinical studies. *Behavioral Therapy,* Vol. 20: pp. 177-198.

Kubany, E.S., Haynes, S.N., Leisen, M.B., et al. (2000). Development and preliminary validations of a brief broad-spectrum measure of trauma exposure: the Traumatic Life Events Questionnaire. *Psychological Assessment,* Vol. 12: pp. 210-224.

Kucukalic, A., Dzubur-Kulenovic, A., Ceric, I., et al. (2005). Regional collaboration in reconstruction of mental health services in Bosnia and Herzegovina. *Psychiatric Services,* Vol. 56: pp. 1455-1457.

Kuljic, B., Miljanovic, B., & Svicevic, R. (2004). Posttraumatic stress disorder in Bosnian war veterans: Analysis of stress events and risk factors. *Military-Medical and Pharmaceutical Review,* Vol. 61: pp. 283-289.

Kulka, R.A., Schlenger, W.E., Fairbank, J.A., et al. (1990). *The National Vietnam Veterans Readjustment Study: Tables of findings and technical appendices.* New York, NY: Brunner/Mazel.

Kulka, R.A., Schlenger, W.E., Fairbank, J.A., et al. (1990). *Trauma and the Vietnam War Generation: Report of Findings from the National Vietnam Veterans Readjustment Study.* New York, NY: Brunner/Mazel.

Labbate, L.A., & Douglas, S. (2000). Olanzapine for nightmares and sleep disturbance in Posttraumatic Stress Disorder (PTSD). *Canadian Journal of Psychiatry,* Vol. 45: pp. 667-668.

Langlois, J.A., Rutland-Bown, W., & Wald, M.M. (2006). The epidemiology and impact of traumatic brain injury: A brief overview. *Journal of Head Trauma Rehabilitation,* Vol. 21: pp. 375-378.

Lapierre, C.B., Schwegler, A.F., & LaBauve, B.J. (2007). Posttraumatic stress and depression symptoms in soldiers returning from combat operations in Iraq and Afghanistan. *Journal of Trauma and Stress,* Vol. 20: pp. 933-943.

Lazarus, R.S., & Folkman, S. (1984). *Stress appraisal and Coping.* New York, NY: Springer.

Lazic, D., & Bojanin, S.S. (1995). New forms of deviant behavior in adolescent refugees. *Psychiatry Today,* Vol. 27: pp. 103-116.

Lew, H.L., et al. (2008) Overlap of mild TBI and mental health conditions in returning OIF/OEF service members and veterans. *Journal of Rehabilitation Research and Development,* Vol. 45: pp. xi-xvi.

Lewin, K. (1943). Defining the "Field at a Given Time." *Psychological Review,* Vol. 50: pp. 292-310.

Lewin, K. (1946). Action research and minority problems. *Journal of Social Issues,* Vol. 2: pp. 34-47.

Lewin, K. (1951). *Field theory in social sciences: selected papers on group dynamics* (Lewin, G.W., ed.). New York, NY: Harper & Row.

Llabre, M.M., & Hadi, F. (2009). War-related exposure and psychological distress as predictors of health and sleep: A longitudinal study of Kuwaiti Children. *Psychosomatic Medicine,* Vol. 71: pp. 776-783.

Lindert, J., von Ehrenstein, O.S., Priebe, S., et al. (2009). Depression and anxiety in labor migrants and refugees - A systematic review and meta-analysis. *Social Science & Medicine,* Vol. 69: pp. 246-257.

Lindorff, M. (2002). After the War is over...:PTSD symptoms in World War II veterans. *The Australian Journal of Disaster and Trauma Study,* Vol. 2: pp.16-21.

Lippei, S., et al. (1986). Preliminary study of Carbamezapine in post-traumatic stress disorder. *Psychosomatics,* Vol. 27: pp. 847-854.

Loncar, M., Medved, V., Jovanovic, N., & Hotujac, L. (2005). Psychological consequences of rape on women in 1991-1995 war in Croatia and Bosnia and Herzegovina. *Croatian Medical Journal,* Vol. 47: pp. 67-75.

Lydiard, R.B. (2003). The role of GABA in anxiety disorders. *Journal of Clinical Psychiatry,* Vol. 64: pp. 21-27.

Macksoud, M.S., & Lawrence, A.J. (1996). The war experience and psychosocial development of children in Lebanon. *Child Development,* Vol. 67:70-88.

Malloy, P.F., Fairbank, J.A., & Kean, T.M. (1983). Validation of a multimethod assessment of post-traumatic stress disorders in Vietnam veterans. *Journal of Consulting and Clinical Psychology,* Vol. 51: pp. 4-21.

Markus, H.R., & Kitayama, S. (1991). Culture and the self: Implications for cognition, emotion and motivation. *Psychological Review,* Vol. 98: pp. 224-253.

Marmar, C.R., Weiss, D.S., Schlenger, W.E., et al. (1994). Peritraumatic dissociation and posttraumatic stress in male Vietnam theater veterans. *American Journal of Psychiatry,* Vol. 151: pp. 902-907.

Marshall, R.D., Olfson, M., Hellman, F., et al. (2001). Comorbidity, impairment, and suicidality in subthreshold PTSD. *American Journal of Psychiatry,* Vol. 158: pp. 1467-1473.

Marshall, E.K. (2006). Cumulative Career Traumatic Stress (CCTS): A pilot study of traumatic stress in law enforcement. *Journal of Police and Criminal Psychology,* Vol. 21: pp. 62-72.

Martin, E.M., et al. (2008). Traumatic brain injuries sustained in Afghanistan and Iraq Wars. *Journal of Trauma Nursing,* Vol. 15: pp. 94-99.

Marx, B.R., Bailey, K., Proctor, S.P., & MacDonald, H.Z. (2009). Association of time since deployment, combat intensity, and posttraumatic stress symptoms with neuropsychological outcomes following Iraq war deployment. *Archives of General Psychiatry,* Vol. 66: pp. 996-1004

McCormick, C. (2010). *McCormick TBI Interview (Military)*. Salisbury VAMC (Cortney.McCormick@va.gov.).

McCrea, M. (2008). *Mild Traumatic Brain Injury and Post-Concussion Syndrome: The New Evidence Base for Diagnosis and Treatment*. New York, NY: Oxford University Press.

McFall, M.E., Smith, D.S., Mackay, P.W., & Tarver, D.J. (1990). Reliability and validity of the Mississippi Scale for combat-related post-traumatic stress disorder. *Psychological Assessment,* Vol. 2: pp. 114-121.

McFall, M.E., Mackay, P.S. & Donovan, D.M. (1991). Combat-related PTSD and psychosocial adjustment problems among substance abusing veterans. *Journal of Nervous and Mental Disease,* Vol. 179 (1): pp. 33 -38.

McFarlane, A.C. (1988). The longitudinal course of posttraumatic morbidity : The range of outcomes and their predictors. *Journal of Nervous Mental Disease,* Vol. 176: pp. 30-39

McFarlane, A.C. (1989) The aetiology of post-traumatic morbidity: predisposing, precipitating and perpetuating factors. *British Journal of Psychiatry,* Vol. 154: pp. 221-228.

McFarlane, A.C. (2009). Military deployment: the impact on children and family adjustment and the need for care. *Current Opinion in Psychiatry,* Vol. 22: pp. 369-373.

Meichenbaum, D. (1994). *A Clinical Handbook/Practical Therapist Manual: for Assessing and Treating Adults with Post-Traumatic Stress Disorder (PTSD)*. Waterloo, Ontario, Canada: Institute Press.

Merrill, L.L., Newell, C.E., Thomsen, C.J., et al. (1999). Childhood abuse and sexual revictimization in a female Navy recruit sample. *Journal of Traumatic Stress,* Vol. 12: pp. 211-225.

Mghir, R. Freed, W., Raskin, A., & Katon, W. (1995). Depression and posttraumatic stress disorder among a community sample of adolescent and young adult Afghan refugees. *Journal of Nervous and Mental Disease,* Vol. 183: pp. 24-30.

Micovic, M., & Cabarkapa, M. (1996). Standardization of the scale for estimating the psychopathological consequences of traumatic stress. *Military-Medical and Pharmaceutical Review,* 53(3): pp. 201-208.

Milic, A. (2003). PTSD in war actors in police forces. *Engram: Journal of Clinical Psychiatry, Psychology and Related Disciplines*, Vol. 25: pp. 63-67.

Miller, G. (2002). Gene's effect seen in brain's fear response. *Science,* Vol. 297 (5580): p. 319.

Miller, K., et al. (2002). Bosnian refugees and the stressors of exile: A narrative study. *American Journal of Orthopsychiatry,* Vol. 72: pp. 341-354.

Miller, K., et al. (2002). The relative contribution of war experiences and exile-related stressors to levels of psychological distress among Bosnian refugees. *Journal of Traumatic Stress,* Vol. 15: pp. 377-387.

Milliken, C.S., Auchterlonie, J.L., & Hoge, C.W. (2007). Longitudinal assessment of mental health problems among Active and Reserve Component soldiers returning from the Iraq War. *Journal of the American Medical Association (JAMA)*, Vol. 298: pp. 2141-2148.

Milosavljevic, B., Savic, J., Gutovic, V., & Kutalac, M. (1996). War, the warfare environment and the syndrome of war psychic trauma in children. *Psychology*, Vol. 29: pp. 465-476

Mollica, R.F., Donelan, K., Svang, T., et al. (1993). The effect of confinement on functional health and mental health status of Cambodians living in Thailand-Cambodia border camps. *Journal of the American Medical Association (JAMA)*, Vol. 270: pp. 581-586.

Mollica, R.F., et al. (1999). Disability associated with psychiatric comorbidity and health status in Bosnian refugees living in Croatia. *Journal of the American Medical Association (JAMA)*, Vol. 282: pp. 433-439.

Mollica, R.F., Caridad, K.R., & Massagi, M. (2007). Longitudinal study of posttraumatic stress disorder, depression, and changes in traumatic memories over time in Bosnian refugees. *Journal of Nervous and Mental Disease*, Vol. 195: pp. 572-579.

Momartin, S., Silove, D., Manicavasagar, V., & Steel, Z. (2004). Complicated grief in Bosnian refugees: Associations with posttraumatic stress disorder and depression. *Comprehensive Psychiatry*, Vol. 45: pp. 475-482.

Momartin, S., Silove, D., Manicavasagar, V., & Steel, Z. (2004). Comorbidity of PTSD and depression: associations with trauma exposure, symptom severity and functional impairment in Bosnian refugees resettled in Australia. *Journal of Affective Disorders*, Vol. 80: pp. 231-238.

Monnelly, E.P., & Ciraulo, D.A. (1999). Risperidone effects on irritable aggression in posttraumatic stress disorder. *Journal of Clinical Psychopharmacology*, Vol. 19: pp. 377-378.

Morgan, I.H. (1916). Outrage upon the honour of women. *German Atrocities: An Official Investigation*. New York, NY: Dutton: pp. 81-83.

Munafo, M.R., Durrant, C., & Flint, L.G. (2009). Gene X environment interactions at the serotonin transporter locus. *Biological Psychiatry*, Vol. 65: pp. 211-219.

Murdoch, M., Polusny, M.A., Hodges, J., et al. (2004). Prevalence of in-service and post-service sexual assault among combat and noncombat veterans applying for Department of veterans Affairs posttraumatic stress disorder disability benefits. *Military Medicine*, Vol. 169: pp. 392-395.

Murphy, D.L., Fox, M.A., Timpano, K.R., et al. (2008). How the serotonin story is being written by new gene-based discoveries principally related to SLC6A4, the serotonin transporter gene, which functions to influence all cellular serotonin systems. *Neuropharmacology*, Vol. 55: pp. 932-960.

Murray, C.K., Reynolds, J.C., Schroeder, J.M., et al. (2005). Spectrum of care provided at an Echelon II medical unit during Operation Iraqi Freedom. *Military Medicine,* Vol. 170: pp. 516-520.

Murthy, R.S., & Lakshminarayana, R. (2006). Mental health consequences of war: a brief review of research findings. *World Psychiatry,* Vol. 5: pp. 25-30.

National Center on Addiction and Substance Abuse at Columbia University. (2009). Brain-injury deaths lower among alcohol users. *Join Together* (September   30): www.jointogether.org/news/research/summaries/2009/brain-injury-deaths-lower.html.

National Collaborating Centre for Mental Health/ (2005). *Post-Traumatic Stress Disorder: The Management of PTSD in Adults and Children in Primary and Secondary Care.* London, England: National Institute for Clinical Excellence.

Nay, A.M. (2008). Health disparities in military veterans with PTSD: Influential sociocultural factors. *Journal of Psychosocial Nursing & Mental Health Services,* Vol. 46: pp. 41-51.

Newman, R.A. (1964) Combat fatigue: A review of the Korean Conflict. *Military Medicine,* Vol. 129: pp. 921-928.

Nikoloski-Koncar, N., Zotovic, M., & Hautekeete, M. (2006). Effects of bombing after five years: Development of early maladaptive cognitive schemas in children. *Psychology,* Vol. 39: pp. 229-246.

Norman, S.B., Stein, M.B., & Davidson, J.R. (2007). Profiling posttraumatic functional impairment. *Journal of Nervous and Mental Disease,* Vol. 195; PP. 48-53.

North, C.S. (2009). Intervention and resilience after mass trauma. *American Journal of Psychiatry,* Vol. 166: pp. 1071-1072.

Norris, F.H., Foster, J.D., & Weisshaar, D.L. (2002). The epidemiology of sex differences in PTSD across developmental, social, and research contexts. *Gender and PTSD* (Kimerling, R., Ouimette, P., & Wolfe, J., eds.). New York, NY: The Guilford Press: pp. 3-43.

Norris, F.H., & Elrod, C.L. (2006). Psychosocial consequences of disaster: a review of past research. *Methods for Disaster Mental Health Research* (Norris, F.H., Friedman, M.J., & Watson, P.J., editors). New York, NY: Guilford: pp. 20-42.

Nutt, D.J., & Malizia, A.L. (2004). Structural and functional brain changes in posttraumatic stress disorder. *Journal of Clinical Psychiatry,* Vol. 65: pp.11-17.

O'Brien, L.S. (1994). What will be the psychiatric consequences of the war in Bosnia? *British Journal of Psychiatry,* Vol. 164: pp. 443-447.

Opalic, P.D. (2000). Research of the dreams of the traumatized subjects. *Psychiatry Today,* Vol. 32: pp. 129-147.

Opalic, P.D. (2000). Psychotherapeutic help to the refugees in Yugoslavia until 1998. *Sociology,* Vol. 42: pp. 637-646.

Opalic, P.D. (2005). Human figure Test in the research of psychopathological state of refugees and somatically traumatized. *Serbian Archives for the Whole Medicine,* Vol. 133: pp. 21-28.

Opalic, P.D. (2008). Disarrangement-dominant symptoms of traumatized people in Serbia. *Sociology,* Vol. 50: pp. 417-432.

Orsillo, S., Raja, S., & Hammond, C. (2002). Gender issues in PTSD with comorbid mental health disorders. *Gender and PTSD* (Kimerling, R., Ouimette, P., & Wolfe, J., ed.s). New York, NY: The Guilford Press: pp. 207-231.

Oruc, L., et al. (2008). Screening for PTSD and depression in Bosnia and Herzegovina: Validating the Harvard Trauma Questionnaire and the Hopkins Symptom Checklist. *International Journal of Culture and Mental Health,* Vol. 1: 105-116.

Ozer, E.J., Best, S.R., Lipsey, T.L., & Weiss, D.S. (2003). Predictors of posttraumatic stress disorder in trauma-exposed adults. *Psychological Bulletin,* Vol. 129: pp. 52-73.

Papageorgiou, V., et al. (2000). War trauma and psychopathology in Bosnia refugee children. *European Child & Adolescent Psychiatry,* Vol. 9: pp. 84-90.

Parson, E., (1984). The reparation of self: Clinical and theoretical dimensions in the treatment of Vietnam combat veterans. *Journal of Contemporary Psychotherapy,* Vol. 14: pp. 4-56.

Parris, C., Roth, C., Roberts, B., & Davies, G. (2009). Assessment of cognitive-communicative disorders of mild traumatic brain injury sustained in combat. *Neurophysiology and Neurogenic Speech and Language Disorders,* Vol. 19: pp. 47-57.

Pavlov, I.P. (1926). *Conditioned Reflexes: An investigation of the physiological activity of the cerebral cortex.* (Anrep, G.V., Trans. & Ed.). New York, NY: Dover Publications.

Pearlin, L.I., & Schooler, C. (1978). The structure of coping. *Journal of Health and Social Behavior,* Vol. 19: pp. 2-21.

Pearrow, M., & Cogrove, L. (2009). The aftermath of combat-related PTSD: Toward an understanding of transgenerational trauma. *Communication Disorders Quarterly,* Vol. 30: pp. 77-82.

Petrovic, V. (2004). Level of psychopathology in children with war related trauma. *Psychiatry Today,* Vol. 36 (1): pp. 17-28.

Petrovic, V. (2004). Level of traumatization in children with war related trauma. *Psychiatry Today,* Vol. 36 (2): pp. 191-226.

Petrunik, M., & Deutschmann, L. (2008). Exclusion-inclusion spectrum in state and community responses to sex in Anglo-American and European Jurisdictions. *International Journal of Offender Therapy and Comparative Criminology,* Vol. 52: pp. 499-519.

Philpott, T. (2005). PTSD case review hit: More meds moving off formulary. (September 29th): *Military.com.*

Pitman, R. K., Altman, B., & MacKlin, M.L. (1989).   Prevalence of
   posttraumatic stress disorder in wounded Vietnam veterans. *American
   Journal of Psychiatry,* Vol. 146: pp. 667-669.
Pitman, R.K. (1989). Post-traumatic stress disorder, hormones, and memory.
   Biological Psychiatry, Vol. 26: pp. 221-223.
Pivac, N., & Kozaric-Kovacic, D. (2006).   Pharmacotherapy of treatment-
   resistant combat-related posttraumatic stress disorder with psychotic
   features. *Croatian Medical Journal,* Vol. 47: pp. 440-451.
Pizarro, J., Silver, R.C., & Prause, J.A. (2006). Physical and mental health costs
   of traumatic war experiences of war experiences among civil war
   veterans. *Archives of General Psychiatry,* Vol. 63: pp. 190-200.
Placko, V. (1999). Disabled veterans of the patriotic war in the Krizevci area
   and the post-traumatic stress disorder.   *Polemos: Journal of
   Interdisciplinary Research on War and Peace.* Vol. 2: pp. 187-206.
Pope, H.S., Butcher, J.N., & Seelen, J. (1993). *The MMPI, MMPI-2, & MMPI-A
   in Court.* Washington, DC: American Psychological Association Press.
Polovina, N., & Divac, L.J. (1992). Posttraumatic stress disorder and
   psychotherapeutic approach. *Military-Medical and Pharmaceutical
   Review,* Vol. 49: pp. 115-126.
Popovic, M. (1994). Some aspects of psychological help to refugees in Serbia.
   Psychiatry Today, Vol. 26: pp. 241-248.
Post, R.M., Rubinow, D.R., & Ballenger, J.C. (1986). Conditioning and
   sensitization in the longitudinal course of affective illness. *British
   Journal of Psychiatry,* Vol. 149: pp. 191-201.
Powell, D.W. (2006). *My Tour in Hell: a Marine's battle with Combat Stress.*
   Ann Arbor, MI: Modern History Press.
Powell, S., & Durakovic-Belko, E. (2004). Sarajevo 2000: the psychosocial
   consequences of war, results of empirical research from the territory of
   former Yugoslavia. *International Journal of Human Sciences,* Vol.1:
   pp. 35-42.
Price, J.L. (2003). Findings from the National Vietnam Veterans' Readjustment
   Study.   *National Center for Posttraumatic Stress Disorder.*
   Washington, DC: United States Department of Veterans Affairs.
   http://www.ncptsd.va.gov/ncmain/ncdocs/fact_shts/fs_nvvrs.
Priebe, S., Gavrilovic, J., Schuetzwohl, M., et al. (2002).Rationale and method
   of the STOP study: Study on treatment behavior and outcomes of
   treatment of people with Posttraumatic Stress following conflicts in ex-
   Yugoslavia. *Psychiatry Today,* Vol. 34: pp. 133-134.
Priebe, S., Jankovic-Gavrilovic, J., Schutzwohl, M., et al. (2004).   Study of
   long-term clinical and social outcomes after war experiences in ex-
   Yugoslavia: Methods of the "CONNECT Project." *Psychiatry Today,*
   Vol. 36: pp. 111-122.
Priebe, S., Matanov, A., Jankovic-Gavrilovic, J., et al. (2009). Consequences of
   Untreated posttraumatic stress disorder following war in former

Yugoslavia: Mobidity, subjective quality of fife, and care cost. *Croatian Medical Journal,* Vol. 50: pp. 465-475.

Priebe, S., Bogic, M,. Ajdukovic, D., et al. (2010). Mental disorders following war in the Balkans. *Archives of General Psychiatry,* Vol. 67: pp. 518-528.

Prins, A., Quimette, P., Kimerling, R., et al. (2004). The Primary care PTSD Screen (PC-PTSD): Development and operating characteristics. *Primary Care Psychiatry,* Vol. 9: pp. 9-14.

Puhalo, S. (2003). Ethnical distance of the citizens of Republika Srpska and the Federation of Bosnia and Herzegovina to the nations of former Socialist Federal Republic of Yugoslavia. *Psychology,* Vol. 36: pp. 141-156.

Pupovac, V. (2004). International therapeutic peace and justice in Bosnia. *Social & Legal Studies,* Vol. 13: pp. 377-401.

Putman, K.M., Lantz, J.I., Townsend, C.L., & Gallegos, A.M. (2009). Exposure to violence, support needs, adjustment, and motivators among Guatemalan humanitarian aid workers. *American Journal of Community Psychology,* Vol. 44: pp. 109-115.

Pynoos, R.S. (1993). Traumatic stress and developmental psychopathology in children and adolescents. *American Psychiatric Press Review of Psychiatry,* Vol. 12: pp. 205-238.

Rabkin, J.G., & Struening, E.L. (1976). Life events, stress and illness. *Science,* Vol. 194: pp. 1013-1020.

Ramet, S.P. (2002). Under the holy lime tree: the inculcation of neurotic & psychotic syndromes as a Serbian wartime strategy, 1986-1995. *Polemos: Journal of Interdisciplinary Research on War and Peace,* Vol. V: pp. 83-97.

Rao, V., & Lyketsos, C. (2000). Neuropsychiatry sequelae of traumatic brain injury. *Psychosomatics,* Vol. 41: pp. 95-103.

Rauch, S.L., Vanderkolk, B.A., Fisler, R.E., et al. (1996). A symptom provocation study of posttraumatic stress disorder using positron emission tomography and script-driven imagery. *Archives of General Psychiatry,* Vol. 53: pp. 380-387.

Reck, C., Pukrop, R., Klosterkotter, J., et al. (2008). Obsessive-compulsive disorder and posttraumatic stress disorder. *Psychopathology,* Vol. 41: pp. 129-134.

Regan, T. (2004). High survival rate for US troops wounded in Iraq. *Christian Science Monitor* (November 29th).

Resnick, H.S., Kilpatrick, D.G., Best, C.L., & Kramer, T.I.. (1992). Vulnerability-stress factors in development of posttraumatic stress disorder. *Journal of Nervous Mental Disorders,* Vol. 180: pp. 424-430.

Resnick, H.S., Kilpatrick, D.G., Dansky, B.S., et al. (1993). Prevalence of civilian trauma and posttraumatic stress disorder in a representative sample of women. *Journal of Consulting and Clinical Psychology,* Vol. 61: pp. 984-991.

Reynolds, M., & Brewin, C.R. (1999). Intrusive memories in depression and posttraumatic stress disorder. *Behavioral Research and Therapy,* Vol. 37: pp. 201-215.

Richardson, F.M. (1978). *Fighting Spirit: A Study of Psychological Factors in War.* London, England: Cooper.

Richardson, J.D., Ellhai, J.D., & Pedlar, D.J., (2006). Association of PTSD and depression with medical and specialist care utilization in modern peacekeeping veterans in Canada with health-related disabilities. *Journal of Clinical Psychiatry,* Vol. 67: pp. 1240-1245.

Ringdal, G.I., Ringdal, K., & Simkus, A. (2008). War experiences and war-related distress in Bosnia and Herzegovina eight years after war. *Croatian Medical Journal,* Vol. 49: pp. 75-86.

Rizvi, S.L., Vogt, D.S., & Resick, P.A. (2009). Cognitive and affective predictors of treatment outcome in cognitive processing therapy and prolonged exposure for posttraumatic stress disorder. *Behaviour Research and Therapy,* Vol. 47: pp. 737-743.

Roberts, M. (2005). Study finds foster care may foster lifelong ills. *The Carter Center* (April 7th). http://www.cartercenter.org/news/documents/doc2065.html.

Roper, G., & Gayranidou, M. (2003). Capacity building in trauma therapy and trauma research in Bosnia and Herzegovina. *New Directions in Youth Development,* Vol. 98: pp. 99-110.

Rosner, R., Powell, S., & Butollo (2003). Posttraumatic stress disorder three years after the siege of Sarajevo. *Journal of Clinical Psychology,* Vol. 59: pp. 41-55.

Rosenheck, R. (1984). Hospital based treatment of malignant post Vietnam stress syndrome. *Psychiatric Quarterly,* Vol. 56: pp. 259-269.

Rosenheck, R., & Fontana, A. (1999). Changing patterns of care for war-related post-traumatic stress disorder at Department of Veterans Affairs Medical Centers: The use of performance data to guide program development. *Military Medicine,* Vol. 164: pp. 795-802.

Rothman, K.J. (2002). *Epidemiology: An Introduction.* New York, NY: Oxford University Press.

Ruef, A.M., Litz, B.T., & Schlenger, W.E. (2000). Hispanic ethnicity and risk for combat-related posttraumatic stress disorder, *Cultural Diversity and Ethnic Minority Psychology,* Vol. 6: pp.235-251.

Sakusic, A., et al. (2009). Intensity of posttraumatic stress disorder symptoms in relation to alcohol use in war veterans-experiences from Bosnia-Herzegovina. *Alcoholism,* Vol. 45: pp. 95-105.

Saunders, J.B., Aasland, O.G., Barbor, T.F., et al. (1993). Development of the Alcohol Use Disorder Identification Test (AUDIT). *Addictions,* Vol. 88: pp. 791-804.

Scaer, R.C. (2005). *Trauma Spectrum: Hidden Wounds and Human Resiliency.* New York, NY: Norton.

Schlenger, W.E., Kulka, R.A., Fairbank, J.A., et al. (1992). The prevalence of post-traumatic stress disorder in the Vietnam generation: A multimethod, multisource, assessment of Psychiatric Disorder. *Journal of Traumatic Stress,* Vol. 5: pp. 333-336.

Schmidt, N.B., Joiner, T.E., Young, J.E., & Telch, M.J. (1995). The Schema Questionnaire: Investigation of psychometric properties and the hierarchical structure of a measure of maladaptive schema. *Cognitive Therapy and Research,* Vol. 19: pp. 295-321.

Schnurr, P.P., et al. (2000). PTSD and utilization of medical treatment services among male Vietnam veterans. *Journal of Nervous and Mental Disease,* Vol. 188: pp. 496-504.

Schnurr, P.P., & Spiro, A. (1999). Combat exposure, posttraumatic stress disorder symptoms, and health behaviors as predictors of self-reported physical health in older veterans. *Journal of Nervous and Mental Disease,* Vol. 187: pp. 353-359.

Schnurr, P.P., Lunney, C.A., Sengupta, A., & Waelde, L.C. (2003). A descriptive analysis of PTSD chronicity in Vietnam veterans. *Journal of Traumatic Stress,* Vol. 16: pp. 545-553.

Schnurr, P.P., Lunney, C.A., & Sengupta, A. (2004). Risk factors for the development versus maintenance of Posttraumatic Stress Disorder. *Journal of Traumatic Stress,* Vol. 17: pp. 85-95.

Schnurr, P.P. (2004). *Trauma and Health: Physical health consequences of Exposure to Extreme Stress.* Washington, DC: Washington, DC: American Psychological Association.

Schooler, J.W., Bendiksen, M., & Ambadar, Z. (1997). Taking the middle line: can we accommodate both fabricated and recovered memories of sexual abuse? *False and Recovered Memories.* (Conway, M., ed.). New York, NY: Oxford University Press.

Schwab, K.A., Ivins, B., Cramer, G., et al. (2007). Screening for traumatic brain injury in troops returning from deployment in Afghanistan and Iraq: Initial investigation of the usefulness of a short screening tool for Traumatic Brain Injury. *Journal of Head Trauma Rehabilitation,* Vol. 22: pp. 377-389.

Scott, M.J. (2006). *Counseling for Post-Traumatic Stress Disorder.* Thousand Oaks, CA: Sage.

Scientific America (1993). *Mind and Brain: Readings from Scientific American.* New York, NY: W.H. Freeman and Company.

Seal, K.H., Bertenthal, D., Miner, C.R., et al. (2007). Bringing the war back home: Mental health disorders among 103,788 US veterans returning from Iraq and Afghanistan seen at Department of Veterans Affairs facilities. *Archives of Internal Medicine,* Vol. 167: pp. 476-482.

Seal, K.H., Bertenthal, D. et al. (2008). Getting beyond "Don't ask; Don't tell": An evaluation of US Veterans Administration postdeployment Mental Health Screening of veterans returning from Iraq and Afghanistan. *American Journal of Public Health,* Vol. 98: pp. 714-720.

Segerstrom, S.C., & Miller, G.E. (2004). Psychological stress and the human immune system: a meta-analysis of 30 years of inquiry. *Psychological Bulletin,* Vol. 130(4): 601-630.

Selakovic-Bursic, S.D., Vuckovic, N.S., & Sekulic-Bartos, O. (2000). Crisis intervention during NATO bombing. *Current Topics in Neurology, Psychiatry and Related Disciplines,* Vol. 8: pp. 1-9.

Selakovic-Bursic, S.D., Sekulic-Bartso, O, Bugarski, V., et al. (2001). Suicidal behavior during NATO bombing in Yugoslavia. *Current Topics in Neurology, Psychiatry and Related Disciplines,* Vol. 9: pp. 1-7.

Selligman, M.E.P. (1975). *Helplessness: On Depression, Development, and Death.* San Francisco, CA: W.H. Freeman.

Selye, H. (1936). A syndrome produced by diverse nocuous agents. *Nature,* Vol. 138: p. 32.

Selye, H. (1946). The General Adaptation Syndrome. *Journal of Endocrinology.* Vol. 6: pp. 117-230.

Selye, H. (1950). Diseases of adaptation. *Wisconsin Medical Journal,* Vol. 49 (6): pp. 515-516.

Selye, H. (1956). *The Stress of Life.* New York, NY: McGraw-Hill..

Serafina, N.M. (2003). *Peacekeeping: Issues of U.S. Military Involvement.* Washington, DC: Congressional Research Service.

Shalev, A.Y., Peri, T., Canetti, L., & Schreiber, S. (1996). Predictors of PTSD in injured trauma survivors: A prospective study. *American Journal of Psychiatry,* Vol. 153: pp. 219-225.

Shalev, A.Y., et al. (2004). Posttraumatic stress disorder as a result of mass trauma. *Journal of Clinical Psychiatry,* Vol. 65: pp. 4-10.

Shay, J. (2002). *Odysseus in America: Combat Trauma and the Trials of Homecoming.* New York, NY: Scribner.

Shay, J. (1994). *Achilles in Vietnam: Combat Trauma and the Undoing of Character.* New York, NY: Athenum.

Shea-Porter, C. (2009). Posttraumatic stress disorder and government initiatives to relieve it. *Health & Social Work,* Vol. 34: pp. 235-236.

Sherif, M. (1966). *Group Conflict and Cooperation: Their Social Psychology.* London, England: Routledge & Kegan Paul.

Shevlin, M., Hunt, N., & Robbins, I. (2000). A confirmation factor analysis of the impact of event scale using a sample of World War II and Korean War veterans. *Psychological Assessment,* Vol. 12: pp. 414-417.

Shin, L.M., et al. (2005). A functional magnetic resonance imaging study of amygdala and medical prefrontal cortex response to overly presented fearful faces in Posttraumatic Stress Disorder. *Archives of General Psychiatry,* Vol. 62: pp. 273-281.

Shore, J.H., Tatum, E.L., & Vollmer, W.M. (1986). Psychiatric reactions to disaster: the Mount St. Helens experience. *American Journal of Psychiatry,* Vol. 143: pp. 590-595.

Shore, J.H., & Manson, S.M. (2004). The American Indian veteran and posttraumatic stress disorder: a telehealth assessment and formulation. *Culture, Medicine and Psychiatry,* Vol. 28: pp. 231-243.

Shore, J.H., Savin, D., Orton, H., et al. (2007). Diagnostic reliability of telepsychiatry in American Indian veterans. *American Journal of Psychiatry,* Vol. 164: pp. 115-118.

Sijbrandij, M.,, Olff, M., Reitsma, J.b., et al. (2007). Treatment of acute posttraumatic stress disorder with brief cognitive behavioral therapy: A randomized controlled trial. *American Journal of Psychiatry,* Vol. 164: pp. 82-90.

Silove, D., Manicavasagar, V., Coello, M., & Aroche, J.. (2005). PTSD, depression, and acculturation. *Intervention,* Vol. 3: pp. 46-50.

Simmons, R.K., Maconochie, N., & Doyle, P. (2004). Self-reported ill health in male UK Gulf War veterans: a retrospective cohort study. *BMC Public Health,* Vol. 4: p 27.

Simpson, G., & Tate, R. (2007). Suicidality in people surviving a traumatic brain injury: prevalence, risk factors, and implications for clinical management. *Brain Injury,* Vol. 21: pp. 1335-1351.

Sloan P., Arsenault, L., Hilsenroth, M., et al. (1995). Rorschach measures of posttraumatic stress in Persian Gulf War veterans. *Journal of Personality Assessment,* Vol. 64: 397-414.

Slone, L.B., & Friedman, M.J. (2008). *After the War Zone: A Practical Guide for Returning Troops and their Families.* Cambridge, MA: Da Capo Lifelong.

Smith, D.W., Frueh, B.C., Sawchuk, C.N., et al. (1999). Relationship between symptom over-reporting and pre- and post-combat trauma history in veterans evaluated for PTSD. *Depression and Anxiety,* Vol. 10: pp. 119-124.

Smith, T.C., Ryan, M.A.K., Wingard, D.L., et al. (2008). New onset and persistent symptoms of post-traumatic stress disorder self reported after deployment and combat exposures: Prospective population based US military cohort study. *British Medical Journal* (online).

Snyder, C., et al. (2005). Social work with Bosnian Muslim refugee children and families: A review of the literature. *Child Welfare,* Vol. 84: pp. 607-630.

Sodic, L., Anticevic, V., Britvic, D., & Ivkosic, N. (2007). Short-term memory in Croatian war veterans with posttraumatic stress disorder. *Croatian Medical Journal,* Vol. 48: pp. 140-145.

Solomon, S.D., Gerrity, E.T., & Muff, A.M. (1992). Efficacy of treatments for post- traumatic stress disorder: An empirical review. *Journal of the American Medical Association (JAMA),* Vol. 268: pp. 633-638.

Solkoff, N., Gray, P., & Keill, S. (1986). Which Vietnam veterans develop posttraumatic stress disorder. *Journal of Clinical Psychology,* Vol. 42: pp. 687-698.

Sonnenberg, S. M. (ed.). (1985). *Trauma of War: Stress and Recovery in Viet Nam Veterans.* Washington, DC: American Psychiatric Press.

Sossou, M-A., et al. (2008). A qualitative study of resilience factors of Bosnian refugee women resettled in the southern United States. *Journal of Ethnic & Cultural Diversity,* Vol. 17: pp. 365-385.

Southwick, S.M., et al. (1993). Trauma-related symptoms in veterans of Operation Desert Storm: A preliminary report. *American Journal of Psychiatry,* Vol. 150: pp. 1524-1538.

Southwick, S.M., Morgan, C.A., Nicolaou, A.L., & Charney, D.S. (1997). Consistency of memory for combat-related traumatic events in veterans of Operation Desert Storm. *American Journal of Psychiatry,* Vol. 154: pp. 173-177

Sparr, L.F. & Pankratz, L.D. (1983). Factitious posttraumatic stress disorder. *American Journal of Psychiatry,* Vol. 140: pp. 1016-1019.

Sparr, L.F., & Atkinson, R.M. (1986). Post-traumatic stress disorder as an insanity defense: Medico-legal quicksand. *American Journal of Psychiatry,* Vol. 143: pp. 608-613.

Sparr, L.F., Reaves, M.E., & Atkinson, R.M. (1987). Military combat, posttraumatic stress disorder, and criminal behavior in Vietnam veterans. *Bulletin of the American Academy of Psychiatry and the Law,* Vol. 15: pp. 141-162

Sparr, L.F.,& Boehnlein, J.K. (1990). Post-traumatic stress disorder in tort actions: Forensic minefield. *Bulletin of the American Academy of Psychiatry and the Law,* Vol. 18: pp. 283-302.

Sparr, L.F., White, R., Friedman, M.F., & Wiles, D.B. (1994). Veterans psychiatric benefits: Enter Courts and Attorneys. *Bulletin of the American Academy of Psychiatry and the Law,* Vol. 22: pp. 205-222.

Sparr, L.F. (1996). Mental defenses and posttraumatic stress disorder: Assessment of criminal intent. *Journal of Traumatic Stress,* Vol. 9: pp. 405-425.

Sparr, L.F., & Boehnlein, J.K. (1997). Posttraumatic Stress Disorder in tort actions: Forensic minefield. *Croatian Society of Expert Witnesses,* Vol. 13: pp. 8-20.

Sparr, L.F. (2005). Mental incapacity defense as the War Crimes Tribunal: Questions and controversy, *Journal of the American Academy of Psychiatry and the Law,* Vol. 33: pp. 59-70.

Sparr, L.F., & Bremner, J.D. (2005). PTSD and memory: Prescient medicolegal testimony at the International War Crimes Tribunal? *Journal of the American Academy of Psychiatry and the Law,* Vol. 33: pp. 71-78.

Spasojevic, J., Heffer, R., & Snyder, D. (2000). Effects of posttraumatic stress and acculturation on marital functioning of Bosnian refugee couples. *Journal of Traumatic Stress,* Vol. 13: pp. 205-217.

Spitzer, C., Barnow, S., Volzke,H., et al. (2008). Trauma and posttraumatic stress disorder in the elderly: Findings from a German community study. *Journal of Clinical Psychiatry,* Vol. 69: pp. 693-700.

Spiric, Z., & Samardzic, R. (2005). Comorbidity of posttraumatic stress disorder and mild closed head injury in war veterans: Endocrinological and psychological profiles. *Military-Medical and Pharmaceutical Review*, Vol. 62: pp. 17-25.

Stajic-Soldatovic, B.S., Borisev, L.D., Drezgic-Vukic, S.M., & Dasovic, A. (1995). Psychiatric disorders of refugees treated at Novi Sad psychiatric clinic. *Current Topics in Neurology, Psychiatry and Related Disciplines*, Vol. 3: pp. 42-47.

Steel, Z., Silove, D., Bird, K., et al. (1999). Pathways from trauma to posttraumatic stress symptoms among Tamil asylum seekers, refugees, and immigrants. *Journal of Traumatic Stress*, Vol. 12: pp. 421-422.

Steel, Z., Chey, T., Silove, D., et al. (2009). Association of torture and other potentially traumatic events with mental health outcomes among populations exposed to mass conflict and displacement. *Journal of the American Medical Association (JAMA)*, Vol. 302: pp. 537-549.

Stein, B., et al. (1999). Prospective study of displaced children's syndrome in wartime Bosnia. *Social Psychiatry & Psychiatric Epidemiology*, Vol. 34: pp. 464-469.

Stein, M.B., & McAllister, T.W. (2009). Exploring the convergence of posttraumatic stress disorder and mild traumatic brain injury. *American Journal of Psychiatry*, Vol. 166: pp. 768-776

Stimpson, N.J., Thomas, H.V., Weighttman, A.L., et al. (2003). Psychiatric disorders in veterans of the Persian Gulf War of 1991: Systematic Review. *British Journal of Psychiatry*, Vol. 182: pp. 391-403.

Stouffer, S.A., et al. (1949). *The American Soldier: Adjustment during Army life* (Vol. I). Princeton, NJ: Princeton University Press.

Stouffer, S.A., et al. (1949). *The American Soldier: Combat and its aftermath* (Vol. II). Princeton, NJ: Princeton University Press.

Strech, H. (1985). Posttraumatic stress disorder among US Army Vietnam and Vietnam-era veterans. *Journal of Consulting Clinical Psychology*, Vol. 53: pp. 935-936.

Summerfield, D. (2003). War, exile, moral knowledge and the limits of psychiatric understanding: A clinical case study of a Bosnian refugee in London. *International Journal of Social Psychiatry*, Vol. 49: pp. 264-268.

Sundquist, K., et al. (2005). Posttraumatic stress disorder and psychiatric co-morbidity: symptoms in a random sample of female Bosnian refugees. *European Psychiatry*, Vol. 20: pp. 158-164

Taber, K.H., & Hurley, R.A. (2009). PTSD and combat-related injuries: Functional neuroanatomy. *Journal of Neuropsychiatry and Clinical Neurosciences*, Vol. 21: pp. iv-4.

Taft, C.T., Monson, C.M., Schumm, J.A., & Watkins, L.E. (2009). Posttraumatic stress disorder symptoms, relationship adjustment, and relationship aggression in a sample of female flood victims. *Journal of Family Violence,* Vol. 24: pp. 389-396.

Taft, C.T., Resick, P.A., Watkins, L.E., & Panuzio, J. (2009). An investigation of posttraumatic stress disorder and depressive symptomatology among female victims of interpersonal trauma. *Journal of Family Violence,* Vol. 24: pp. 407- 415.

Tanielian, T., Jaycox, L.H., Schell, T.L., et al. (2008). *Invisible Wounds of War: Summary and Recommendations for Addressing Psychological and Cognitive Injuries* (document no. MG-720/1-CCF). Santa Monica, CA: Rand Corporation.

Terzic, J., Mestovic, J., Dogas, Z., et al. (2001). Children war casualties during the 1991-1995 wars in Croatia and Bosnia and Herzegovina. *Croatian Medical Journal,* Vol. 42: pp. 156-160.

Thompson, M. (2009). The dark side of recruiting. *Time,* Vol. 176 (April 13th issue): pp. 34-38.

Thompson, M. (2009). An Rx for the Army's wounded minds. *Time,* Vol. 176 (August 16th issue): pp. 20-23.

Thompson, R.F. (2000). *The Brain: A Neuroscience Prima.* W.H. Freeman.

Thulesius, H., & Hakansson, R. (1999). Screening for posttraumatic stress disorder symptoms among Bosnian refugees. *Journal of Traumatic Stress,* Vol. 12: pp.167-174.

Thurman, D.J., Sniezek, J.E., Johnson, D., et al. (1995). *Guidelines for Surveillance of Central Nervous System Injury.* Atlanta, GA: Center for Disease Control and Prevention.

Torinek, T., Katic, M., & Kern, J. (2005). Morbidity of native, immigrant, and returned refugee populations in family medicine practice in Croatia after 1991-1995 war. *Croatian Medical Journal,* Vol. 46: pp. 990-995.

Traumatic Brain Injury Task Force. (2007). *Report to the Surgeon General.* Washington, DC: U.S. Government Printing Office.

Triffleman, E.G., Marmar, C.R., Delucchi, K.L., et al. (1995). Childhood trauma and posttraumatic stress disorder in substance abuse patients. *Journal of Nervous Mental Disorders,* Vol. 183: pp. 172-176.

Trlaja, L., Kostic, P., & Dedic, G. (1997). Post-traumatic stress disorder of war casualties. *Psychology,* Vol. 30: pp. 425-436.

Tsigos, C., & Chrousos, G.P. (1996). *Handbook of stress, medicine and health.* Boca Ratun, Fl: CRC Press.

Tsigos, C., & Chrousos, G.P. (2002). Hypothalamic-pituitary-adrenal axis, neuroendocrine factors, and stress. *Journal of Psychosomatic Research,* Vol. 53: pp. 865-871.

Tuerk, P.W., Grubaugh, A.L., Hamner, M.B., & Foa, E.B. (2009). Diagnosis and treatment of PTSD-related compulsive checking behaviors in veterans of the Iraq War: The influence of military context on the expression of PTSD symptoms. *American Journal of Psychiatry,* Vol. 166: pp. 762-767.

Tulving, E., & Thomson, D.M. (1973). Encoding specificity and retrieval processes in episodic memory. *Psychological Review,* Vol. 80: pp. 352-373.

Turjacanin, V. (2004). Ethnic stereotypes among Bosniak and Serbian youth in Bosnia and Herzegovina. *Psychology,* Vol. 37: pp. 357-374.

Turner, S. (2000). Psychiatric help for survivors of torture, *Advances in Psychiatric Treatment,* Vol. 6: pp. 295-303.

Turner, S.W., Bowie, C., Dunn, G., et al. (2003). Mental health of Kosovan Albanian refugees in the UK. *British Journal of Psychiatry,* Vol. 182: pp. 444-448.

Ursano. R.J., Fulerton, C., Kao, T., & Bharitya, V. (1995). Longitudinal assessment of posttraumatic stress disorder and depression after exposure to traumatic death. *Journal of Nervous and Mental Disease,* Vol. 183: pp. 36-42.

Ursano, R.J., et al. (1999). Posttraumatic stress disorder and identification in disaster workers. *American Journal of Psychiatry,* 156: pp. 353-359.

Ursano, R.J. (2002). Post-traumatic stress disorder. *New England Journal of Medicine,* Vol. 346: pp.130-132.

Ursano, R.J., et al. (2004). Practice guideline for the treatment of patients with cute stress disorder and posttraumatic stress disorder. *American Journal of Psychiatry,* Vol. 161 (Suppl. 11): pp. 3-31.

Ursano, R.J., et al. (2006). The impact of disasters and their aftermath on mental health. *Journal of Clinical Psychiatry,* 67: pp. 7-14

Van der Kolk, B.A. (1987). *Psychological Trauma.* Washington, DC: American Psychiatric Press.

Van der Kolk, B.A. (1988). The trauma spectrum: The interaction of biological and social events in the genesis of the trauma response. *Journal of traumatic Stress,* Vol. 1: pp. 273-290.

Van der Kolk, B.A. (1994). The body keeps the score – memory and the evolving psychobiology of Posttraumatic Stress. *Harvard Review of Psychiatry,* Vol. 1: pp. 253-265.

Van der Kolk, B.A., et al. (1994). Fluoxetine in posttraumatic-stress disorder. *Journal of Clinical Psychiatry,* Vol. 55: pp. 517-522.

Van der Kolk, B.A., & Fisler, R. (1995). Dissociation and the fragmentary nature of traumatic memories – overview and exploratory study. *Journal of Traumatic Stress,* Vol. 8: pp. 505-525.

Van der Kolk, B.A., et al. (1996). Dissociation, Somatization and affect dysregulation: The complexity of adaptation to trauma. *American Journal of Psychiatry,* Vol. 153: pp. 83-93.

Van Ommeren, M., de Jong, J., Sharma, B., et al. (2001). Psychiatric disorders among tortured Bhutanese refugees in Nepal. *Archives of General Psychiatry,* Vol. 58: pp. 475-484.

Varsek, I. (1999). Problems connected with return of refugees and displaced persons. *Polemos: Journal of Interdisciplinary Research on War and Peace,* Vol. 2: pp. 171-217.

Vasterling, J.J., (ed.). (2005). *Neuropsychology of PTSD: Biological, Cognitive, and Clinical Perspectives*. New York, NY: Guilford Press.

Vasterling, J.J., Proctor, S.P., Amoroso, P., et al. (2006). Neuropsychological outcomes of army personnel following deployment to the Iraq War. *Journal of the American Medical Association (JAMA)*, Vol. 296: pp. 519-529.

Vermetten, E., Vythilingam, M., Southwick, S.M., et al. (2003). Long-term treatment with Paroxetine increases verbal declarative memory and hippocampal volume in Posttraumatic Stress Disorder. *Biological Psychiatry*, Vol. 54: pp. 693-702.

Wagner, A.W., Wolfe, J., Rotnitsky, A., et al. (2000). An investigation of the impact of posttraumatic stress disorder on physical health. *Journal of Trauma and Stress*, Vol. 13: pp. 41-55.

Walters, J., Bisson, J.I., & Shepherd, D. (2007). Predicting post-traumatic stress disorder: Validation of the Trauma Screening Questionnaire in victims of assault. *Psychological Medicine*. Vol. 37: pp. 143-150.

Warden, D. (2006). TBI during the Iraq and Afghanistan wars. *Journal of Head Trauma Rehabilitation*, Vol. 21: pp. 398-402.

Weathers, F.W., Kearne, T.M., & Davidson, J.R. (2001). Clinicians administered PTSD scale: a review of the first ten years of research. *Depression and Anxiety*, Vol. 13: pp. 132-156.

Weine, S.M., Becker, D., McGlashan, T., et al. (1995). Adolescent survivors of "ethnic cleansing": Observations on the first year in America. *Journal of the American Academy of Child and Adolescent Psychiatry*, Vol. 34: pp. 1153-1159.

Weine, S.M., Kulenovic, A.D., Pavkovic, I., et al., (1998). Testimony psychotherapy in Bosnian refugees: a pilot study. *American Journal of Psychiatry*, Vol. 155: pp. 1720-1726.

Weine, S.M. (1998). Bosnian student survivors at home and in exile: Findings and reflections. *Psychiatric Times*, Vol. 15: p. 5.

Weine, S.M., et al. (1998). PTSD symptoms in Bosnian refugees 1 year after resettlement in the United States. *American Journal of Psychiatry*, Vol. 155: pp. 562-564.

Weine, S.M., et al. (2000) Profiling the trauma related symptoms of Bosnian refugees who have not sought mental health services. *Journal of Nervous and Mental Disease*, Vol. 188: pp. 416-421.

Weine, S.M., et al. (2001). PTSD among Bosnian refugees: A survey of providers' knowledge, attitudes and service patterns. *Community Mental Health Journal*, Vol. 37: pp. 261-271.

Weine, S.M., et al. (2004). Family consequences of refugee trauma. *Family Process*, Vol. 43: pp. 147-169.

Weine, S.M., Ware, N., & Klebic, A. (2004). Converting cultural capital among teen refugees and their families from Bosnia-Herzegovina. *Psychiatric Services*, Vol. 55: pp. 923-927.

Weiss, D.S., Marmar, C.R., Schlenger, W.E., et al. (1992). The prevalence of lifetime and partial post-traumatic stress disorder in Vietnam theater veterans. *Journal of Traumatic Stress,* Vol. 5: pp. 365-376.

Wessely S. (2005). The London attacks-aftermath: victimhood and resilience. *New England Journal of Medicine,* Vol. 353: pp. 548-550.

White, G. (1998). Trauma treatment training for Bosnian and Croatian mental health workers. *American Journal of Orthopsychiatry,* Vol. 68: pp. 58-62.

WHO (2001). *The Athens Declaration on Mental Health and Man-made Disasters, Stigma and Community Care.* Athens, Greece: World Health Organization.

Williams, R.M. (1984). Field observations and surveys in combat zones. *Social Psychology Quarterly,* Vol. 47: pp. 186-191.

Williams, R.M. (1989). The American soldier: An assessment, several wars later. *Public Opinion Quarterly,* Vol. 53: pp. 155-174.

Wilson, J.P. (ed.) (1997). *Assessing Psychological Trauma and PTSD.* New York, NY: Guilford Press.

Winick, C., & Kinsie, P.M. (1971). *The Lively Commerce.* Chicago, IL: Quadrangle.

Wolfgang, M., & Ferracuti, F. (1967). *The Subculture of Violence.* London, England: Travistick.

Wright, S.C., & Taylor, D.M. (2003). The social psychology of cultural diversity: Social stereotyping, prejudice, and discrimination. *The Sage handbook of Social Psychology* (Hogg, M.A., & Cooper, J., eds.). London, England: Sage.

Yehuda, R., Southwick, S.M., & Giller, E.L. (1992). Exposure to atrocities and severity of chronic posttraumatic stress disorder in Vietnam combat veterans. *American Journal of Psychiatry,* Vol.149: pp. 333-336.

Yehuda, R., et al. (1995). Low urinary cortisol excretion in Holocaust survivors with posttraumatic stress disorder. *American Journal of Psychiatry,* Vol. 152: pp. 982-986.

Yehuda, R., Boisoneau, D., Lowy, M.T., & Giller, E.L. (1995). Dose-response changes in plasma-cortisol and lymphocyte glucocorticoid receptors following Dexamethasone administration in combat veterans with and without posttraumatic stress disorder. *Archives of General Psychiatry,* Vol. 52: pp. 583-593.

Yehuda, R.,& McFarlane, A.C. (1995). Conflict between current knowledge about posttraumatic stress disorder and its original conceptual basis. *American Journal of Psychiatry,* Vol. 152: pp. 1705-1713.

Yehuda, R., Blair, W., Labinsky, E., & Bierer, L.M. (2007). Effects of parental PTSD on the cortisol response to Dexamathasone administration in their adult offspring. *American Journal of Psychiatry,* Vol. 164: pp. 163-166.

Young, J.E. (1990). *Cognitive Therapy for Personality Disorders: A Schema focused Approach.* Sarasota, FL: Professional Resource Exchange.

Young, J.E., Klosko, J., & Weisshar, M.E. (2003). *Schema Therapy: A practitioner's guide.* New York, NY: Guildord.

Zaidi, L.,& Foy, D. (1994). Childhood abuse experiences and combat-related PTSD. *Journal of Traumatic Stress,* Vol. 7: pp. 33-42.

Zatzick, D.F., Kang, S.M., Muller, H.G., et al. (2002). Predicting posttraumatic distress in hospitalized trauma survivors with acute injuries. *American Journal of Psychiatry,* Vol. 159: pp. 941-946.

Zayfert, C., & Becker, C.B. (2008). *Cognitive-Behavioral Therapy for PTSD: a Case Formulation Approach.* New York, NY: Guilford.

Zlotnick, C., et al. (2001). Gender differences in patients with posttraumatic stress disorder in a general psychiatric practice. *American Journal of Psychiatry,* Vol. 158: pp. 1923-1925.

Zotovic, M. (2005). PTSD and depression after the NATO air campaign: Individual differences in stress reactions. *Psychology,* Vol. 38: pp. 93-109.

Endnotes

Chapter One

1. See, L. Coser 1955, *The Functions of Social Conflict,* The Free Press.

2. See, T. Ben-Zeev, et al., 2005, Arousal and stereotyping threat, *Journal of Experimental Social Psychology,* 41, 174-181; J. Platania, & G.P. Moran, 2001, Social facilitation as a function of the mere presence of others, *Journal of Social Psychology,* 14, 190-197.

3. See, W.W. Holland, 1993, *European Community Atlas of Avoidable Death,* (2nd ed.), Vol. 2, Oxford University Press.

4. See, World Health Organization, 1992, *International Statistical Classification of Diseases and Related Health Problems,* 10th revision, Vol. 1, Geneva: WHO; & *WHO, Historical Collection – Disease Classification and Nomenclature Doctrines,* www.who.int/library/collections/historical/en/indexl.html.

5. See, D. McGuffin, The history of the diagnostic & statistical manual of mental disorders-DSM, www.@how.com/facts_5583594_history-manual-mental-disorders-dsm; & F. Mesle, 1996, Reconstructing long-term series of causes of death, *Historical Methods,* 29, 72-87.

6. See, M. Fishbein, 1947, *History of the American Medical Association , 1847-1947,* Saunders; & F. Champion, 1984, *The AMA and U.S. Health Policy since 1940,* Chicago Review Press.

7. See *APA History,* www.psych.org/MainMenue/EducationCourseDevelopment/Library/APAHistory.aspx.

8. See, A.C. Houts, 2000, Fifty years of psychiatric nomenclature: Reflections on the 1943 War Department Technical Bulletin, Medical 203, *Journal of Clinical Psychology,* 6, 935-967.

9. Op cited #.

10. See, G.E. Berrios, & R. Porter, 1995, *The History of Clinical Psychiatry,* Athlone Press; & I.B. Syed, 2002, Islamic medicine: 1000 years ahead of its time, *Journal of the International Society for the History of Islamic Medicine,* 2, 2-9.

11. See, C. Alexander, 2010, The shock of war, *Smithsonian,* 41, 8-66; & J. Pizarro, et al., 2006, Psychical and mental health costs of traumatic war experiences among Civil War veterans, *Archives of General Psychiatry,* 63, 193-200.

12. See, A brief history of the VA, *United States Department of Veterans Affairs,* www4.va.gov/about_va/vahistory.asp; *The World Health Organization (WHO),* www.who.int/ ; D. McGuffin, 2011. *The History of the Diagnostic & Statistical Manual of Mental Disorders DS .*

13. See, S.A. Stouffer, et al., 1949. *The American Soldier: Adjustment during Army life* (Vol. I); & *The American Soldier: Combat and its Aftermath* (Vol. II), Princeton University Press; & G. Myrdal, 1944, *An American Dilemma,* Harper & Brothers.See, D.A. Goslin, 1969, *Handbook of Socialization Theory and Research,* Russell Sage Foundation, Rand McNally & Company.

14. See, D. McGuffin, op cited #12.

15. See, APA, 2002, *Diagnostic and Statistical Manual of Mental Disorders – Fourth Edition – Text Revision* (DSM-IV-TR), American Psychiatric Association.

16. *Mortality and Burden of Disease Estimates for WHO Member States in 2004,* www.who.int/entity/healthinfo/global_burden_disease/gbddeathdalycountryestimates200 4.xls.

17. See, J.L. Prince, *Findings from the National Vietnam Veterans' Readjustment Study,* ncptsd.va.gov/ncmain/ncdocs/facts_shts/fs_nvvrs.html?

Chapter Two

1. See, S. Freud, 1937/1968, *The Ego and the Mechanisms of Defense,* Hogarth Press; Institute of Psychoanalysis.

2. See, L.J. Friedman, 1999, *Identity's Architect: A Biography of Erik H. Erikson,* Scribner Book Company.

3. See, E.H. Erikson, 1975, *Life History and Historical Moment,* Norton.

4. See, Selye Hans, *The Canadian Encyclopedia,* The Historica-Dominion Institute.

5. See, H. Selys, 1946, The General Adaptation Syndrome, *Journal of Endocrinology,* 6, 177.

6. See, L.A. French, 2000, *Addictions and Native Americans,* Praeger Press.

7. See, *Servicemen's Readjustment Act (1944),* www.ourdocuments.gov.

8. See, L.A. French, & M. Manzanarez, 2004, Comparative education among NAFTA partners (Cpt. 8), *NAFTA & Neocolonialism* (French & Manzanarez), University Press of America, 195-225.

9. Irma related her story to the author, L.A. French, while he was a Fulbright Scholar at the University of Sarajevo from September 2009 – June 2010.

10. Lidija is the co-author of the book and worked with L.A. French on the psychological and forensic needs of Serbian war trauma victims while French was a Fulbright Scholar in 2009-2010.

11. See, S. Brownmiller, 1975, *Against our Will: Men, Women, and Rape,* Simon and Schuster.

12. See, H. Shudo, 2005, *The Nanking Massacre: Facts versus Fiction,* Sekai Shuppan, Inc. (ISBN 4-916079-12-4).

13. See, L.A. French, 1997, Suicide: A biopsychosocial review, *The Forensic Examiner,* 6, 11-15.

14. See, L.A. French, & B. deOca, 2001, The neuropsychology of impulse control: New insights into violent behaviors, *Journal of Police and Criminal Psychology,* 16, 25-32.

15. See, APA, 2002, Sexual Disorders, *Diagnostic and Statistical Manual – Fourth Edition – Text Revision* (DSM-IV-TR), American Psychiatric Press; & French & deOca, 2001, ibid.

16. See, L.L. Amowitz, et al., 2003, A population-based assessment of women's mental health and attitudes toward women's human rights in Afghanistan, *Journal of Women's Health,* 12, 577-587; & A. Raj, et al., 2008, Driven to a fiery death – the tragedy of self-immolation in Afghanistan, *New England Journal of Medicine,* 358, 2201-2203.

17. See, E. Durkheim, 1951, *Suicide: A Study in Sociology,* Free Press.

18. See, L.A. French, *Addictions and Native Americans,* op cited #6.

19. See, S. Palmer, 1962, *The Psychology of Murder,* Apollo.

20. See, J. Gibbs, 1968, *Suicide,* Harper & Row; & L.A. French, & F. Bryce, 1978, Suicide and female aggression, *Journal of Clinical Psychiatry,* 39, 761-765.

21. See, J.A. Humphrey, et al., 1974, The process of suicide: The sequence of disruptive events in the lives of suicide victims, *Diseases of the Nervous System,* 3, 275-277.

22. See, L.A. French, 1985-86, Forensic suicides and attempted suicides, *Omega,* 16, 335-345.

23. See, H. Engelberg, 1992, Low serum cholesterol and suicide, *Lancet,* 339, 727-729; & M.F. Muldoon, et al,. 1990, Lowering cholesterol concentrations and mortality: A quantitative review of primary prevention trials, *British Medical Journal,* 301, 309-314.

Chapter Three

1. See, M.I. Posner, 1996, New images of the mind, *General Psychologist,* 32, 79-84.

2. See, J.E. Edgerton, 1999, *American Psychiatric Glossary,* American Psychiatric Press.

3. See, R. Kolb, & I.Q. Whishaw, 2008, *Fundamentals of Human Neuropsychology,* W.H. Freeman.

4. See, Posner, op cited #1.

5. See, R.F. Thompson, 2000, *The Brain: A Neuroscience Prima.* W.H. Freeman.

6. See, H. Selye, 1956, *The Stress of Life,* McGraw-Hill.

7. See, L.A. French, & B. deOca, 2001, The neuropsychology of impulse control: New insights into violent behaviors, *Journal of Police and Criminal Psychology,* 16, 25-32.

8. See, G. Aston-Jones, et al., 2000, Locus coeruleus and regulation of behavioral flexibility and attention, *Progressive Brain Research,* 126, 165-182; & C.W. Berridge, & E.D. Abercrombie, 1999, Relationship between locus coeruleus discharge

rates and rates of norepinephrine release within neocortex as assessed by in vivo microdialysis, *Neuroscience,* 93, 1263-1270.

9.   See, APA, 2002, Axis I Major Clinical Disorders, *Diagnostic and Statistical Manual of Mental Disorders – Fourth Edition – Text Revision* (DSM-IV-TR), American Psychiatric Press.

10.   Ibid, Axis II – Personality Disorders.

11.   See, L.A. French, 1991, Neuropsychology of violence, *Corrective and Social Psychiatry,* 37, 12-17; & French & deOca op cited #7.

12.   See, D. Charney, 2004, Psychobiological mechanisms of resilience and vulnerability: Implications for successful adaptation to extreme stress, *American Journal of Psychiatry,* 161, 195-216.

13.   See, H.J. Grabe, at al., 2009, Serotonin transporter gene (SLC6A4) promoter polymorphisms and the susceptibility to posttraumatic stress disorder in the general population, *American Journal of Psychiatry,* 166, 926-934.

14.   See, J. Preston, et al., 2004, *Handbook of Clinical Psychopharmacology for Therapists,* New Harbinger.

15.   See, L.A. French, 1997, Suicide: A biopsychosocial review, *The Forensic Examiner,* 6, 11-15.

16.   See, B.A Van der Kolk, 1988, The trauma spectrum: The interaction of biological and social events in the genesis of the trauma response, *Journal of Traumatic Stress,* 1, 271-290; B.A. Van der Kolk, & R. Fisler, 1995, Dissociation and fragmentary nature of traumatic memories – overview and exploratory study, *Journal of Traumatic Stress,* 8, 505-525; C.A. Byrne, et al., 2001, Comparisons of memories for traumatic events and other experiences, *Applied Cognitive Psychology,* 15, 119-133; C. Parrish, et al., 2009, Assessment of cognitive-communicative disorders of mild traumatic brain injury sustained in combat, *Neurophsiology and Neurogenic Speech and Language Disorders,* 19, 47-57; K.H. Taber, & R.A. Hurley, 2009, PTSD and combat-related injuries: Functional neuroanatomy, *Journal of Neuropsychiatry and Clinical Neurosciences,* 21, iv-4; & R.R. Das, et al., 2005, Traumatic brain injury in the war zone, *New England Journal of Medicine,* 353, 633-634.

Chapter Four

1.   See, A.E. Cowdrey, 1985, MASH vs M*A*S*H*: The mobile Army surgical hospital, *Medical Heritage,* 1, 4-11; & T.H. Wilson, Jr., 1969, New concepts in the management of trauma (Vietnam War), *American Surgeon,* 32, 104-106.

2.   See, J.W. Chambers II, 1976, Draftees or volunteers: A documentary history of the debate over military conscription in the United States, 1787-1973, *The Oxford Companion to American Military History,* Oxford University Press; & M. Kestinbaum, 2000, Citizenship and compulsory military service: The Revolutionary origins of conscriptions in the United States, *Armed Forces & Society,* 27, 7-36.

3.   See, G.Q. Flynn, 1993, *The Draft, 1940-1973,* University of Kansas Press.

4.   See, J.K. Mahon, 1983, *History of the Militia and the National Guard,* The Potowmack Institute, www.pototwmack.org/mahanch4.html.; & B.M. Stentiford, 2008,

The meaning of a name: The rise of the National Guard and the end of a town militia, *Journal of Military History*, 72, 727-754.

5.   See, *The National Guard Bureau Heritage Collection*, www.ngh.army.mil/gallery/heritage/index.asp.

6.   Ibid.

7.   See, G. Barzilai, 1993, *The Gulf Crisis and its Global Aftermath*, Routledge.

8.   See, A. Munro, 2006, *Arab Storm: Politics and Diplomacy behind the Gulf War*, I.B. Tauris; & M.M. Motale, 2006, *The Origins of the Gulf Wars*, University Press of America.

9.   See, M.T. Klare, 2001, *Resource Wars: The New Landscape of Global Conflict*, Metropolitan Books.

10.   See, Persian Gulf War, *Gale Encyclopedia of U.S. History*, www.answers.com/topic/gulf-war; E.L. Benjamin, & M.J. Mazarr, 1994, *Turning Point: The Gulf War and U.S. Military Strategy*, Westview Press; W. Head, & E.H. Tilford, 1996, *The Eagle in the Desert: Looking back on U.S. Involvement in the Persian Gulf War*. Praeger.

11.   See, VFW, 2011, *Persian Gulf War – Special 20th Anniversary Issue*, VFW, 99; & N.L.W. Hoffman, 2011, Operation Desert Shield and Desert Storm, *Leatherneck*, XCIV, 28-31.

12.   See, M.R. Gordon, 2006, *Cobra II: The inside story of the invasion and occupation if Iraq*, Pantheon; & T.E. Ricks, 2006, *Fiasco: The American military adventure in Iraq*, Penquin.

13.   See, S.M. Maloney, 2005, *Enduring the Freedom: A rogue historian in Afghanistan*, Potomac Books.

14.   Ibid; & E. O'Connell, 2008, *Counterinsurgency in Iraq, 2003-2006*, RAND.

15.   See, R. North, 2009, *Minister of Defeat: The British war in Iraq, 2003-2009*, Continuum.

16.   See, T. Tanielian, & L.H. Jaycox (ed.s), 2008, Preface, *Invisible Wounds of War*, RAND, ivi-iv.

17.   Ibid, The Wars in Afghanistan and Iraq – An overview, 19-31; E. Krenke, 2010, Army relegates guard to combat in First Gulf War, *National Guard Bureau*, www.dvidshub.net/news/printable/59390; & R. Powers, 2005, Deployment rates, *About.com Guide – U.S. Military*.

18.   See, S. Curphey, 2003, 1 in 7 U.S. military personnel in Iraq is female, *We.news, Womens@news.org*, http://www.womens@new.org/print/4757.

19.   See, D. Ephron, & P. Wingert, 2006, Top of her class, *Newsweek* (October 9), 43; S. fainaru, 2005, Battle knows no gender lines, *Washington Post* (June 26); & M. Thompson, 2011, Air Boss, *Time*, 177, 36-38.

20.   Op cited # 16, The Stress-Diathesis Model, 121.

21.   See, R.J. Rona, et al, 2007, Mental health consequences of overstretched in the UK armed forces, *British Medical Journal*, 335.

22.   See, A.C. McFarlane, 2009, Military deployment: The impact on children and family adjustment and need for care, *Current Opinion in Psychiatry*, 22, 369; M.

Madgalena Liabre, & F. Hadi, 2009, War-related exposure and psychological distress as predictors of health and sleep: A longitudinal study of Kuwaiti children, *Psychosomatic Medicine,* 71, 776; & C. Panter-Brick, et al., 2009, Violence, suffering, and mental health in Afghanistan: A school-based survey, *The Lancet,* 374, 807-907.

23. Op cited #16, Marriage, Parenting, and Child Outcomes, 111-126.

24. Ibid, Substance Abuse, 134-136.

25. See, M.E. McFall, et al., 1992, Combat-related posttraumatic stress disorder and severity of substance abuse in Vietnam veterans, *Journal of Studies in Alcohol and Drugs,* 53, 357-363.

26. See, NIDA, 2007, Teen Marines allowed to drink, *Join Together* (May 21); UPI, 2011, Marines wrestle with alcoholism, *United Press International,* (January 2), www.jointogether.org.

27. See, NIDA, 2007, Substance use among young military personnel differs from civilians, *Join Together* (May 3), www.jointogether.org.

28. See, NIDA, 2008, Veterans bill addresses addiction, mental health, *Join Together* (June 6), www.jointogether.org.

29. See, NIDA, 2010, Drinking a big problem for British troops in Afghanistan and Iraq, *Joint Together* (May 17); & J.I. Bisson, 2007, Post-traumatic stress disorder, *British Medical Journal,* 334, 789-793.

30. Op cited #24.

31. See, D.M. Hughes, et al., 2007, Modern-day comfort women: The U.S. military, transnational crime, and the trafficking of women, *Violence against Women,* 13, 901-926.

32. See, J. Ellison, 2011, The military's secret shame, *Newsweek* (April 11), 40-43.

33. See, 2003, The real story of Jessica Lynch, *Time,* 162, 32; & A. Mulrine, 2008, Out of the spotlight: Five years on, Jessica Lynch and ex-POW comrades look back, *U.S. News and World Report,* 144, 12-14.

34. See, M. Thompson, 2011, Service members sue Pentagon over rapes, *Time,* 177, 26.

35. See, *Military Sexual Trauma (MST),* Department of Veterans Affairs, www.va.gov.

36. See, AP, 2011, Air Force chief pleads guilty to sexual misconduct, *Associated Press,* (January 25).

37. See, S. Thorne, 2010, Military leaders "disappointed", *The Daily Gleaner* (July 13), A7 (Fredericton, New Brunswick, Canada).

38. See, M. Babbage, 2010, Col. Williams headed to Kingston pen, *The Canadian Press,* ca.news.yahoo.com/s/capress/101021/national/colonel_murder_charge?; F. Thornhill, 2010, Canadian Air Force colonel jailed for sex murders, *Reuters,* ca.news.yahoo.com/s/reuters/101022/canada_us_murder?

39. See, NIDA, 2007, One of three war vets have mental-health problem; & Alcohol problems among U.S. Soldiers in Iraq tied to violence, *Join Together* (March 14); & L.C. Baldor, 2008, More convicted felons enlisted in Army, Marines, *Associated Press* (April 22).

40. See, BBC, 2006, The rape & murder scene of Mahmudiyah, *BBC documentary* (August 7); & Mahmudiyah incident, *Opentopia Encyclopedia.*

41. See, L. Myers, 2010, U.S. soldier to face court-martial in Afghan slayings, *Reuters* (October 16), ca.news.yahoo.com/s/reukters/101016/n_top-news/cnews_us_usa_soldiers_crime?; & A. Moran, 2011, 5 U.S. soldiers accused of randomly targeting Afghan civilians, *Digital Journal* (August 26), www.digitaljournal.com/article/296620.

42. See, *Jeremy Michael Boorda, Admiral, United States Navy Chief of Naval Operations,* www.arlingtoncemetery.net/borda.htm.

43. Op cited #16, suicide, 128-129.

44. See, AP, 2008, Most vet suicides among Guard, Reserve troops (February 12); P. Jelinek, 2008, Army suicide up as much as 20 percent, *Associated Press,* www.defenselink.mil.

Chapter Five

1. See, E.J. Erickson, 2003, *Defeat in Detail: The Ottoman Army in the Balkans, 1912-1913,* Praeger; R. Hall, 2000. *The Balkan Wars, 1912-1913: Prelude to the First World War,* Routledge.

2. See, E.C. Stowell, 2009, *The Diplomacy of the War of 1914: The Beginnings of the War (1915),* Kessinger Publishing; L. Albertini, 2005, *Origins of the War of 1914,* (Vol. I), Enigma Books; R. Belfield, 2005, *The Assassination Business: A History of state-sponsored murder,* Carrol & Graf; & V. Dedijer, 1966, *The Road to Sarajevo,* Simon and Schuster.

3. See, L. Benson, 2001, *Yugoslavia: A concise history,* Palgrave Macmillan; J.R. Lampe, 2000, *Yugoslavia as history: Twice there was a country,* Cambridge University Press; & S.P. Ramet, 2006, *The Three Yugoslavias: State-building and legitimization, 1918-2005,* Indiana University Press.

4. See, S.P. Ramet, op cited.

5. See, J. Gow, & C. Carmichael, 1999, *Slovenia and the Slovenes,* Hurst.

6. See, L. Silber, & A. Little, 1995, *The Death of Yugoslavia,* Penguin; & T. Ripley, 2001, *Conflict in the Balkans, 1991-2000,* Osprey Publishing.

7. See, USA State Department, 1995, *Dayton Peace Accords on Bosnia* (March 30); & D. Chandler, 2005, From Dayton to Europe, *International Peacekeeping,* 12, 336.

8. See, P.C. Latawski, & M.A. Smith, 2003, *The Kosovo Crisis and the evolution of post-Cold War European security,* Manchester University Press; M. Mandelbaum, 2000, *The New European Diasporas: National minorities and conflict in Eastern Europe,* Council on Foreign Relations; & M. Buckley, & N. Sally, 2002, *Kosovo: Perceptions of War and its aftermath,* Continuum Press.

9. See, B. Allen,, 1996, *Rape Warfare: The hidden genocide in Bosnia-Herzegovina and Croatia,* University of Minnesota Press; & Landmark verdicts for rape, torture, and sexual enslavement: Criminal Tribunal convicts Bosnian Serbs for Crimes against Humanity, *Human Rights News-Bosnia* (February 2, 2001), www.hrw.org/en/news/2001/02/22/bosnia-landmark-verdicts-rape-torture-and-sexual-enslavement.

10. See, N. Henisberg, et al., 2001, Stressor characteristics and post-traumatic stress disorder symptom dimensions in war victims, *Croatian Medical Journal,* 42, 133-139.

11. See, D. Begic, & N. Jokie-Begic, 2007, Heterogeneity of posttraumatic stress disorder symptoms in Croatian war veterans: Retrospective study, *Croatian Medical Journal,* 48, 133-139.

12. See, D. Kozaric-Kovaciv, et al., 2001, Posttraumatic stress disorder and depression in soldiers with combat experiences, *Croatian Medical Journal,* 42, 16-170.

13. See, D. Britvic, et al., 2006, Long-term dynamic-oriented group psychotherapy of posttraumatic stress disorder in war veterans: Prospective study of five-year treatment, *Croatian Medical Journal,* 47, 76-84.

14. See, I. Dijanaic-Plasc, et al., 2007, Psychiatric heredity and posttraumatic stress disorder: Survey study of war veterans, *Croatian Medical Journal,* 48, 146-156.

15. See, L. Sodic, et al., 2007, Short-term memory in Croatian war veterans with posttraumatic stress disorder, *Croatian Medical Journal,* 48, 140-145; & V. Placko, 1999, Disabled veterans of the patriotic war in the Krizevic area and the post-traumatic stress disorder, *Polemos: Journal of Interdisciplinary Research on War and Peace,* 11, 187-206.

16. See, E. Avdibegovic, et al., 2008, Mental health care of pscyhotraumatized persons in post-war Bosnia-Herzegovina – experiences from Tuzla Canton, *Psychiatria Danubina,* 20, 474-484.

17. See, B. Kuljic, et al., 2004, Posttraumatic stress disorder in Bosnian war veterans: Analysis of stress events and risk factors, *Military-Medical and Pharmaceutical Review,* 61, 283-289.

18. See, A.A. Jovannovic, et al., 2009, Predicting violence in veterans with posttraumatic stress disorder, *Military-Medical and Pharmaceutical Review,* 66, 13-21; & L. Trlaja, et al., 1997, Post-traumatic stress disorder of war casualties, *Psychology,* 30, 42-436.

19. See, M. Basoglu, 2005, Psychiatric and cognitive effects of war in former Yugoslavia, *Journal of the American Medical Association (JAMA),* 294, 580-590.

20. See, M. Definis-Gojanovic, et al., 1997, Influence of war on frequency and patterns of homicides and suicides in south Croatia (1991-1993), *Croatian Medical Journal,*38, 59-63.

21. Op cited #16.

22. See, G.I. Ringdal, et al., 2008, War experiences and war-related distress in Bosnia-Herzegovina eight years after the war, *Croatian Medical Journal,* 49, 75-86.

23. See, P.D. Opalic, 2008, Disarrangement-dominant symptoms of traumatized people in Serbia, *Sociology,* 50, 417-432.

24. See, J.J. Gavrilovic, et al., 2005, Association of posttraumatic stress and quality of life in civilians after air attacks, *Journal of the Association of Posttraumatic Stress on Quality of Life,* 37, 297-305.

25. See, Z. Steel, et al., 2009, Association of torture and other potentially traumatic events with mental health outcomes among populations exposed to mass conflict and displacement, *Journal of the American Medical Association (JAMA)*, 302, 537-549.

26. See, S. Priebe, et al,. 2004, Study of long-term clinical and social outcomes after war experiences in ex-Yugoslavia: Methods of the "CONNECT Project", *Psychiatry Today*, 36, 111-122.

27. See, D. Silove, et al., 2005, PTSD, depression, and acculturation, *Intervention*, 3, 46-50.

28. See, D. Donev, et al., 2002, Refugee crisis in Macedonia during the Kosovo conflict in 1999, *Croatian Medical Journal*, 43, 184-189.

29. See, M. Klavic, et al., 2007, Psychological consequences of war trauma and postwar social stressors in women in Bonsnia-Herzegovina, *Croatian Medical Journal*, 48, 167-176.

30. See, M. Loncar, et al., 2005, Psychological consequences of rape on women in 1991-1995 war in Croatia and Bosnia and Herzegovina, *Croatian Medical Journal*, 47, 67-75.

31. See, M. Ajdukovic, 1995, Children in war in Croatia, *Croatian Journal of Social Policy*, 2, 295-304.

32. See, S. Ceranic, 2003, Psycho-social consequences in adolescents: Victims if landmines, *Journal of Clinical Psychiatry, Psychology and Related Disciplines*, 25, 49-54; J. Terzic, et al., 2001, Children war casualties during the 1991-199 wars in Croatia and Bosnia and Herzegovina, *Croatian Medical Journal*, 42, 156-160.

33. See, B. Milosavljevic, et al., 1996, War, the warfare environment and the syndrome of war psychic trauma in children, *Psychology*, 29, 465-476.

34. See, A. Barath, 2002, Psychological status of Sarajevo children after war: 1999-2000 survey, *Croatian Medical Journal*, 43, 213-220.

35. See, M. Klavic, et al., 2008, Psychological problems in children of war veterans with posttraumatic stress disorder in Bosnia and Herzegovina, *Croatian Medical Journal*, 49, 491-498.

36. See, V. Petrovic, 2004, Levels of psychopathology in children with war-related trauma, *Psychiatry Today*, 36, 17-28.

37. See, A. Barath, 2002, Children's well-being after the war in Kosovo survey, 2000, *Croatian Medical Journal*, 43, 199-208.

38. See, S. Puhalo, 2003, Ethnical distance of the citizens of Republika Srpska and the Federation of Bosnia-Herzegovina to the nations of former Yugoslavia, *Psychology*, 36, 141-156; & V. Turjacamin, 2004, Ethnic stereotypes among Bosniak and Serbian youth in Bosnia and Herzegovina, *Psychology*, 37, 37-374.

39. See, M. Biro, & P. Milin, 2005, Traumatic experiences and the process of reconciliation, *Psychology*, 38, 133-148.

40. See, H. Hjort, & A. Frisen, 2006, Ethnic identity and reconciliation: Two main tasks for the young in Bosnia-Herzegovina, *Adolescence*, 41, 141-163.

Chapter Six

1. See, A. Anastasi, & S. Urbina, 1997, Reliability (Chapter 4), *Psychological Testing,* Prentice Hall.

2. Ibid., A. Anastasi, & S. Urbina, Validity: Basic Concepts (Chapter 5).

3. See, P.T. Trzepacz, &R.W. Baker, 1993, *The Psychiatric Mental Status Examination* Oxford University Press.

4. See, D.J. Robinson, 2000, *The Mental Status Exam Explained,* Rapid Psychier Press; & R.L. Strub, & W.F. Black, 2000, *The Mental Status Examination in Neurology,* F.A. Davis.

5. See, 309.81 Posttraumatic Stress Disorder, DSM-5: The Future of Psychiatric Diagnosis, www.dsm5.org/pages/sefault.aspx.

6. See, R. Rogers, 2001, *Handbook of Diagnostic and Structured Interviewing,* Gilford Press; & T.F. Babor, & M.B. First, 2009, Structured clinical interview for DSM-IV (SCID), *Encyclopedia of Drugs, Alcohol, and Addictive Behavior,* www.encyclopedia.com.

7. See, J.R. Graham, 2000, *MMPI-2: Assessing Personality and Psychopathology,* Oxford University Press; & R.L. Green, 2000, *The MMPI-2: An Interpretive Manual,* Allyn & Bacon.

8. See, L.A. French, 2003, Police culture and the MMPI, *International Journal of Comparative Criminology,* 3, 63-67; L.A. French, 2002, Assessing law enforcement personnel: Comparative uses of the MMPIs, *The Forensic Examiner,* 11, 21-28; & R.R. Sewell, et al., 2006, The MMPI-2 restructured clinical scales, *Journal of Personality Assessment,* 87, 139-147.

9. See, A. Anastasi, & S. Urbina, 1997, op cited #1: Projective Techniques (Chapter 15), 410-442; W.B. Walsh, & N.E. Betz, 1995, The Assessment of Personality (Part II), *Tests and Assessment,* Prentice Hall, 87-148.

10. Ibid., W.B. Walsh, & N.E. Betz, 144-145; National Center for Posttraumatic Stress Disorders – Assessments, *United States Department of Veterans Affairs,* ncptsd.va.gov/ncmain/ncdocs/assmnts.

11. See, McCormick, *TBI Interview(Military),* developed at Salisbury VAMC by Courtney McCormick (VISN G MIRECC).

12. See, APA, 2011, *American Psychologist – Special Issue: Comprehensive Soldiers Fitness,* 66, 1-86.

13. Op cited #7.

14. Op cited #8.

15. See, A. Poolos, 2002, Yugoslavia: Environmental damage lingers three years after NATO bombing, *Radio Free Europe – RadioLiberty* (May 7), www.rferl.org/articleprintview/1099628.html.

16. See, L.A. French, & N. Picthall-French, 1998, The role of substance abuse among rural youth by race, culture and gender, *Alcohol Treatment Quarterly,* 16, 101–108; & L.A. French, & N. Picthall-French, 1996, Assessing three adolescent groups in New Mexico using the Problem-Oriented Screening Instrument, *Psychological Reports,* 79, 242.

17. See, D.K Snyder, 1979, *Marital Satisfaction Inventory,* Western Psychological Services; & D.K. Snyder, et al., 1981, Empirical validation of the Marital Satisfaction Inventory: An actuarial approach, *Journal of Counseling and Clinical Psychology,* 49, 262-268.

18. See, VA expects surge in 'Agent Orange' claims, *Caltrap,* 2011, 57, 3.

19. See, Vets to protest for better war injury benefits, *The Canadian Press* (November 6, 2010), http://ca.news.yahoo.com/s/capress/101106/national/vets.

20. See, T. Tanielian, & I.H. Jaycox, 2008, Part IV, Conclusions and Recommendations, *Invisible Wounds of War,* RAND Corporation, 431.

21. Ibid.

22. See, M.A. Bornovalova, et al., 2009, Testing gender effects on the mechanisms explaining the association between post-traumatic stress symptoms and substance use frequency, *Addictive Behaviors,* 34, 685-692.

23. See, D. Meichenbaum, 2009, Core psychotherapeutic tasks with returning soldiers: A case conceptualization approach, *Living and Surviving in Harm's Way* (Freeman, Moore, Freeman, ed.s), Routledge – Taylor & Francis Group.

24. See, P.A. Resick, & M.K. Schnicke, 1992, Cognitive processing therapy for sexual assault victims, *Journal of Consulting and Clinical Psychology,* 60, 748-756.

25. See, T. Cavic, et al., 2008, Post-traumatic stress disorder and coping strategies in psychotraumatized refugees, *Medical Review,* 61, 11-15.

26. See, M. Sijbrandij, et al., 2007, Treatment of acute posttraumatic stress disorder with brief cognitive behavioral therapy, *American Journal of Psychiatry,* 164, 82-90.

27. See, D.R. Johnson, et al., 1996, Outcome of intensive inpatient treatment for combat-related posttraumatic stress disorder, *American Journal of Psychiatry,* 153, 771-777.

28. See, L.A. French, 1993, Adapting projective tests for minority children, *Psychological Reports,* 72, 15-18.

29. See, A. Barath, 1996, Creative therapies for war-traumatized children: 1991-95 Croatian experience, *Croatian Medical Journal,* 37, 355-368.

30. See, P.D. Opalic, 2005, Human figure test in the research of psychopathological state of refugees and somatically traumatized, *Serbian Archives for Whole Medicine,* 133, 21-28.

31. See, S. Morgillo, et al., 2009, Myths and realities of pharmacotherapy in the military, *Living and Surviving in Harm's Way, op cited* #23, 329-346.

32. See, N. Pivac, & D. Kozaric-Kovacic, 2006, Pharmacotherapy of treatment-resistant combat-related posttraumatic stress disorder with psychotic features, *Croatian Medical Journal,* 47, 440-451.

33. See, C.J.Hildreth, 2009, Tracing the flow of knowledge: Geographic variability in the diffusion of Prazosin use for the treatment of posttraumatic stress disorder nationally in the Department of Veterans Affairs, *Journal of the American Medical Association (JAMA),* 301, 2310; & I. Harpaz-Rotem, & R.A. Rosenheck, 2009, Geographic variability in the diffusion of Prazosin use for the treatment of posttraumatic

stress disorder nationally in the Department of Veterans Affairs, *Archives of General Psychiatry,* 66, 417-421.

34. See, G.A. Fava, et al., 2005, Sequential treatment of mood and anxiety disorders, *Journal of Clinical Psychiatry,* 66, 1392-1400.

35. See, K.J. Reivich, et al., 2011, Master resilience training in the U.S. Army, *American Psychologist, op cited* #12, 25-34.

36. See, A-R Blais, et al., 2009, The development and validation of the Army Post-Deployment Reintegration Scale, *Military Psychology,* 21, 365-381.

37. See, D. Meichenbaum's Care Conceptualization Model, *op cited* #23.

38. See, D. Kozaric-Kovacic, et al., 2002, Psychiatric help to psychotraumatized persons during and after war in Croatia, *Croatian Medical Journal,* 43, 221-228.

Index